CHRONICLES
IN
STONE

A volume in the NIU Series in
SLAVIC, EAST EUROPEAN, AND EURASIAN STUDIES
Edited by Christine D. Worobec

For a list of books in the series, visit our website at cornellpress.cornell.edu.

CHRONICLES IN STONE

Preservation, Patriotism, and Identity in Northwest Russia

VICTORIA DONOVAN

NORTHERN ILLINOIS UNIVERSITY PRESS
AN IMPRINT OF
CORNELL UNIVERSITY PRESS
ITHACA AND LONDON

First published 2019 by Cornell University Press

Printed in the United States of America

ISBN 978-1-5017-4787-8 (cloth : alk. paper)
ISBN 978-1-5017-4789-2 (pdf)
ISBN 978-1-5017-4788-5 (epub/mobi)

Book and cover design by Yuni Dorr

Librarians: A CIP record is available with the Library of Congress.

For

JOHN AND SUE DONOVAN,

LOVERS OF KNOWLEDGE
and
PATRIOTS OF THEIR TOWN

CONTENTS

ILLUSTRATIONS

Unless otherwise stated, all images are the author's own.

ACKNOWLEDGMENTS

This book has benefited from the expertise of numerous generous colleagues and friends. The first among these is Catriona Kelly, my former DPhil supervisor, whose formidable knowledge, inspiring dedication, and professional lightness of touch have shaped my work in invaluable ways. An important role in this project was played by Edith Clowes, who offered generous support and advice at critical stages in this book's publication. My other closest readers have been Andrei Zorin, Philip Bullock, and Karl Leydecker, my colleagues at St Andrews, Katharine Holt, Claire Whitehead, and Emily Finer, and friends and fellow Russianists, Anna Lordan and Elizabeth Stern. Shura Collinson, Andy Byford and Stephen Lovell also read parts of this book and offered constructive criticism. I am grateful to my PhD student Darya Tsymbalyuk, whose work on Donbas migrant memory inspired me to think further about the theory of oral history research. I am likewise deeply indebted to Dmitrii Shatalov and Galina Scott for their patient verification of the Russian text and assistance in untangling the handwriting of local *chinovniki*. This book could not have been written without the kindness and support of my partner, David Hill, to whom I am forever indebted.

In the course of writing this book, I have benefited a great deal from conversations with uniquely knowledgeable colleagues at a number of international conferences and seminars. Particularly helpful were the audiences at the Russian and East European Cities between Past and Present seminar series at St Antony's College, Oxford, organized by Uilleam Blacker; the Russian and Eurasian Studies seminar series at Mount Holyoke College, organized by Carolin Roeder and Peter J. Scotto; and the conference "Centrifugal Forces: Reading Russia's Regional Identities and Initiatives" at the University of Virginia, organized by Edith Clowes, Gisela Erbslöh, and Ani Kokobobo. My attendance at the latter resulted in the contribution of a book chapter to the organizers' edited collection *Russia's Regional Identities: The Power of the Provinces* (2018). I would like to thank Routledge for granting permission to reproduce some of the material from that chapter in this book. I also thank the editors of *Slavic Review*, in particular Mark D. Steinberg, for allowing me to present here some material that has already appeared in a different form in that journal.

I could not have conceived of, researched, or written this book without the goodwill and enthusiasm of many Russian friends and associates. Dmitrii Nechiporuk, Yury Basilov, Margarita Tkachenko, Alena and Valentina Gorodilova, Natal'ia Shvetsova, Svetlana Podrezova, and Irina Soboleva provided invaluable help gathering materials, creating networks of contacts in the Northwest, and tying up loose ends, not to mention demonstrating warm hospitality each time I visited their hometowns. Dmitrii Baranov and Evgeniia Guliaeva helped me to become initiated at the Novgorod archives and have offered much appreciated advice and friendship during my years of research in Russia. For their enlightening discussion and insightful reflections I am grateful to Dmitrii Mukhin, Iurii Ganichev, and Tat'iana Kos'ianenko. Finally, and most warmheartedly, I thank Valentina Vladimirovna, who shared her lunch and her wonderful conversation with me for several months at the Novgorod Museum Archive.

This book draws on doctoral research carried out as part of the AHRC-funded project "National Identity in Russia from 1961: Traditions and Deterritorialization." I acknowledge with much gratitude the support of the AHRC, without which it would have been impossible to carry out such thorough research in the Russian Northwest or to air the arguments in this book at international conferences. I am also very grateful for the support of the Wingate Scholarship, the Scatcherd European Scholarship, and the Peter Fitzpatrick Scholarship, which provided me with the means to reflect on and write up my research in my fourth year of doctoral study. A number of invaluable research trips to Russia were also made possible by the financial support of the Ilchester Fund, Santander Travel Grants, and University of St Andrews research and travel grants, for all of which I am most thankful.

FIGURE 1. Map of the Russian Federation, based on UN map (Russian Federation, map no. 3840, rev. 2, January 2004).

FIGURE 2. Detail of the Russian Northwest, based on UN map (Russian Federation, map no. 3840, rev. 2, January 2004).

Architectural monuments are likened to stone chronicles. And, on the whole, this association is correct. But these particular chronicles have not survived intact. Over the course of their lives, their "pages" have been torn, damaged and defaced.

—Iurii Spegal'skii, *Pskov* (1978)[1]

The reason we don't preserve the past is not because there is so much of it, or because there are so few of us who value the past's beauty, so few patriots who love their native history and native art, but because we are in too much of a hurry, we're racing for the next immediate "return," we don't believe in the slow virtues of the soul.

—Dmitrii Likhachev, "Kraevedenie as Science and Practice" (1987)[2]

INTRODUCTION

The onion-domed churches, kremlin walls, and austere monasteries of the Russian Northwest today constitute iconic visions of Russianness. Images of this architecture adorn embassy walls and tourist guidebooks, providing material expression for the ideals of military strength and Orthodox spirituality that underpin the Russian national idea. One may reasonably assume that the elevation of this architecture to the status of national heritage was a post-Soviet development—part of the recovery of national traditions after 1991. In reality, the Northwest has provided the symbols for imagining the Soviet and Russian nations since the end of World War II. This book is a study of the forms of internal cultural appropriation that provided the basis of Soviet nation-building from 1945 to 1991. It reveals the centrality of the Northwest to the Soviet and Russian national ideas, drawing on oral history and participant observation work to explore the impact of identity politics on local communities and the way they view both themselves and the nation as a whole.

The central argument of this book is that the Soviet state exploited the architectural heritage of the Russian Northwest, and specifically the towns of Novgorod, Pskov, and Vologda, to craft visions of Russified Sovietness that could stimulate popular patriotic consciousness. In the decades after World War II, the Soviet Union encountered a series of political challenges: the recovery from the material and psychological devastation of war in the late 1940s and 1950s; the political disorientation that resulted from Stalin's death; and the destabilizing influence of ethnic nationalism, including Russian nationalism, during the last decades of Soviet power. At each of these junctures, the architectural heritage of the Northwest was used to craft nationally unifying patriotic narratives about the Soviet people's genius, heroism, and strength. The impact of this process on the local landscape, the formation and politics of local elites, and the self-perception of local communities are the subjects of this book.

A valuable point of comparison in this regard is Alon Confino's seminal study of German nationalism and "Heimat," or homeland. Confino notes that the understanding of nationalism as something produced by ruling elites and imposed upon the masses is misleading. Instead, we need to study "the way people devise a common denominator between their intimate, immediate, and real local place and the distant, abstract, and not-less-real national world."[3] Confino reserves a special place within this process for what he calls "the Heimat idea," a spatial concept that mediates between the local and the national. The Heimat idea aroused sentiments of patriotism, sacrifice, and sacredness normally associated with nations, while at the same time becoming a fundamental part of the everyday life of the German people through entertainment, vacations, and tourism.[4]

The notion of Heimat is a valuable one for thinking about the Russian Northwest and its role in imagining Soviet-Russian nationhood. Novgorod, Pskov, and Vologda served as symbolic homelands for the Soviet and post-Soviet Russian nations, mediating between the local, national, and transnational. Following the war, the state marketed the region's cultural heritage to the nation as the symbols of Russified Soviet identity linked to myths of sacredness, sacrifice, and patriotism. Like the Heimat idea, the idea of the Northwest was placed at the center of everyday life, emerging as a center of tourism and cultural activity in the 1960s to 1980s. The region thus formed "a vehicle for internalizing the impersonal nation by placing it within the familiar local world," or a site where local and national memory could be fused.[5]

Novgorod, Pskov, Vologda

The three towns at the center of this study functioned similarly to Heimat in that they relied on myths of sacredness (and its secular Soviet equivalent, democracy), sacrifice, and patriotism. The myth of Novgorod was founded on the town's medieval incarnation as the Democratic Republic of Novgorod, an entity that endured from 1136 to 1478. The republic's abiding feature in Russian cultural memory was its system of "veche" parliaments, a network of district and neighborhood assemblies that was responsible for the election of magistrates and other local officials and that aimed to prevent the emergence of tyranny.[6] The repression of these "democratic" institutions following the republic's defeat and annexation by Muscovy in 1478 became the stuff of local legend. The Massacre of Novgorod by Ivan IV and his troops became known as a turning point in Russian history, leading Russia off the enlightened path of democracy and justice and down the dark road of autocracy and tyranny.

Novgorod's story of thwarted democracy appeared in many different iterations in the centuries that followed. Of particular note among these was the tale of the Veche Bell of the St. Sophia Cathedral, which was said to have smashed itself on the hills of Valdai as the tsar attempted to transport it from Novgorod to Moscow. Legend had it that the bell's pieces transformed of their own accord into miniature bells, which were then transported by carriage drivers around Russia to spread Novgorod's message of democracy and freedom. The myth was preserved in *byliny*, medieval epic poems featuring freedom-loving figures such as Sadko and Vasilii Buslaev, and reproduced in the romantic poetry of Alexander Pushkin and Mikhail Lermontov. The tale's democratic credentials also made it appealing to the revolutionary Decembrist movement and agrarian populists; indeed, the title of Alexander Hertzen's influential revolutionary journal *The Bell* gives a nod to the the legend of the Novgorod bell.

Despite sharing much of Novgorod's political history, Pskov was not celebrated in the same way as a repository of democratic traditions. The myth of Pskov was rather one of sacrifice, heroism, and military might. Pskov was a fortress town and defender of Russian interests against marauding foreign forces. In the pre-Muscovite period this identity was linked to the actions of the Lithuanian King Daumantas of Pskov (the son-in-law of the mighty Russian warrior Alexander Nevsky), whose triumphs against the Lithuanians and the Livonian Order were celebrated in national historiography.[7] The town's foundation myth, however, was undoubtedly the Siege of Pskov, which took place during the first stage of the Livonian War (1558–1583). The successful repulsion of the Polish-Lithuanian forces, led by Stephen Báthory, was attributed largely to the will and strength of the Pskov people, who reputedly fought side by side with Russian soldiers throughout the blockade to defend their beloved town.

Pskov's myth of patriotic self-sacrifice was immortalized in the romantic art and literature of the nineteenth century. Karl Briullov's 1843 *Siege of Pskov*, for example, depicted a motley crew of priests, women, and children surging forward through the damaged kremlin walls to defend their town against Báthory's unseen forces. Similarly, Boris Chorikov's illustration of the siege from his *Picturesque Karamzin, or Russian History in Pictures*, portrayed the local clergy and towns-folk valiantly battling with a heavily fortified and overwhelming Polish army.[8] The ultimate tribute to Pskov's grassroots heroism, however, was recorded by the Russian historian Nikolai Karamzin in his encyclopedic *History of the Russian State* (1816–1829). In his account of the siege, Karamzin tacitly acknowledged the efforts of the local population, whose contribution, he suggested, had helped to secure Russian victory over the Poles:

> Pskov, like a mighty bastion, checked Stefan's invincibility; having taken Pskov, Báthory would not have satisfied Livonia; he would not have stopped at Smolensk, nor at the northern territories, he would perhaps have taken even Novgorod. . . . So truly, Pskov or Shuiskii saved Russia from a great danger, and the memory of this great service will not fade in our history, so long as we do not lose the love for our fatherland and its name.[9]

The myth of Vologda stands in contrast to that of both Novgorod and Pskov. Neither a "cradle of Russian democracy" nor a "fortress city" that had sacrificed itself for the defense of the Motherland, Vologda tended to be presented in lyrical rather than epic terms as a center of spirituality, unadulterated Russian nature, and authentic national culture. The cultural purity of Vologda was frequently associated with the fact that the city had avoided the imperialist influence of foreign invaders. This perception was reinforced by the region's strong oral folk culture, which had survived relatively intact as a result of Vologda's remote location and the fact that it had been spared the worst effects of serfdom in the tsarist period.[10]

The patriotic mythologization of Vologda was in a large part the consequence of the literary output of the *narodnik* writers who migrated or were exiled to the region in the second half of the nineteenth century. Among these were the social critic Petr Lavrov, who wrote his *Historical Letters* while living in exile in the region between 1867 and 1870, and the literary critic Nikolai Shelgunov, who penned articles for the revolutionary journal *Russian Word* while traveling among the impoverished settlements of the region. The most notable literary dedication to Vologda's spiritual value was perhaps *The Wooded Kingdom* (1878), by the Velikii Ustiug-born writer Pavel Zasodimskii. This work drew on the writer's experience traveling around the Zyriansk area, then part of the Vologda gubernia, to paint a vivid picture of local life, arts, and crafts. The work in many ways anticipated the culturally conservative writings of the "Vologda School" of

Village Prose authors, many of whom found similar inspiration in the region's heritage and traditions.[11]

Democracy, sacrifice, and patriotism thus formed the foundation stones of the Northwest's mythopoetics. It should come as no surprise, then, that the postwar Soviet state chose to focus its nation-building efforts on the region, elevating its heritage and traditions to the status of symbols of national identity. After the collapse of Soviet power, the powerful and pervasive myth of the Northwest continued to function as a means of asserting Russia's uniqueness and cultural primacy. As the country declined into elected authoritarianism in the twenty-first century, neoconservative thinkers began to celebrate the region as a site of spiritual strength and integrity—an alternative to the "cosmopolitan" and morally impoverished capital. This book locates the origins of these chauvinistic tendencies in the politics of the postwar period, when the link between the Northwest's heritage landscape and the Russian national idea was established. By offering an alternative lens through which to view the rise of Russian patriotic consciousness in the twentieth and twenty-first centuries, the book demonstrates the value of regional scholarship in understanding identity debates in Russia today and contributes to a growing corpus of region-based scholarship reflecting on questions of Russian national identity.[12]

Northwestern Architecture and Its Preservation in the Soviet Period

Given this book's focus on architectural heritage and its preservation, it makes sense at this juncture to offer a brief overview of the architectural history of the Northwest and the legislative milestones that contributed to the transformation of its heritage objects into symbols of national identity.

Many of Novgorod's most notable historical buildings date from the era of Kievan Rus', when the city thrived as the second most important urban center in the political confederation. The most significant structure to be erected at this time was the Cathedral of St. Sophia (1045–1050), which was dedicated to the Holy Wisdom of God in imitation of the Hagia Sophia Cathedral in Constantinople. The iconic five-domed structure was commissioned by Prince Vladimir of Novgorod, son of Yaroslav the Wise, and replaced an even older, thirteen-domed wooden church, which had been built around 989 by Novgorod's first bishop. Other notable buildings to be commissioned at this time included the St. Nicholas Cathedral (1113), which from 1136 became Novgorod's most important veche cathedral, and the St. George's Monastery Cathedral (1119) and the Cathedral of the Nativity of Our Lady (1119) in the St. Anthony's Monastery, both of which, in their cubic solidity and laconic decoration, constituted outstanding examples of the early Novgorodian style.

With the creation of the Veche Republic in 1136, Novgorod expanded as a center of international commerce. As traders flocked to the town, residential areas arose and merchant estates, until then built in isolation, began to be connected by roads and pedestrian thoroughfares. It became commonplace at this time for wealthy residents to commission the construction of churches whose composition reflected the identity and social status of their patrons. The St. John the Baptist Church on Opoki (1127–1130), for example, was erected by a society of merchants who specialized in the production of wax and honey. A number of other onion-domed structures were built with commercial purposes in mind. Many churches on Yaroslav's Yard (*Iaroslavogo dvorishche*), the complex of historic monuments located on the town's "trade side," included capacious ground floors, allowing the buildings to function both as sacred spaces and storehouses for merchandise.

Following Novgorod's annexation by Muscovy in 1478, the city was developed as a military stronghold. In 1484–1490, restructuring work was carried out on the medieval kremlin complex, resulting in the addition of a number of features that characterize the fortress today: its red-brick facing, the wooden roofs on the towers, and the swallow-tail "teeth" that crown the kremlin walls. Muscovite princes and tsars commissioned further construction, including the Church of St. Nicholas the Martyr, which was built on the orders of Ivan IV in 1560. The buildings from this era reveal the influence of Muscovite tastes and preferences. The Cathedral of the Virgin of the Sign (1688), for example, contrasted sharply with buildings in the early Novgorodian tradition, most notably through its ornate decoration and grandiose proportions.

From the eighteenth century, Novgorod acquired the architectural trappings of civic life. The Travelers Palace (1771), Metropolitan Chambers (1770), and Public Offices (1778) were all built in the Petersburg style, while residential quarters of neoclassical buildings were erected on Great Palace Street, Great Moscow Street, and St. Nicholas Street, among others. A number of monumental gateways were added to the city walls at this time to control entry and direct exiting traffic to Moscow, St. Petersburg, and Pskov. Enhancements to civic life, which included the creation of parks, squares, and sculptural monuments, continued throughout the nineteenth century. One of the most notable additions to the local landscape at this time was the Millennium of Russia Monument (1862), a composition in the form of Monomakh's Cap that marked the thousand-year anniversary of the foundation of the Russian state.

Architectural developments in Pskov followed a somewhat different trajectory. Forming part of the Novgorod Republic until the mid-thirteenth century, Pskov was heavily influenced by the architectural traditions of its dominant north-western neighbor. One of the first churches to be built in the Pskov region, the Transfiguration of the Savior Cathedral (pre-1156), located within the Mirozhsk Monastery complex, thus echoed the Novgorodian structures of the same period in its Byzantine floor plan and graceful domed roof. After Pskov gained independence in 1348, local church architecture acquired more specific characteristics that came to be associated with the "Pskov School" of architectural construction: many of the ecclesiastical structures from this period were built from the regional flagstone and plastered with a textured whitewash solution that gave the buildings a recognizable "sculptural" form.

In 1461, the Pskov Republic, like its neighboring territories, was absorbed into the Muscovite sphere of influence. As the town was an important military stronghold within the medieval Russian state, emphasis was placed on its defensive architecture and in particular on the nucleus of local military life—the medieval citadel, or *krom*. Over subsequent decades defensive walls were added to the main fortress structure to protect the town from foreign incursions. These additions included Boris the Posadnik's walls (1309), the walls of the Middle Town (1375), and the walls of the Surrounding Town (1460s–1480s). In places of perceived vulnerability, fortress towers were constructed, among them the Middle Tower (1400–1417), the Kutekrom Tower (1400), and the Flat Tower (1500). At its most extensive, the fortress was reputed to have included a total of thirty-five towers, the large majority of which were removed or destroyed in the centuries that followed.

While functioning primarily as a military outpost, Pskov, like Novgorod, grew in prominence as a center of trade and commerce over the sixteenth and seventeenth centuries. This experience left its mark on the architectural landscape in the form of impressive stone mansions, commissioned by affluent local merchants. The most outstanding examples of this architectural tradition were the Pogankin, Menshikov, and Syrnikov Palaces (mid-17 c.), which reflected in their scale and composition the prestigious status of their merchant patrons. The mansions were typically formed of three stories: two lower ones, reserved for the storage of merchandise and animals, and a residential floor—including entrance hall, reception rooms, and sleeping quarters—heated by decoratively tiled enamel stoves.

Construction in Pskov continued throughout the eighteenth and nineteenth centuries, though, as in Novgorod, the architecture of this period was mostly

derivative of developments in the new northern capital. One important project, however, was the Cathedral of the Annunciation (1836), a neoclassical, sin-
gle-domed structure built inside the historic kremlin complex close to the iconic
Trinity Cathedral (1682–1699). The cathedral fell victim to the Stalinist anti-
religious campaigns of the 1930s when, following its exclusion from the category
of "architectural monuments," it was mined with dynamite and demolished. A
number of other churches from this era, such as the Church of the Assumption
of Our Lady from Polonishche (1810–1811) and the Church of the Nativity of the
Virgin (1833), escaped this fate—presumably as a result of their less prominent
locations in the city suburbs—and survived in radically adapted forms into the
post-Soviet period.

Compared to Novgorod and Pskov, Vologda was a younger city whose oldest
historical monuments dated from around the sixteenth century. It was at this time,
during the reign of Ivan IV, that Vologda became a major transit point for trade
and commerce between Moscow and Arkhangelsk, and strategic interest in the
region grew. Legend had it that the Russian tsar intended to make Vologda the
center of his secret police state, the Oprichnina, and the country's second capital,
and with that purpose in mind he commissioned the construction of an extensive
kremlin complex and the St. Sophia Cathedral (1568–1570). In 1571, however,
the construction work was brought abruptly to a halt, presumably in connection
with the tsar's decision to abolish the Oprichnina. Parts of the incomplete fortress
structure were later strengthened with wooden walls, which remained in place
until the nineteenth century, when they were disassembled by the city authorities
and used as construction materials by local residents.

A number of historic buildings nevertheless date from this period, including
the Savior Church (1537–1542) at the Savior of Priluki Monastery, one of the
oldest religious complexes in the Russian Northwest. Vologda witnessed its most
intensive period of church construction in the seventeenth and eighteenth centuries, however, when the Church of St. John the Baptist in Roshchen'e (1618), the
Cathedral of the Shroud on Kozlenskaia Street, (1713–1720), and the Church of
Demetrius of Priluki on Navolok (1618), among other notable structures, were
built. Still, Vologda's most valuable architectural monuments were undoubtedly
its wooden noble, merchant, and bourgeois mansions, products of the town's
vibrant trading life in the late Imperial period. A number of these buildings serve
as unique models of the "wooden Empire style": examples include the Zasetskii
House (1790s), a two-story decorative wooden mansion with a mezzanine floor;
the Levashov House (1829), complete with eight-columned ionic portico; and the

Volkhov House (early 19 c.), a classically proportioned mansion decorated with pilasters and architectural scrolls.

Soviet attitudes toward the preservation of Russia's historic architecture varied over time.[13] In the immediate postrevolutionary period, prominent figures such as Maxim Gorky, as head of the self-appointed Commission for Artistic Affairs, and Anatoly Lunacharsky, the new Commissar for Enlightenment, spoke out in favor of the preservation of Russia's prerevolutionary heritage, relating conservation to the new conditions of social equality in the Bolshevik state.[14] The association of heritage with late Imperial nationalism, however, made this position ideologically tenuous. Therefore early Soviet legislation focused on preventing iconoclasm and damage to historic buildings rather than celebrating and promoting the relics of the prerevolutionary past.[15] Conversely, emphasis was placed on creating new symbols of communist identity, as evidenced in the April 14, 1918, decree "On the Removal of Monuments Erected to Honor the Tsars and Their Servants and the Creation of Plans for Monuments of the Russian Socialist Revolution" and the famous "Plan of Monumental Propaganda," adopted later the same year, which proposed employing visual art—and specifically, a sculptural pantheon of the Revolution's heroes—as a means of propagating communist ideas.

During the Stalinist First Five Year Plan (1928–1932), the exigencies of forced industrialization and the ideological drive to create the "model socialist town" generated mass demolition of heritage objects, and particularly churches.[16] Among the high-profile demolitions to be enacted around this time were the destruction of the Church of the Annunciation in Leningrad (demolished to make way for a tramway line in 1929), the Alexander Nevsky Cathedral in Rostov-on-Don (demolished in 1930 and replaced with the Square of Soviets), and the Kazan Cathedral in Moscow (demolished in 1936 and replaced by a public toilet). The crash modernization of the church-studded Northwest likewise involved the "liquidation" of a number of inconvenient historical monuments. As noted above, late Imperial churches proved particularly vulnerable to the whims of "socialist planning": in Vologda, about a dozen churches were destroyed, among them the Athanasius of Alexandria Church (late 17 c.) and St. Nicholas Church on Haymarket Square (1713–1777), both of which were removed to create the town's new Soviet centerpiece, Revolution Square.[17]

The wartime destruction of the Northwest had the effect of infusing local heritage objects with new cultural significance. Most influential in determining the region's primacy in postwar preservation was the November 1945 declaration "On Measures to Reconstruct the Towns of the USSR Destroyed by the Nazi Invaders" and the May 22, 1947, decree of the Council of Ministers of the RSFSR "On the Preservation of Architectural Monuments." The latter made explicit reference to "Old Russian" architecture as a category worthy of preservation, effectively securing the fate of the historic region.[18] The August 30, 1960, resolution of the Council of Ministers of the RSFSR "On the Further Improvement of Work for the Preservation of Cultural Monuments in the RSFSR" instigated the creation of the first lists of federally protected monuments. In line with the 1947 decree, local authorities placed emphasis on medieval Russian architecture while excluding later Imperial buildings, such as Vologda's nineteenth-century wooden estates, from the privileged canon of "heritage."

As a number of critics have noted, the Khrushchev regime marked a particularly difficult period in the history of Soviet preservation.[19] With the shift in governmental priorities from postwar recovery to urban growth, and the revival of the war against religion, the cause of conservation ceased to be a focus of cultural politics. The budget for historical restoration shrank steadily from the end of the 1950s and was cut drastically in 1962 to 50 percent of the level of funding allocated in previous years.[20] The result was the exclusion of historical buildings from lists of architectural monuments, with the brunt of this change being borne by the heritage of the late Imperial period. Buildings removed from the list of protected monuments in Novgorod at this time included the White Corpus in St. Anthony's Monastery (18–19 c.), the Western Corpus and Orlov Corpus in St. George's Monastery (19 c.), and the former monastery hospital (19 c.).[21] While some notion of the inviolability of heritage persisted in these years, preservationist voices nevertheless tended to be drowned out in a celebratory discourse of transformative modernization.[22]

The mid-1960s marked a turning point in official attitudes toward cultural heritage. The formation in 1965 of the All-Russian Society for the Preservation of Historical and Cultural Monuments (VOOPIiK) transformed the preservation of heritage from a discrete concern of an outspoken cultural elite into a mainstream activity in which Soviet citizens could—and, indeed, were expected to—participate. The decree "On the Conditions and Means for Improving Historical and Cultural Monuments of the RSFSR," which followed in May 1966, advanced the most comprehensive package of legislation pertaining to the preservation of monuments since the Declaration and Instructions of 1948 and 1949. The remaining decades of Soviet rule were consequently characterized by a more sympathetic approach to preservation. While preservationist critics launched far-reaching criticisms of VOOPIiK's shortcomings in the 1980s,[23] architectural heritage would never again be subjected to systematic violence and denigration as it had in the Stalin and late Khrushchev eras.

Official endorsement of preservationist arguments has been linked by some scholars to the rise of Russian ethno-nationalism and the existence of a so-called "Russian Party" (*Russkaia partiia*) within the late Soviet government.[24] The view from the regions, however, reveals a more nuanced picture of preservation as a field of activity in which actors from all walks of cultural life and political backgrounds were involved. While the ranks of regional preservationists contained some conservative and even chauvinistic elements (particularly in the later years of Soviet rule), enthusiasts of local heritage were more likely to express views that were anti-Soviet or anti-communist in nature. Indeed, heritage preservation, if anything, constituted a unifying force for the late Soviet intelligentsia. Defending the country's architectural and cultural traditions provided a means of asserting difference from the political center and crafting alternative social identities in the late socialist era.[25]

Region, Province, Periphery

The Russian vocabulary of territory is notoriously slippery. *Oblast'*, *okrug*, and *krai*, official administrative subdivisions of the Russian Federation, tend to disappear in the cracks between the terms "province," "region," and "district" upon crossing the linguistic border into English. The reasons for this definitional blurring are historically rooted. The territorial restructuring that followed the two revolutions of the Soviet twentieth century caused the country to fragment and recoalesce in different administrative forms. Terms that had once held authority were replaced by overlapping but subtly distinct territorial concepts. While not attempting to sketch the landscape of Russian regionalism in its complicated entirety, this introduction thus includes a definition of key concepts that will inform the discussion in later chapters.

Oblasts are the most relevant administrative subdivisions to this study of Russian regionalism and form the layer of government above district or municipal authorities that is referred to throughout this work as "regional." Oblasts were the main subnational units of the Soviet Socialist Republics and form one of the six constituent entities or federal subjects that comprise the Russian Federation today. It is worth clarifying in this context the difference between oblasts and republics, which might helpfully be compared to the English-language territorial categories of "regions" and "countries." While oblasts are arbitrarily defined territories whose largest demographic constituent is ethnic Russians (the Novgorod, Pskov, and Vologda oblasts, for example), republics are areas of predominantly non-Russian ethnicity and distinct national entities (the Chuvash or Sakha republics, for example).

Okrugs and krais do not feature prominently in this study, though the latter have nominative relevance to the discipline of *kraevedenie*, discussed in detail in chapter 2. Okrugs were subnational entities in the tsarist period that were phased out during the Soviet administrative reforms of the 1920s and 1930s. A new category of national okrugs (from 1977 autonomous okrugs) was introduced in the Stalin era to provide relative autonomy to indigenous peoples in the Russian North. Krais were likewise imperial constructs that survived as administrative anachronisms in the Soviet Union. Historically, krais were large territories along the edge of Russia (hence the word *krai*, meaning "edge" or "border"). The relevance of the category to the field of Soviet local study is indirect. Krai in this context has the broader meaning of "region" or "territory" as opposed to the historical association of "edgeland."[26]

The more abstract concepts of periphery and province, along with their specific Russian-language connotations, also warrant clarification. As Stephen Lovell points out, *periferiia* had particular political associations in the Soviet period. The term was Sovietspeak, "designed to avoid the undesirable connotations of conquest, subjugation, and benightedness that were present in words like 'provinces' and 'colonies,' but at the same time [leaving] little doubt that outlying regions were subservient to the designs of the state and had some catching up to do."[27] Edith Clowes notes that center and periphery remain the leading metaphors with which post-Soviet Russia defines itself and is defined by others. The Russian periphery is not always "a politically disenfranchised, impoverished 'outback,'" however.[28] As Clowes reminds us, peripheries have become a source of creative renewal and innovation for Russian thinkers and artists in the twenty-first century, from the Eurasianism of Aleksandr Dugin to the literary art of Liudmila Ulitskaia.[29]

Provinces, by contrast, can be understood in neutral terms, as Catherine Evtuhov suggests in her study of Nizhnii Novgorod, as territorial entities that are *not* the capital. As Evtuhov explains:

> *Provintsiia*, in Russian as in English, denotes the opposite of "capital" or "center." "Province" can thus refer to every space that is not one of the two capital cities, St. Petersburg and Moscow (although . . . even those cities can potentially contain "provincial" aspects).[30]

This understanding is useful given the value judgments involved in the other usage of provincialism to mean a condition or state opposed to urbanity, sophistication, and worldliness. An important caveat should be added here: what is now considered a province may not have been one previously. If province is defined as a non-capital region, then Venice can be seen as a modern-day province with a capital's cultural heritage. This point has particular relevance for many Russian provinces—such as Kazan and Novgorod—that were pre-Muscovite centers of politics and culture.

What, then, is the value of studying regions, peripheries, and provinces? What new perspectives can the "view from below" provide on the traditional questions asked by scholars of nationalism? In many ways, this is the wrong question to ask since studies of nations are already regional studies with greater degrees of abstraction. The historian of the nation sifts through and condenses regional detail in the process of crafting a national narrative. Such work is important given the current primacy placed on the nation-state as the foremost political entity in international relations. Regional studies therefore provide the means necessary to make broader claims about processes and developments relevant to the national experience. This is the approach endorsed by Evtuhov, who states that "the [Russian] province needs to be studied not for its own sake (the pursuit of kraevedenie or local history) but as an integral and indispensable part of a larger historical narrative."[31]

If we move from history to anthropology and sociology, the need to speak to the national experience becomes less urgent. From these disciplinary perspectives the study of regions is valuable not just as a means of constructing the national experience, but in its own right as a means of understanding a specific configuration of political, social, and cultural conditions. Here the scholarly impetus moves in the opposite direction, away from the nationally generalizable and politically productive to the culturally specific and experientially exceptional. This more discrete focus can allow for degrees of abstraction beyond the nation to the transnational or, more broadly, the human experience. The study of regions thus becomes a means to understand social networks, institutions, and experiences in less obvious places than the nation-state.[32]

The study of peripheries has attracted considerable attention from postcolonial scholars, who, drawing on the work of Homi Bhabha, among others, have focused on the "marginal" or "silenced" voices excluded from existing historical narratives.[33] In recent years, the most prominent proponent of these ideas has been the oral historian of Soviet and Russian identities Svetlana Alexievich, who in her 2015 Nobel Lecture described herself as a "human ear" taking in the unheard stories of the Soviet experience.[34] In fact, social historians of Russia have been engaged in the excavation of Soviet identities for several decades. Beginning with the "revisionist" movement of the 1970s and 1980s, scholars rejected the idea of a single totalitarian experience and set about excavating Soviet society's embedded subjectivities.[35] The result was a wealth of criticism focusing on social, ethnic, and gendered "de-centered" experiences. This scholarship informs the approach of this book, one of the central objectives of which is to represent and integrate local voices and experiences that have traditionally been excluded from Russian studies.

Constructing the Russian Regions

Scholars and critics have taken a selective view of Russian regionalism. As Evtuhov has pointed out, the American literature of recent decades has tended to fixate on borderlands, peripheries, and non-Russian nationalities, revealing something like an "obsession . . . with the problems of empire."[36] By contrast, the Russian-language discipline of kraevedenie has distanced itself from theory—an understandable reaction to decades of ideologization under Soviet rule—resulting in what Denis Kozlov has called a "factographic" approach to historical knowledge.[37] The result has been something of a disconnect between the wealth of locally produced detail and the selective, theoretically informed representation of this detail in English-language scholarship. As Susan Smith-Peter has put it, in the West we see "theory without the local," while in Russia we see "the local without theory."[38]

This book is not primarily concerned with the questions of colonialism that have traditionally preoccupied scholars of the non-Russian regions. Nor is it interested in studying the provincial experience for its own sake. Its aim is rather to explore regional subjectivities in noncosmopolitan Russia in order to enhance our current understanding of Russian identities. As such, it is closely aligned with a number of recent socio-anthropological studies—Serguei Oushakine's *Patriotism of Despair*, Catriona Kelly and Mark Bassin's *Soviet and Post-Soviet Identities*, and Hilary Pilkington et al.'s *Punk in Russia*, for example—which have explored Russian identities away from the capitals.[39] Like the authors of this scholarship, I argue that there is value in studying the Russian experience outside of Moscow and St. Petersburg. I maintain, as they do, that the view from the noncosmopolitan

Russian provinces revises and renews our understanding of identities in Russia, past and present.

Recent work has successfully refuted the notion that the Russian provinces were places of cultural stagnation and administrative sclerosis, asserting in its place a reality of multiple circulations of ideas and knowledge. As Evtuhov explains in the introduction to *Portrait of a Province*, the intellectual history of Nizhnii Novgorod "points at once to a *different chronology* as well as to the existence of a provincial intelligentsia whose passionate engagement with things local provides a *significant counterpoint* to the apparent progression of Russian thought over the nineteenth century."[40] Studying the provinces offers a means of challenging established notions of Russia's intellectual evolution through the careful documentation of the genesis, flow and reception of ideas.

Historians and critics of Soviet Russia have also begun to challenge the established understanding of regional culture as an inferior copy of intellectual life in the capitals. Mark Lipovetsky's work on perestroika-era Sverdlovsk thus reverses the capital-province dichotomy to reveal the Urals region as a cradle of "cultural revolution" and artistic innovation in the 1990s.[41] Likewise, in his online project *Far From Moscow*, David MacFadyen has illustrated the unexpected flow of musical influence from periphery to center through the meticulous analysis of online data pertaining to music streaming and production across Eastern Europe.[42] This work fundamentally challenges established thinking about Russian and Soviet culture, revealing the existence of new directions of cultural flow and networks of influence.

This book complements these studies while also engaging with another dynamic area of academic debate: the scholarship dedicated to Russian nationalism and its evolution over the Soviet twentieth century. In recent years, this criticism has focused on the relationship between the forms of transnational but Russified "official" patriotism promoted by the Stalinist state and the ethnic Russian nationalism that emerged during the last decades of Soviet rule.[43] The 1930s and 1940s have been interpreted as years of "Russo-centric etatism," when the Stalinist regime drew strategically on the power of ethnic nationalism in order to strengthen social solidarity during the difficult years of war and postwar reconstruction.[44] The 1960s to 1980s, moreover, have been understood as an era of "inclusionary politics" when the Brezhnev government co-opted the arguments of an emergent nationalist elite in order to enforce stability in the ailing communist state.[45]

The scholarship of these developments has, quite understandably, focused on political and cultural elites in Moscow—that is, the agents responsible for "imagining" the Soviet and Russian "nations." Emphasis has consequently been placed on the discursive dimension of Soviet-Russian nationhood, or, to put it another way, the stories told by elites about the communities they claim to represent. What has been left out of this explanation, however, is the matter of how these nation-imagining discourses were disseminated around the country, how they were received and—to use Alon Confino's term—"internalized" by the Russian people.[46] This is the additional dimension that this study of the Russian regions can add to the discussion. By offering the view from below, regional narratives can reveal the reach, relevance, and impact of debates about national identity throughout Russia.

Patriotism, Nationalism, Ethnocentrism

In this context, the preference in this book for the term "patriotism" over "nationalism," "ethnocentrism," or a number of other vexed signifiers in circulation in the literature on Russian identities deserves further comment. "Patriotism" and "nationalism" have quite distinct associations for the American and British English-language reader. While historically interchangeable as terms denoting a general love for one's country, "nationalism" acquired an exclusionary aspect in the nineteenth century, that of exalting one nation above all others and promoting its culture and interests to the detriment of other nations or groups. "Nationalism," etymologists note, is thus often modified by specific movements, particularly those of an aggressively political persuasion (white nationalism, British nationalism, etc.), while "patriotism" has tended to be employed more frequently in conjunction with perceived civic virtues, such as bravery, valor, duty, and devotion.[47] The distinction is an important one for the current study. While Russian chauvinistic tendencies emerged around heritage politics in the Soviet and post-Soviet periods, other more socially affirmative consequences of preservation for local and national communities are the focus here—namely, familiarity with one's history and culture, appreciation for art and architecture, and a sense of identity and respect for the cultural environment. Patriotism, and local patriotism in particular, is not automatically dismissed as a senseless or risible phenomenon but is examined seriously as a valid search for self in an unstable and, frequently, unpredictable socio-political context.

The terms *patriotizm* and *patrioty* have a separate set of political associations in the Soviet and post-Soviet Russian-language contexts. Condemned in the post-revolutionary era as "an extremely reactionary ideology, the task of which is to justify imperialist bestiality and deaden the proletariat's class consciousness,"[48] Soviet patriotism was rehabilitated in the 1930s as a central tenet of the Stalinist state's mobilization ideology.[49] Recognizing the limited appeal of Marxist-Leninist theory for a marginally educated citizenry, the Stalinist regime, David Brandenberger argues, attempted "to foster a maximally accessible, populist sense of Soviet social identity through the instrumental use of russocentric appeals."[50] The notions of a proletarian "Motherland" (*Rodina*) and "Fatherland" (*Otechestvo*), previously dismissed by Leninist internationalists as ideological heresy, formed core components in this campaign to raise Soviet patriotic consciousness. As *Pravda* editorialized in 1935: "Soviet patriotism is a burning feeling of boundless love, a selfless devotion to one's motherland and a profound responsibility for her fate and defense, which issues forth like mighty spring waters from the depths of our people."[51]

The Stalinist notion of "Soviet patriotism," Ronald Grigor Suny notes, "attempted not to descend into ethno-nationalism, yet the lines between patriotism and nationalism were not merely blurred but impossible to draw."[52] The peculiar amalgamation of Soviet and Russian identities that informed Stalinist nation-building became even more marked during wartime, when historians began to mine Russian history for inspirational material that would spur the Soviet people forward in their struggle against Nazism.[53] The Soviet "nation" was instructed at this time to take pride in the "valiant example of our ancestors," a pantheon of ethnic Russian defenders of the Fatherland that included Alexander Nevsky, Dmitrii Donskoi, and Mikhail Kutuzov. "Old Russian" architecture was likewise held up as Soviet (rather than Slavic) heritage and its destruction at the hands of the German occupiers as an insult to national pride. After 1943, this "supranational but Russified patriotism" gave way to a more extreme nationalistic line on the Russian people's ethnic primacy within Soviet society.[54] This was revealed, most famously, by Stalin's May 1945 toast to the Russian people as the "first among equals" of nations forming the Soviet Union.

The death of Stalin in 1953, and the ascent to power of the neo-Leninist Khrushchev, brought the notion of "Soviet patriotism" under renewed scrutiny. Like Stalin, Khrushchev employed patriotic narratives pragmatically, as a means to strengthen social solidarity and allegiance to the Communist Party in the USSR at a time of political restructuring and destabilization.[55] Rather than drawing on the symbols of Russian national identity, many of which were in any case compromised through their association with Stalin and his cult of personality, Khrushchev reached back to recent history—the achievements and triumphs of the first half of the socialist twentieth century. The Revolution and World War II replaced the Battles of Borodino and Kulikovo as the central sites of Soviet memory, and proletarian heroes were substituted for the nation-building tsars as the idols of national history.[56]

In contrast with Stalinist state patriotism, Khrushchev's patriotic politics were remarkably decentered. Rather than limiting patriotic discourse to a centrally determined canon of myths and heroes, local elites were empowered to craft their own narratives of Soviet identity. The rehabilitated discipline of "local studies" (*kraevedenie*) was an important vehicle in this process.[57] Following the revival of several *kraevedcheskie* publications in 1956, the movement grew throughout the 1960s to form a developed institutional infrastructure for the production of local knowledge. Within the forums provided by the movement, local populations were encouraged to turn inward to examine the particular role their locality had played in national events and to celebrate their local heroes and heroines. This process was instrumental in the formation of Soviet patriotic consciousness, which, from the mid-1950s onward, derived form and content from both local and national sources.[58]

The relationship between Brezhnev-era Soviet patriotism and the Russian ethno-nationalism that emerged in intelligentsia circles in the last decades of Soviet power has been vigorously debated by scholars of Russian nationalism.[59] According to the literature of the "Russian revival," the Brezhnev regime co-opted the claims of Russian nationalists concerning the preservation of patrimony and traditions in a bid to win favor for its policies of revitalizing Soviet agriculture and strengthening the country's military-industrial base.[60] Nikolai Mitrokhin argues that the strategic inclusion of nationalist arguments within the realm of permissible criticism resulted in the coalescence of the nationalist movement, which by the 1970s had organized itself into a "Russian Party" with institutional representation in a variety of political and cultural spheres.[61] Marlène Laruelle perceives the roots of the post-Soviet Russian far right in the politics of this era. Denouncing not only censorship and the failures of cultural preservation, nationalist criticism hardened and radicalized, she argues, incorporating conspiratorial theories of foreign plots against the USSR and propagating a view of the Russian people as victims of the Soviet experiment.[62]

The story of Russian nationalism's victory over Soviet patriotism has proved compelling, particularly for those detractors of communism who have seen in it evidence of the irremediable structural dysfunctions of the Soviet project. It should be noted, however, that the nationalists' "politics of culture" failed to move beyond intelligentsia circles in the late Soviet period, and, with the reemergence of civil society under Gorbachev, failed to resonate in the context of mass politics.[63] Indeed, the appeal of Russian chauvinist claims about the preservation of cultural heritage, voiced by civic associations such as "Motherland," "Memory," and the "Russian Club" in the 1980s, was limited in the Russian regions, where Soviet patriotic narratives of wartime resistance and postwar reconstruction continued to have potency.[64] Extreme nationalism, or "fascism," as it came to be labeled in the 1990s, remained marginal to political life even after the collapse of communism. By contrast, pride in the achievements of socialism and the sacrifices of war continued to inform Russians' sense of collective identity, demonstrating the successes of Soviet nation-builders in forging affective links between members of the multi-ethnic state.[65]

The implementation of violent and destabilizing political and economic reforms in the 1990s nevertheless divided the Russian political elite. National-patriotic thinking fragmented and coalesced into new forms at this time, surfacing in the xenophobic arguments of Vladimir Zhirinovsky's Liberal Democratic Party of Russia, the neo-imperialist esotericism of Aleksandr Prokhanov's political activism, and the Great Russian chauvinism of Eduard Limonov and Aleksandr Dugin's Nationalist Bolshevik Party, among other movements.[66] The ideological polarization of these years, and the political instability that resulted, gave rise to what Laruelle has called the "patriotic centrism" of the Putin era.[67] Following in the Soviet tradition, Putin monopolized the discourse on the nation, espousing a vocabulary of "Great Power" (*velikoderzhavnost'*) and "statehood" (*gosudarstvennost'*) in an effort to boost popular affiliation with the political regime.[68] The hyper-militarized, anti-Western patriotic discourse that characterized Putinist politics in the twenty-first century proved remarkably effective as a form of mobilizational propaganda: from the annexation of Crimea in 2014 to the retributive expulsion of British diplomats from Russia in 2018, patriotic posturing created spikes in popularity for the Russian president, distracting from compromising economic and social conditions at moments of strategic necessity.

Putinist state patriotism carefully distinguished itself from Russian nationalism in an effort to draw support from all parts of the multi-ethnic, multilingual Russian Federation. The introduction to the program for the "Patriotic Education of Russia's Citizens, 2001–2005," the first phase in an official campaign to boost recruitment to and the reputation of the Russian Army, thus bemoaned the deterioration of Russian society's patriotic consciousness and the rise of unhealthy Russian "nationalism."[69] Indeed, the militarized patriotism of the Putin era, rooted in the cultural memory of World War II, resembled more closely the state patriotism of the Brezhnev era than the rabid ethno-nationalism at the margins of political life in twenty-first century Russia.[70] While utilizing contemporary media—Internet forums rather than pioneer meetings—the values promoted in this patriotic work remained unchanged: a defensive love for the Motherland; respect for the Russian military; and hostility to Western interference in Russia's sphere of geopolitical influence.

This book's focus on "patriotism" is thus aimed not so much at the Russian ethno-nationalist ideas that emerged in connection with cultural preservation in the twentieth and twenty-first centuries, but rather at Soviet and post-Soviet identity politics and their consequences for local communities. Indeed, the former has already received sufficient attention in the extant scholarship, with the result that heritage preservation is now broadly understood as a realm of ethno-national mobilization in the late Soviet era.[71] In contrast to scholarship with an ethno-nationalist focus, this study centers on the ways that Russian architectural heritage was exploited in the official campaign to raise patriotic consciousness among the Soviet population after the war and how it was made to work for socialist ends and signify socialist values. In addition, the book's focus on the implementation of a Soviet patriotic agenda in the Russian regions allows another, lesser-known part of the story of Soviet preservation to be told: that of the state-sponsored affirmation and evolution of local patriotic consciousness, its relationship of coexistence and conflict with other forms of Soviet and Russian identity.

Methods and Sources

The structure of this book reflects its fundamentally interdisciplinary approach to the themes of identity politics and historical memory. Following the social historian Raphael Samuel, this approach defines history as "a social form of knowledge" created by a multitude of different actors in a variety of cultural spheres.[72] According to this view, historical narratives emanate from public institutions and compete for dominance in the field of public representations of the past. Yet, knowledge of the past is also produced in the course of everyday life, through a "common sense of the past" generated and perpetuated in oral narrative and social ritual.[73] This book strives to reflect this reality by engaging not only with the authoritative voices of archives, but also with local voices, documented in letters and memoirs and recorded in oral testimony. These voices are positioned as mutually clarifying frames of reference.

The first three chapters of this book draw primarily on local archival sources and Russian-language reference materials to explore the questions of architectural preservation and heritage tourism in the Russian Northwest in the first four decades after the war (1945–1985). Approaching these topics through the local archives allows a privileged view of the practicalities of implementing preservationist policy on the ground. While central policy is extremely well documented in existing Russian-language guides, less is known about the institutional and cultural implications of state-sponsored preservation for local communities. What this book's approach brings to the fore, then, are local voices: the voices of regional officials who attempted, at different moments, to fulfill or resist the exacting requirements of central preservationist policy; those of the local preservationist community, including members of restoration workshops and museum-reserves, who battled with the regional authorities to implement their visions of architectural preservation; and those of local residents, who, exploiting the participatory politics of the post-Stalin era, expressed their approval or condemnation of preservationist decisions in letters, commentaries, and complaints. From these voices a lesser-known story of Soviet preservation emerges: it appears not as the exclusive domain of Russian chauvinism, as some studies have suggested, but as a space in which different identities and patriotisms competed and collided.

Another valuable source in the first half of the book comprises the published architectural and tourist guides to the towns. Many of these detailed references to the region's historic architecture were written by members of the local restoration workshops and informed by different politico-cultural agendas. On the one hand, they reflected the preservationist preoccupations of those working in the restoration sphere in the postwar period; on the other, their presentation of the relationship between historic architecture and modern socialist construction was dictated by the shifting political priorities of the time. The opinions expressed by the restorer-authors of these guides in connection with preservationist shortcomings and planning mistakes in the historic region reveal the parameters of permissible criticism at different moments in the postwar period. The guides thus have value not only as the preservationist philosophies of some of the most important figures in local cultural life but also as records of the internal politics of the local cultural sector.

In its focus on preservationist debates and conflicts, the first half of the book contributes to a growing body of literature that has mined local and central archives to document the contested processes of postwar reconstruction of the country's most important urban centers. Karl Qualls's study of Sevastopol, for example, has detailed the competing visions for restoration in the historic region after the war, tracing the complicated negotiations between the Soviet planners at the center and periphery, on the one hand, and the preferences of local civic movements and residents, on the other.[74] In his study of reconstruction in postwar Leningrad, Steven Maddox has adopted a similar approach, drawing on a wealth of archival sources to explain the motivational ideology behind the late Stalinist campaign to rebuild the tsarist capital.[75] These studies demonstrate the value of archives in tracing policy development and implementation in the sphere of architectural preservation. Their meticulous analyses of the minutes of planning meetings and preservationist assemblies successfully highlight the competing agendas for preservation in historic Soviet towns, along with the ways that these agendas changed in line with the political exigencies of the postwar period.

While it shares an interest in many of these same questions, this book is not a complementary history of preservationist policy in the northwest region. It is rather a study that privileges local voices over elite debates and political wrangling in an effort to understand the human consequences of architectural reconstruction. In this sense it is closely aligned with Lisa Kirschenbaum's and Catriona Kelly's studies of preservation and local identities in Leningrad/St. Petersburg.[76] These scholars have adopted an interdisciplinary approach to their subjects, combining archival explorations of heritage policy with socio-anthropological and oral history work to place architectural preservation within a broader "landscape of [local] memory."[77] Kelly's pioneering use of oral evidence, on which she draws to add detail and depth to the Soviet boilerplate so often encountered in the archives, has particular relevance for the current study. Like Kelly's work, this book places value on oral testimony and participant observation work as a means of accessing the lived experience of Soviet politics and culture that resides outside of the archive in collective memory.

In the course of researching this book, I lived for a year and a half in the Russian Northwest, sharing accommodation with local residents, some of whom became close friends and colleagues. In each of the three towns, I lived in a Khrushchev-era flat in the city's residential periphery and traveled every day by bus or on foot past the towns' many impressive architectural monuments to the historic centers where I conducted my research in archives and libraries. On weekends, I often accompanied the families with whom I was staying on excursions to local monasteries or historic estates, crowding in with other tourists and listening to improbably knowledgeable tour guides explain the origins and intricacies of various buildings. I also took enthusiastic part in local festivals and celebrations, watching historic reconstructions, participating in folk craft workshops, and wandering through historic centers that came alive on these occasions with color, noise, and movement.

During this time, I had many formal and informal conversations about preservationist matters with people from all walks of local cultural life. A number of these interactions were facilitated by the landladies (*khoziaiki*) of the rooms that I rented in the towns. In Pskov and Vologda, these women organized meetings with teachers, tractor drivers, politicians, hairdressers, soldiers, and scientists in a bid to further my research.[78] The interviews that I conducted took place around heaving dining tables, in noisy cafés, during walks with grandchildren, and even in churches. From these discussions, a varied and at times surprising picture of local preservationist opinion emerged. It is from this personal archive that I draw to discuss the impact of preservationist politics on local patriotic consciousness in the second half of the book.

Oral history and socio-anthropological methods afford privileged access to local communities, allowing us to ask a different set of questions about preservation, patriotism, and identity. These include, but are by no means limited to, the following: How did residents react to official efforts to market their regions' architecture as the symbols of national identity? How did they feel about their towns being turned into tourist attractions and the mediated subjects of patriotic self-admiration? What strategies emerged among local communities to retain ownership over heritage objects in response to their cultural appropriation by the political center? And how did perceptions of local identity and center-region relations change with shifts in preservationist politics after the collapse of socialism? In addressing these questions, the book shifts attention away from political ideology toward the formation of social identities, linking with the research carried out by scholars of Soviet subjectivities.[79] As such, it gives insight into not only the motivations and actions of Soviet policymakers in the sphere of preservation but also the ways in which these policies informed a sense of local and national selfhood, both in the Soviet past and in Russia today.

Outline of the Book

The book has two parts that pivot on the collapse of Soviet power in 1991. The chapters that comprise these two parts employ a range of disciplinary approaches in an attempt to understand not just the official discourses of cultural identity projected onto the localities of the Northwest but also the ways in which these discourses were internalized, revised, and resisted by the communities living in the region. The discussion of postwar heritage politics in Part 1 draws primarily on archival materials but foregrounds the lived experience of communities in the historic towns through personal correspondence and public commentary. Part 2 draws more directly on the methods of social anthropology, incorporating participant observation work and oral history research to explore the social legacy of heritage debates in twenty-first-century Russia.

Part 1 examines the ways in which the heritage of the Northwest was exploited for political ends in the postwar Soviet Union. Chapter 1 focuses on the postwar reconstruction of the formerly occupied territories of Novgorod and Pskov and the debates about heritage preservation that emerged in the first decade after 1945. The reconstructionist agenda of the late Stalin regime emerges here as part of the state-sponsored drive to "forget" the experience of Nazi occupation and to assert a Soviet patriotic "myth of war" in its place. Particular attention is paid in this chapter to debates between central and local actors about the composition of the postwar heritage landscape. Localist agendas that were seen to privilege particularistic narratives of the past were regarded with suspicion at this time, and the actors who advocated them were vulnerable to political repression.

Chapter 2 addresses the role of cultural heritage in the drive to strengthen social solidarity and national unity in the ideologically unstable era of de-Stalinization. During the second, reconstitutive phase of de-Stalinization after 1961, the heritage of the Northwest played a strategic role in "imagining" the post-Stalin Soviet nation, a community founded on the political principles of socialist democracy, collectivism, and internationalism. The chapter shows how the creation of a touristic infrastructure in the region served as a means of exhibiting the heritage of the Northwest to the Soviet people. A key component in this enterprise is the body of touristic and kraevedenie materials focusing on the region's historic architecture: these texts reinforced a politically correct understanding of heritage as an integral part of Soviet modernity.

Chapter 3 shifts the focus to regional folk heritage, with a particular emphasis on developments in Vologda in the 1960s to 1980s. It presents the strategic affirmation of folk culture in the region through the lens of the Brezhnev-era "Russian revival," the emergence of a Russian patriotic intelligentsia in the mid-1960s with a particular interest in the fate of Russian rural traditions. The state-sponsored promotion of folk heritage, which included the creation of museums of folk architecture in Novgorod and Vologda, is understood as an expression of Brezhnev-era "inclusionary politics," a strategy to contain rising ethno-nationalism through the strategic promotion of Russian themes. The chapter explores how this policy led to the promotion of an aestheticized vision of northwestern folk culture as the epitome of the "national style."

Part 2 deals with the restructuring of heritage politics after socialism and the social legacy of heritage debates in the twenty-first century regions. Chapter 4 draws on newspaper publications, radio and television broadcasts, and legal documents to explore local heritage politics during the economic and cultural liberalization of the Yeltsin years. Public debates at this time reveal a bitter struggle for control over heritage between local cultural elites and new actors of influence in post-Soviet society, from clergymen to supermarket barons. The partial privatization of the heritage economy, which resulted in the commodification of many historic buildings as sites of elite entertainment and recreation, struck a particularly dissonant chord with local preservationists. The criticisms advanced by these lobbies with regard to developments in the heritage sphere reveal a profound sense of displacement and disillusion with the conditions of postsocialist life.

The role of heritage objects as props in the performance of national identity is the focus of Chapter 5, which draws on participant observation work at local festivals and commemorative ceremonies to expose the way heritage objects have been incorporated into new rituals and traditions in the Putin era. These cultural practices reflect an increasingly chauvinistic understanding of the local and national self. The chapter details in particular the initiative led by the ultranationalist critic and writer Aleksandr Prokhanov to establish a new historic monument in Pskov as a focus of nationalistic reflection and performance after the annexation of Crimea. The project is understood as an elite-driven attempt to perform national identity on the local stage, reinforcing traditional associations of the region with ideas of sacredness and self-sacrifice.

Chapter 6 draws on oral testimony and participant observation work conducted in the 2000s and 2010s to explore how Soviet and Russian patriotic discourses rooted in the heritage landscape were internalized by communities living in the historic towns. It focuses on the different oral modes employed by residents to speak about local heritage: the routinized discourse of kraevedenie lectures and touristic excursions and the more intimate language associated with memories of childhood, family festivities, and domestic traditions. The chapter examines the human consequences of the shifts in heritage politics that followed the collapse of communist rule. According to its findings, the experience of living among architectural monuments gave rise to proprietorial feelings about heritage, provoking a range of emotions, from pride to frustration, and even melancholy in connection with the contemporary fate of these buildings.

The historic buildings of the Russian Northwest have been referred to as "stone chronicles," the pages of which bear the imprint of past events.[80] This metaphor gestures at an important characteristic of this heritage: its status as a cultural construct, a set of objects whose meaning has been negotiated by a range of different actors. The region's historic buildings were not always the symbols of Russian strength and spirituality. In the postwar years, they became signifiers of Soviet resilience in the face of foreign aggression and postwar renewal, rising like phoenixes from the ashes of total war. Later they were conceptualized as "architectural monuments," evidence of the cultural genius and democratic spirit of the Soviet nation. After communism the meanings attributed to local architecture proliferated. This book traces the shifting discursive parameters of this heritage, revealing the ways in which the region's "stone chronicles" were written, rewritten, and read over time.

Part 1

THE NORTHWEST IN
THE SOVIET IMAGINATION

1.

PHOENIXES FROM THE ASHES

Postwar Reconstruction as a Patriotic Duty

The occupation and recapture of the Russian Northwest during World War II resulted in the catastrophic devastation of the region's architectural landscape. The iconic onion domes crowning Orthodox churches and cathedrals were punctured by bombing and stripped of their gold leaf, thick medieval walls were pitted by gunfire, and, in some cases, entire monastery complexes were reduced to ashes and rubble. On returning to the region after the war, Soviet officials and restorers were consequently confronted with a difficult decision. At a time of grave political and economic crisis, when residents all over the Soviet Union were in dire need of housing, food, and warmth, could the restoration of old buildings be justified? And, if so, what was to be built in place of the churches and monasteries that had been destroyed? New monuments to the victorious communist regime? Pastiches of old buildings? Or, most expensive and time-consuming of all, scientific reconstructions of the Orthodox architecture that had for centuries defined the historic region?

The Northwest was not alone in facing the dilemmas of postwar reconstruction. The first decades after 1945 saw politicians across Europe debate the merits of heritage objects and their place on the historic landscape. Political authorities in "liberated" Poland thus upheld the need to "de-Germanize" city silhouettes, removing "foreign" structures and foregrounding the relics of alternative Polish, Baltic, or Dutch pasts.[1] The delicate question of heritage preservation in postwar Germany provoked a variety of responses, from modernization in the West to the preservation of historic ruins in the more conservative South.[2] Within the Soviet Union itself strategies of reconstruction varied considerably: the Belarusian capital of Minsk, where wartime bombing had destroyed 70 percent of the housing stock and 80 percent of the urban infrastructure, was rebuilt as an entirely new city, with little acknowledgment of the former structure and architectural content of the prewar town.[3] War-ravaged Sevastopol, by contrast, became a high-profile urban reconstruction project. As Karl Qualls has shown, the political center wished to transform the city into an open-air museum of military victory, though this vision was resisted and reshaped by local architects and officials.[4]

The formerly occupied territories of Novgorod and Pskov, however, presented a special case. During the late Stalinist era of Russocentric Soviet patriotism, the reconstruction of the historic region became a flagship project to bolster social solidarity and national unity within the war-ravaged communist state.[5] Despite the financial exigencies of reconstruction, local restoration workshops were established as soon as the war was over. The workshops were tasked with rebuilding the towns and restoring them to their former architectural glory. Historic monuments, rising from the ashes of conflict, were to constitute symbols of popular defiance against the perceived intentions of the Nazis to destroy all traces of Slavic culture. The Northwest was to form a focus of postwar patriotism that exhibited both the primacy of Russian culture and traditions and the resilience and heroism of the postwar Soviet state.

Heritage under Enemy Occupation

The specificities of postwar reconstruction must be seen through the lens of wartime occupation. Both Novgorod and Pskov were invaded by Nazi forces in summer 1941, during the first phase of the German "Operation Barbarossa," and recaptured by the Red Army in January and July 1944, respectively. Novgorod's location for the duration of the war was catastrophic in terms of the preservation of its architectural landscape. During its two-and-a-half-year occupation, the town was located just two kilometers from the front line beyond the Malyi Volkhovets River, where the Red Army had retreated in 1941.[6] This position on the very edge of the Eastern Front meant that the town's historic buildings were adapted for the purposes of battle: belfries became lookouts for approaching enemy attacks, while the thick walls of medieval churches created ramparts against incoming fire.[7]

Pskov was occupied in July 1941, following the Nazi Army Group North's attack on the Soviet Northwestern Front, the primary objective of which was the capture of Leningrad. Following the establishment of the Leningrad Blockade, Pskov became the "North" Group's command center, housing a number of strategic military facilities, including the unit's administrative inspectorate, hospitals, and military intelligence schools.[8] The town remained a strategic stronghold throughout the war, providing a base for German field marshals and generals who were housed in the medieval Snetogorsk Monastery several kilometers from the center.[9] As in Novgorod, the town's historic architecture was adapted for military purposes: the Snetogorsk Monastery, for instance, was fitted with a modern sanitation system, along with luxuries such as fireplaces, a wine cellar, and even a shooting range.[10]

Architectural heritage was immediately invoked in the propaganda war between the Soviet and Nazi military forces. The region's numerous medieval churches, whose spiritual role had been suspended following the Bolshevik Revolution, became the focus of German efforts to win the sympathies of the local population. The German propagandist publication "Northern Word" in Novgorod thus painted the Nazis as the "saviors of Christian values from the Bolshevik barbarians" and asserted that the church architecture that had been ravaged by the Soviets would be properly maintained under German rule.[11] The Red Army likewise seized on the mobilizational potential of Russia's historic heritage. Partisan-distributed publications instructed locals not to believe the "fascist lies" and to look instead at the harm caused by the occupiers to the St. Sophia Cathedral and other historic buildings to determine the Germans' real appreciation of local culture and traditions.[12]

In Pskov, an important role in the propaganda war was played by the "Pskov Orthodox Mission," a Riga-based operation headed by the Exarch of the Russian Orthodox Church in the Baltic States, Metropolitan Sergii (Voskresenskii).[13] The mission collaborated with the occupying Nazi forces with the ostensible aim of reviving spiritual life in the lands that had been "liberated" from Bolshevik rule. During its two-and-a-half-year residency in Pskov, the mission restored and reopened many of the churches and shrines that had been closed and desecrated by the Bolshevik regime. Indeed, according to Johannes Due Enstad, 220 churches were reopened in the region within the first year of the mission's arrival in Pskov.[14] Locals were reported to have participated enthusiastically in this activity, offering donations in the form of building materials, liturgical articles, and vestments that they had hidden for safekeeping from the atheist Soviet state.[15]

It should be noted that the destruction of local heritage in Novgorod and Pskov was not the exclusive result of Nazi efforts to "wipe Russian culture from the face of the earth," as postwar Soviet historians would later have it.[16] Unlike the British raids on Lübeck and Rostock, described as the first "overt indiscriminate bombing of a town centre with little military or industrial significance,"[17] or the Luftwaffe's retaliatory Baedeker raids on Exeter, Bath, Canterbury, and other locations, the damage inflicted on the heritage of the Northwest was largely incidental. Indeed, Soviet forces themselves caused much harm to local monuments in their efforts to free the region from Nazi control.[18] This fact, however, would be strategically forgotten in the process of crafting a triumphalist narrative of war in the first decades after 1945. The war-ravaged heritage of the Russian Northwest would emerge at this time as a symbol of collective suffering and resilience in the face of Nazi brutality and barbarism.

Graveyards without Headstones

The architectural devastation of the occupied Northwest was nearly total by the end of the war. The sustained fighting and violence that had accompanied the region's invasion by German forces and recapture by the Soviets had wrecked local infrastructure and razed the historic landscape. In a report on conditions in postwar Novgorod published in 1944, it was consequently noted that just forty out of 2,346 residential buildings had been left unscathed by fighting.[19] A General Act of March 1945 confirmed the extent of local damage, reporting that all of the town's hospitals, schools, libraries, and museums had been destroyed, as had all local industry, waterworks, and power plants.[20] Retreating German troops had even mined the infrastructural hubs around the central Great Moscow Street and the bridge across the Volkhov River leading to the kremlin, completing the picture of destruction.[21]

The most shocking aspect of Novgorod's occupation, however, was the nearly total devastation of the town's heritage landscape. According to one report produced by local authorities, sixty-five architectural monuments had been destroyed or badly damaged as a result of wartime bombing, while many other historic buildings were in a state of severe dilapidation by the end of the war.[22] The ruination of the town's medieval landscape made Novgorod unrecognizable to many who returned home from evacuation after 1944. The medieval historian Dmitry Likhachev, an enthusiast for Novgorod's culture and architecture, visited the town soon after its liberation.[23] In an article-memoir written some decades later, he described the impression created by the city's landscape of eviscerated medieval monuments:

> [Novgorod] was covered by a deafening silence. A dead silence stopped my ears. It seemed to me that I was not only deaf, but blind as well. I no longer saw the town once so familiar to me. Under the tragically large sky there was just a flat plain, overgrown with high grass. It was a graveyard without headstones! Here and there, there was the odd remnant of an ancient church. Their thick walls were deeply wounded, but they had survived, stood their ground. The churches and monasteries in the wide ring surrounding Novgorod were not so lucky—they had been flattened on the battlefield. Volotovo, Kovalevo, Skovorodka—so many names familiar to the art historian. All had perished![24]

Pskov's experience of wartime occupation, unlike that of Novgorod, had been relatively peaceful. Located away from the front line, and serving as a strategic outpost for the German army, the city was well preserved until the moment of its recapture from Nazi occupation.[25] In the fighting that accompanied the Red Army's advance on the region in 1944, however, much of the city was engulfed by fire. Many of the town's administrative buildings were destroyed at this time, including the House of the Red Army, the Pskov State Museum building, the city's main hotel, several schools and colleges, the Pushkin Theater, and two cinemas.[26] As they had done in Novgorod, the retreating German troops mined hubs of local infrastructure. The town's main railway station, two railway administration buildings, and the bridges over the River Velikii and the River Pskov were all destroyed as a result.[27]

Pskov likewise experienced severe damage to its heritage landscape during its years of wartime occupation. Among the architectural victims of wartime fighting were the town's seventeenth-century merchant palaces: the Pogankin Palaces, Pechenko House, and Tiunsk Palace, the latter of which was completely destroyed by fire. Shelling damaged the valuable fresco paintings of the twelfth-century Mirozhsk Monastery and reduced to ruins the St. John's Monastery Cathedral (1243), among others.[28] During their retreat from Pskov German troops had likewise mined the area around the Trinity Cathedral, though meticulous deactivation by Soviet forces prevented further damage. The final tally of the destruction was staggering. On visiting the town in 1945, a Soviet commission estimated that 3,748,957,130 rubles worth of damage had been caused to the city's monuments, while the total cost of wartime fighting was calculated at a massive 26,376,128,531 rubles.[29]

Ruins as Wartime Propaganda

The Soviet state was quick to capitalize on the ruins of war as a means of mobilization for political purposes. As early as 1942 the revealingly named Emergency State Commission for the Investigation of the Villainy of the German-Fascist Occupiers was established to monitor and document the material damage inflicted on the occupied territories. The commission was made up of academics, writers, journalists, and museum workers, who visited the occupied regions of Novgorod, Pskov, and Kiev, among others, photographing and reporting on the localities' damaged historical monuments.[30] Commission reports were packaged for public consumption in the form of exhibitions, lectures, and glossy publications. Gutted medieval churches and disfigured kremlin walls were established at this time as the symbols of Soviet suffering at the hands of the barbaric occupying regime. For obvious reasons, no mention was made of the damage inflicted by Soviet forces on the heritage landscape.[31]

The Soviet authorities were, however, careful not to present too bleak an image of war to domestic populations. As Andreas Schönle has pointed out, visions of wartime devastation exhibited to Leningraders during the Blockade were restricted to scenes conducive to bolstering military operations and popular morale. Rather than evoking bombed-out houses and piles of corpses, wartime artists produced aestheticized representations of ruination that recalled the romantic treatment of classical ruins in the eighteenth and nineteenth centuries. Schönle nevertheless notes a distinction between the ruination propaganda exhibited to domestic populations and the images addressed to troops. Soldiers were more likely to be exposed to extreme images of material and human devastation in a bid to galvanize them into acts of violent retribution.[32]

Visions of architectural destruction in the Northwest were similarly ambiguous. Among the most iconic representations of the region's wartime suffering was the art collective Kukryniksy's *Flight of the Fascists from Novgorod* (1944–46). The socialist realist tableau depicted the Millennium of Russia Monument, a sculptural composition honoring the Russian nation's mythical founders and historic heroes, following the monument's demolition by retreating German forces. The painting made explicit the association between material and human devastation that Schönle has noted as characteristic of wartime propaganda:[33] effigies of historic Russian figures appeared corpse-like, strewn around the kremlin grounds. A more optimistic note was struck by the image of the St. Sophia Cathedral in the painting's background. The church was shown standing damaged but proudly intact, a symbol of Russian resilience and strength.

It is remarkable, then, that the years immediately following the war marked a total about-face in terms of the official appreciation of historic ruins. From national symbols designed to galvanize populations in defense of the Motherland, ruins became a political embarrassment, evidence of the catastrophic losses incurred by Stalin's failure to heed repeated warnings of German attacks. As historians of postwar Leningrad have noted, the decision to preserve virtually no ruins in the northern capital can be understood as a policy of "enforced forgetting" that tallied with other measures curbing particularistic memories of the war in the late 1940s.[34] Reconstruction in the Russian Northwest can likewise be interpreted as an act of selective remembrance. The restoration of the region's historic buildings provided a means to obscure the shameful experience of foreign conquest and assert in its place a Russocentric myth of wartime heroism and victory.

Healing the Wounds of War

As soon as the war was over, measures were taken to create a network of preservationist institutions that could manage the complicated and politically fraught task of rebuilding the country's historic architecture. At the center of this institutional nexus was the Committee for Architectural Affairs (CAA), a body established by a declaration of the Council of People's Commissars in 1943 with the aim of ensuring the state control of architectural and planning work in connection with the war-damaged monuments of the formerly occupied zone.[35] In December 1943, the Main Authorities for the Preservation of Monuments (GUOP), a union-level body responsible for the registration, inspection, and restoration of historic architecture, was established under the auspices of the CAA. GUOP comprised a number of notable Soviet artists and architects: Petr Baranovskii, an esteemed restorer of Old Russian architecture, and Igor' Grabar', a famous Russian artist and art historian, were among the Soviet celebrities who served on the Scientific Advisory Board.[36]

These federal-level institutions were responsible for making broad policy decisions on architectural reconstruction, allocating funds for restoration work across the country and administering major restoration projects in the regions. The regional bodies responsible for the day-to-day implementation of preservationist policy, however, were the Sections of Architecture and the Inspectorates for the Protection of Architectural Monuments located within the Regional Executive Committees. In addition, there existed another regional-level authority for architectural restoration in the form of the Central Project Restoration Workshops (TsPRM), which were created by GUOP between 1944 and 1950 to supervise individual restoration projects on the ground. The overlapping spheres of influence of these regional organizations created an environment that was ripe for institutional competition and confrontation; the blurred lines of responsibility between the local preservationist bodies provided opportunities for strategic maneuvering in connection with the implementation (or strategic avoidance) of federal-level policy and decisions.[37]

The distribution of authority between central and local preservationist organs varied considerably from region to region. As Catriona Kelly and Stephen Bittner have demonstrated in their studies of Leningrad and Moscow, respectively, arrangements in Russia's two most important cities were unique in terms of the level of responsibility granted to local monuments offices. Leningrad, by contrast with other Soviet cities, had its own Department for the Preservation of Monuments as early as the 1920s, and the Leningrad Inspectorate was sufficiently established by the postwar period to extend patronage to other conservation offices in Russia.[38] Similar levels of indigenous mobilization were in evidence in Moscow, where the Moscow Section of the Union of Architects, which Bittner describes as "a community of shared expertise and culture that became a surrogate for an autonomous public sphere after 1953," was able to use its popular mandate to influence decisions on preservation.[39] Elsewhere in Russia, however, conditions for preservation were less auspicious. Local workshops, where these existed at all, were entirely dependent on Regional Executive Committees, the members of which were frequently unsympathetic to preservationist arguments, considering these an anathema to the Stalinist ideas of social transformation and urban modernization that formed the basis of their socialization.[40]

With the liberation of the occupied territories, the central authorities for restoration issued orders to concentrate reconstruction efforts on the Russian Northwest. Writing in the journal *Soviet Art* in November 1944, Igor' Grabar' asserted restoration in the war-damaged territories as an objective equal in patriotic importance to the provision of housing or transportation in the postwar Soviet Union: "Now that the Red Army has driven the last fascist aggressors from our country, the time has come to think of the restoration of those fine monuments of art and antiquity, which the German vandals outraged in a malicious frenzy," Grabar' polemicized. Accompanying the article were illustrations of Novgorod's Savior on Nereditsa Church, which had been destroyed by German bombing. The restorer gave categorical instructions for such masterpieces of Russian architecture to be raised from the ashes: "Some few items have been restored. Of various other monuments, which astonished the world by their perfection, nothing is left but their foundations, but we can and must recreate at any cost whatever has in any degree survived. Never before has the world witnessed a restoration task of such grandiose dimensions as faces our country in the next decades."[41]

In line with Grabar"s wishes, architectural reconstruction in the historic Northwest was prioritized as an objective of postwar legislation. A declaration of November 1945, "On Measures to Reconstruct the Towns of the USSR Destroyed by the Nazi Invaders," underlined the need for urgent restoration work to "historically and architecturally important buildings" in Russia's fifteen oldest towns: Novgorod, Pskov, Smolensk, Viaz'ma, Rostov-on-Don, Novorossiisk, Sevastopol, Voronezh, Velikie Luki, Kalinin, Briansk, Orel, Kursk, Krasnodar, and Murmansk.[42] The declaration was followed by two other legislative milestones—the 1948 decree "On the Means to Improve the Preservation of Cultural Monuments" and the 1949 short instructions "On the Procedure for Recording and Registering the Contents of Architectural Monuments."[43] Both rulings placed primacy on the restoration of "Old Russian" architecture, establishing the Northwest, the region with the highest concentration of war-damaged medieval monuments in Russia, as the principal focus of postwar restoration efforts.

Novgorod: "A Monument of Russian Antiquity"

In the first days after the liberation of Novgorod, several high-profile commissions of architectural experts visited the historic town. The first was the Commission on Damage to Historical Buildings and Monuments, including such auspicious figures as the Head of the Leningrad Inspectorate for the Preservation of Architectural Monuments Sergei Davydov, the Head of the Department for Old Russian Art at the Russian Museum Iurii Dmitriev, and the Chair of the Leningrad Executive Committee Mikhail Iudin. The commission worked assiduously between February and April 1944, documenting the wartime damage inflicted on the region's architectural heritage. Following its departure, a second party, including Igor'

Grabar' and the acclaimed Soviet architect Aleksei Shchusev, surveyed the town. On the basis of the documents compiled by these working groups, a series of legislative measures was drawn up for the reconstruction of the historic region.[44]

In the years that followed, the Soviet Council of People's Deputies issued a number of important rulings that underlined the political significance of Novgorod's restoration. These included the declaration of August 1, 1944, "On Measures for the Restoration of Novgorod," and the declaration of December 13, 1944, "On Measures for the Restoration of the Novgorod Kremlin." The latter contained specific instructions to the Novgorod Executive Committee regarding the reconstruction of the historic fortress, detailing requirements to create a special project-restoration workshop and construction trust, as well as a vocational college with a two-year program to train future restoration specialists.[45] Instructions on the "Fundamental Principles for the Restoration of the Novgorod Kremlin," released in August 1944, provided further directions about the nature of the repair and restoration work to be carried out to the medieval fortress. This document, issuing from the highest levels of the Soviet government, stressed the historic significance of the Kremlin and introduced the idea of the complex as a "preservation zone" of restricted construction in which historic buildings could be used only for museum purposes.[46]

The Novgorod Special Project-Restoration Workshop, foreseen in the 1944 legislation, was created on March 16, 1945, by Order of the CAA. The workshop, archival documents suggest, was the first in the country, predating the workshops in Leningrad, Vladimir, and Pskov, which were established in May 1945, December 1945, and February 1946, respectively.[47] Sergei Davydov was appointed the prestigious role of workshop head and proceeded to recruit a number of high-profile colleagues with whom he had worked at the Leningrad Inspectorate. Among the restoration masters to relocate from Leningrad to the historic province at this time were Iurii Dmitriev, a national specialist in preservation and restoration of medieval fresco paintings, and Aleksandr Udalenkov, an acclaimed restorer with specialist knowledge of Novgorod's monuments, who had carried out major reconstruction work in the region in the 1920s and 1930s.[48]

Given the political profile of Novgorod's reconstruction, an Expert Research Council was established under GUOP to supervise all work carried out in the region. The presence of this council, comprising prominent Soviet academicians, architects, artists, and historians, was influential for the workshop's methodological development; regular interactions with the most knowledgeable architectural specialists of the period broadened the collective's horizons and improved the quality of the research and practical work carried out in the region.[49] In May 1945, Davydov invited Liubov' Shuliak, a Leningrad-trained specialist in northern Russian architecture, to join the team as a Senior Architect-Restorer. Shuliak had worked with the renowned prerevolutionary architect Petr Pokryshkin and was an important influence on the next generation of restorers who came to prominence in Novgorod. As Iadryshnikov remarks, Shuliak "was a binding link between the mighty prerevolutionary restorers and the talented and energetic youth of the 1950s."[50]

The postwar legislation placed unequivocal emphasis on the restoration of the region's "Old Russian" architecture. A declaration of the Soviet Council of People's Deputies of July 18, 1945, "On Urgent Measures to Preserve and Restore Architectural and Artistic Monuments in Novgorod and its Surrounding Regions," singled out the objects to be prioritized in the restoration effort. In addition to the medieval kremlin complex, a number of "Old Russian" churches were identified as priorities for reconstruction—the St. Nicholas Cathedral (1113), the St. George Monastery Cathedral (1119), the Savior on Il'in Street Church (1374), the Theodore Stratelates on Ruch'e Church (1361), the Peter and Paul on Sinich Hill Church (1192), the Dmetrius of Thessaloniki Church (1462), the St. Blaise the Martyr Church (1111), and the John the Baptist Church (1127).[51] Most important, however, was project to restore of the town's architectural centerpiece and symbol of national identity, the St. Sophia Cathedral. The cathedral had suffered extensive damage during wartime; a report from 1944 had recorded the destruction of large parts of the building's external and internal walls, damage to the drums and their fresco paintings, and the loss of all interior decoration and crosses.[52] Despite the fact that much of this damage had been caused by Soviet artillery fire, responsibility for the cathedral's condition was laid squarely at the feet of the German occupiers. The project to restore the church in its historically authentic entirety was consequently flagged as an exercise in Soviet patriotic reconstruction, an act of defiance against the attempts of the "Fascists" to desecrate and destroy the country's heritage.[53]

The Sophia Cathedral was considered a national treasure, equal in historical importance to the Moscow Kremlin or the Winter Palace in Leningrad. Accordingly, restoration work on the church was closely monitored by the central restoration authorities. Nikolai Brunov, a corresponding member of the Soviet Academy of Architecture, was responsible for researching the different phases of the cathedral's reconstruction and establishing the "optimum date" for its restoration.[54] The absence of historical materials pertaining to the church's twelfth-century design, however, prevented the restorer from returning the build-ing to its "authentic" medieval form. Supervised by Davydov, and with contribu-tions from Udalenkov, thoroughgoing restoration work was nevertheless carried out to Sophia's drums, arches, arched gables, and central apses between 1944 and 1947.[55] By the end of the decade, the cathedral's glimmering gold and silver cupo-las, the region's most famous cultural icons, once more formed part of the town's historic panorama.

FIGURE 3. The St. Sophia Cathedral and Millennium of Russia Monument.

Between 1944 and 1949 an impressive amount was achieved by the Novgorod restoration collective. In accordance with central legislation, strengthening and restoration work was carried out on the large part of the Kremlin's monuments, including extensive repair work to the Vladimir, Savior, and Intercession Towers.[56] Moreover, and in addition to the state-sanctioned restoration of "Old Russian" churches in the historic center, the workshop developed a number of projects on its own initiative. These included the reconstruction of medieval churches in the surrounding region—the Savior on Nereditsa Church, the Church of St. Nicholas on Lipno Island (1292), the Savior of the Transfiguration on Il'in Street Church (1374), and Peter and Paul in Kozhevniki Church (1406)—whose extreme dilapidation, restorers contended, necessitated urgent measures.[57]

The allocation of financial resources from the state budget for restoration underlined the political significance attributed to the project for Novgorod's architectural reconstruction. Restoration in the historic region was budgeted at 1,200,000 rubles, or 13 percent of the total budget for restoration in 1945, compared with 100,000 rubles (1 percent) in Leningrad and 800,000 rubles (8 percent) in Moscow.[58] It is worth underlining that the large part of this money was spent on the restoration of Orthodox architecture, buildings that only a decade earlier had been condemned as "refuges of delusion" (*ochagi durmanstva*). The shift in the official understanding of these objects, from the relics of an obscurantist belief system to the symbols of Soviet-Russian national identity, was reflected in local publications. As one journalist wrote in *Novgorod Pravda* some years later, in 1961, "The architectural monuments of this medieval town, once associated with the saccharine smell of incense and the irritating clanging of bells, are now interpreted very differently. Freed from their putrid religious contents, they are seen today as magnificent works of Russian architecture."[59]

In the first five years after the war, the agendas of the central preservation authorities, the local administration, and the restoration workshop in Novgorod were closely aligned. The political value attached to the reconstruction of the region's historic architecture resulted in a high level of official scrutiny of local preservationist activities, creating the impetus for local politicians to facilitate restoration on the ground. The correspondence between the Soviet state's agenda for reconstruction and the preferences of local preservationists was further reflected in debates surrounding the creation of Novgorod's General Plan in 1945. This official blueprint for the town's urban development attributed a privileged position to historic architecture, revealing the unique status of the Northwest in national politics and the political will to preserve its architectural monuments as the symbols of patriotic identity.

Novgorod's 1945 General Plan

As Karl Qualls has noted in connection with his study of architectural preservation in post-war Sevastopol, competing visions for the reconstruction of the Soviet Union's historic periphery existed after 1945.[60] While the Soviet government endorsed a patriotically inspired ideal of architectural preservation in the historic Northwest, local officials and planners were influenced by more pragmatic concerns: the urgent need for construction of housing, schools, and hospitals, and the renovation of local transport infrastructure. Preservationist policy in the first decades after the war was consequently the subject of political negotiation as local authorities attempted to dilute and deflect the requirements enforced on them from above. As a consequence of this activity, politicians and planners in the regions attracted sharp criticism from preservationist elites, who through their coordinated activism and writings began to take shape at this time as a lobby for the interests of local architectural heritage.

As Iuliia Kosenkova has noted, two models for urban planning in the USSR's historic localities were advanced after the war. The first was the physical separation of old and new architecture through the creation of protected zones (*zapovedniki*) of historic monuments;[61] the second was the combination of historic and contemporary architecture through the active inclusion of the former in the modern development of the town.[62] Between 1944 and 1945, General Plans were produced for over two hundred historic Soviet towns in which the zoning principle was roundly rejected as too conservative a vision of Soviet urban life.[63] While acknowledging the value of architectural heritage, planners routinely showed a preference for the modernization, or, as it came to be known, the "rejuvenation" of the historic periphery.[64]

In this context, Novgorod's General Plan must be seen as a notable outlier. The Committee for Architectural Affairs considered two proposals for the town's postwar reconstruction, the first authored by "Lengiprogor," a team of engineers and architects from Leningrad specializing in urban planning, the second by the workshop of the acclaimed Soviet architect and planner Aleksei Shchusev. Lengiprogor, as Larry Cothren has noted, was an inherently socialist institution whose ideas about urban planning had been formed by the debates of the 1920s, such as the "Garden City" concept and Leonid Sabsovich's "Urbanism" proposals of the 1930s.[65] The Leningrad team consequently advocated a "progressive" socialist model for Novgorod's urban development: according to its proposal, the town's new administrative center, including government offices and administrative buildings, would be located inside the walls of the historic Kremlin complex, "[resolving] organically the problem of creating a general town center."[66]

Lengiprogor's proposal attracted criticism from, among others, the Stalinist architect and native Novgorodian L. V. Rudnev. Participating in a discussion of the two proposals at the CAA in 1945, Rudnev asserted the uniqueness of the

Novgorod case and the need to take special measures to ensure the preservation of the town's historic landscape: "Novgorod seems to me to be a town of such standing that it is worth setting it apart [*chto imeet pravo byt' vydelennym*]," Rudnev argued. "My suggestion would be the following: to develop the idea of Novgorod as 'a monument of Russian antiquity' and to relocate here a number of cultural institutions. Put the regional center in another part of the town."[67]

Shchusev's proposal, by contrast, took a more accommodating line to the question of architectural preservation. The Kremlin, it suggested, would be transformed into an architectural-historical museum reserve, while the new administrative center would be constructed near it, but not in the immediate vicinity. Victory Square, as the new Soviet center was to be called, would accommodate the largest buildings in the town, the House of Regional Soviets and Party Organizations, the theater, and the House of Culture. Critically, however, the square would preserve the visual integrity of a medieval fortress.[68] Making use of the political parlance of the time, Shchusev explained that this approach, which ultimately won the approval of the CAA, would ensure "organic continuity" between the established traditions of Novgorodian architecture and new Soviet construction.[69]

Shchusev's preservationist plan for Novgorod revealed the privileged status accorded to local heritage in the state-sponsored drive to boost national morale and patriotic identity in the immediate postwar period. However, as political priorities shifted at the end of the decade, official enthusiasm for this vision began to wane. With the liquidation of the CAA in 1949 and the transference of its preservationist functions, first to the Ministry for Urban Economy and then to the short-lived Ministry for Urban Construction, the fate of Novgorod's historic monuments and the workshop that protected them was called into question.[70] According to Iadryshnikov, the political fallout from the "Leningrad Affair," which resulted in the repression of the political elite in Novgorod, impacted negatively on the cause of local heritage preservation.[71] The new regional authorities opposed the preservationist vision enshrined in Shchusev's General Plan and raised objections to the workshop's unauthorized work on war-damaged monuments at the town's periphery.[72] Sergei Davydov, who had presided over the most intensive period of architectural reconstruction in Novgorod's history, might also have fallen the victim to the vicissitudes of late Stalinist politics. According to local historians, the restorer's dismissal following an investigation into financial irregularities at the workshop in the 1950s was politically motivated: while principled preservationists had been essential to the campaign to raise Novgorod's monuments from the ashes of war, by the mid 1950s, "stubborn" academics of Davydov's sort were more likely to be considered an annoying obstacle to socialist progress.[73]

The death of Stalin in 1953 and the advent of the neo-Leninist Khrushchev regime saw a conceptual devaluation of Novgorod's heritage from the privileged symbols of Russified Soviet identity to mere component parts of the socialist land-scape. In line with this shift in cultural values, local administrators in Novgorod were able to subvert Shchusev's preservationist plans for the town with relative impunity. Citing the exigencies of socialist construction, the regional authorities passed amendments to the plan in the mid 1950s, which targeted in particular the architect's notion of zones of restricted construction.[74] A new General Plan, released in 1966, proposed even more radical changes in line with the local admin-istration's intention to construct 2,700,000 square meters of residential housing by 1971.[75] In order to fulfill this requirement, Shchusev's specification that only low-rise housing be constructed within the historic center was abandoned. The result was the chaotic construction of residential housing in close proximity to heritage objects and the erection of buildings in the most heterogeneous styles, from the ascetic to the excessively ornate.

Such an insensitive approach to the region's heritage provoked criticism from local restorers. In his architectural guide to Novgorod, published in 1966, the architect and restorer Il'ia Kushnir pointed out a number of planning "mistakes" that had been made in the historic town. As Kushnir explained, these mistakes included the construction of high-rise housing near the Church of the Twelve Apostles (1454), which had "lessened the compositional role of this interest-ing monument." Another target of his criticism was a new block of flats along Bolshevik Street that "impaired the visibility of a group of interesting monuments for those arriving in the town from the direction of Moscow."[76] In the years that followed, Kushnir's criticisms were amplified in the writings of Russia's most famous and well-respected defender of architectural heritage, Dmitry Likhachev. Throughout the 1960s and 1970s, Likhachev wrote scathing criticisms of Soviet preservation, singling out Novgorod and Pskov as key instances of bad practices. The medievalist pilloried Soviet planners for their disingenuous claims to have "rejuvenated" these historic cities: "Do you really think that all of our country's towns should look like each other?," he wrote in an article published in the *Literary Journal* in 1965. "Are you really under the impression that all our ancient cities need is a 'second birth'?"[77] In the view of Likhachev, Soviet modernization had undermined the architectural integrity of "Old Russian" towns, transforming them from unique examples of medieval culture and art into derivative Soviet cityscapes.

Pskov: "A Monument of Our History"

Like Novgorod, Pskov was singled out in the immediate postwar period as a site for the patriotic reconstruction of historic Russian architecture, which was to rise phoenix-like from the ashes of total war. In May and June 1944, Aleksei Shchusev visited the newly recaptured town as part of a commission of preservationist experts responsible for reviewing the architectural damage inflicted on the territory during wartime. Following the group's investigations, Shchusev delivered an impassioned speech at the Pskov House of Soviets in which he underlined the superlative value of the region's cultural patrimony:

> Pskov is an extremely valuable ancient monument [*bogateishchii pamiatnik stariny*]. It is the pride of our country and is admired throughout the entire world. We must keep this fact in mind as we go about the task of reconstructing the city. Pskov must be attributed its former status of city-museum. We must approach its reconstruction wisely, binding together old and new.[78]

As in Novgorod, the commission's findings were used to compile key legislation on the restoration of Pskov's war-damaged monuments, the most important of which was the declaration of the Council of People's Commissars of the RSFSR of November 20, 1945, "On Urgent Measures to Preserve Architectural Monuments in Pskov and the Pskov Region." This far-reaching legislation foresaw the allocation of 1,500,000 rubles to Pskov's Regional Executive Committee for emergency restoration work to local heritage; the creation a special-restoration workshop by the first quarter of 1946; and the provision of fifty qualified construction workers for the implementation of the workshop's proposals. The declaration contained detailed instructions regarding the exploitation of local monuments, stipulating the purposes for which certain buildings could and could not be used. The town's most valuable monuments—the Mirozhsk Monastery Cathedral, the Snetogorsk Monastery Cathedral, St. John's Monastery, and the seventeenth-century merchant palaces—were reserved exclusively for the purposes of museum exhibition, while less prestigious monuments were prohibited from being used as housing, manufacturing works, or warehouses. Finally, the declaration required the Executive Committee to work together with the Authorities for Architectural Affairs to establish the boundaries of preservation zones around local monuments.[79] This last specification was one of the earliest iterations of the "preservation zone" principle that would become a major point of contention in local preservationist debates in years to come.

The history of Pskov's postwar reconstruction is intimately interwoven with the personal biography of the town's most famous preservationist and restorer, Iurii Spegal'skii. A member of the noble Pechenko family, Spegal'skii was raised in the seventeenth-century merchant mansion Pechenko House, about which he later wrote in his dissertation on the town's seventeenth-century civic architecture.[80] Spegal'skii entered the Leningrad Higher Artistic and Technical Institute (LVKhTI) in 1928 and completed his studies, following the restructuring of this organisation, at the Leningrad Institute of Engineers of Municipal Construction. After graduating in 1936, he worked for the Leningrad Department for the Preservation of Monuments and remained in the city, helping to preserve Leningrad's historic buildings, throughout the difficult years of the Blockade between 1941 and 1944.[81]

With the end of the war, Spegal'skii seized the initiative to return to Pskov and begin working on his native city's war-damaged monuments. Indeed, he wrote to I. E. Grabar' at the Central Restoration Workshop in Moscow with a request to this effect in 1943, before Pskov had even been recaptured from German occupation.[82] Spegal'skii was made head of the Pskov Inspectorate for Architectural Monuments in 1944 and immediately began work on the historic buildings in the most urgent need of restoration. With characteristic disregard for administrative red tape, he began to restore single-handedly some of the town's most valuable monuments, scaling the roofs of the Trinity Cathedral and the Church of Christ's Transfiguration in the Mirozhsk Monastery complex to carry out urgent repairs. The restorer's refusal to delay this work while processing the required documentation elicited sharp criticism from preservationist authorities. Spegal'skii, in turn, showed unguarded contempt for Soviet bureaucracy, which he considered a senseless obstacle to the urgent and necessary task of saving Russia's cultural heritage.[83]

Like Novgorod, Pskov was one of the first historic localities in the postwar Soviet Union to benefit from a restoration workshop (1946), the task of which was to reconstruct the town's most patriotically significant architectural monuments. The creation of the workshop was also intended to introduce a more professional, state-regulated phase in local restoration activity, which until this point had been governed by the individual priorities and preferences of Iurii Spegal'skii. Plans drawn up by the Executive Committee thus promised the workshop construction materials, a qualified labor force, premises at the Sutotsk House and Menshikov Chambers, and a budget of 400,000 rubles for work on a total of fifteen monuments.[84] In reality, however, chronic shortages of construction materials and qualified laborers across the country, combined with the opposition of local politicians and planners to questions of heritage preservation, meant that little of what was promised materialized.[85] As in Novgorod, the patriotic ideal of historic preservation endorsed by the central Soviet government collided with stubborn resistance on the part of local *chinovniki* whose vision of the Pskov's postwar development differed radically from that of Soviet ideologues and local preservationists.

Spegal'skii, more than any member of the restoration elite in Novgorod, was prepared to speak about this unsatisfactory situation. In September 1946, for example, he penned an angry letter to the head of Pskov's Executive Committee, V. D. Semin, in which he condemned in no uncertain terms the local administration's preservationist failings:

> No one has done anything—the Workshop is falling apart because of lack of workers and the absence of suitable premises. It is blindingly obvious that the declaration of the Soviet Government about the preservation of monuments of ancient architecture is being undermined as a result of unacceptably indifferent attitudes towards the implementation of the government's orders; these could have been fulfilled, but the will to do so was simply lacking.[86]

This was one of many such letters. Spegal'skii's willingness to call local officials to account perhaps stemmed from his personal investment in the preservation of Pskov's architectural landscape—his family home, Pechenko House, was, after all, among those monuments whose survival was imperiled by local bureaucracy. Yet, his impassioned defense of local heritage was also motivated by a distaste for Soviet urban modernization and rationalization, policies that ran contrary to the preservationist's inherently conservative philosophical and cultural outlook. Spegal'skii's vociferous denunciation of these policies, combined with his fundamentalist beliefs about the principles of Pskov's architectural restoration, would eventually bring him into conflict with the political authorities.

Despite material shortages and administrative hurdles, the Pskov Workshop produced an impressive number of restoration projects in the first years of its existence. These projects involved meticulous archival research, physical examinations, and carefully documented proposals to restore a number of the town's most valuable seventeenth-century merchant mansions and medieval churches, including the Church of Sts. Cosmas and Damian on Gremiach Hill and the St. Nicholas On-the-Dry-Spot Church.[87] Work on the latter was conducted by Spegal'skii between 1945 and 1947 and involved extensive archival research, including consultation of ancient ceramics, icons, and wood carvings on iconostases to establish the building's original design and structure.[88] On the basis of this work, Spegal'skii established an "optimum date" for the building's restoration of 1553, and set about "relieving" the structure of its seventeenth and eighteenth-century inter-polations.[89] This radical restoration project, initially endorsed by GUOP, was later halted as a result of Spegal'skii's failure to submit the supporting documentation to the relevant authorities.[90] Spegal'skii's actions prompted criticism from the high-est reaches of the Soviet restoration authorities, including from Petr Baranovskii, who condemned the project for its overreliance on "personal opinion rather than evidence on the basis of which others could judge."[91]

Spegal'skii's Project for Architectural Zoning in Pskov

As in Novgorod, the project to develop a General Plan for Pskov's postwar urban development proved controversial. The debate surrounding the place of archi-tectural heritage in the modern urban realm revealed a gulf in understanding between local preservationists and regional administrators. While the central authorities continued to endorse architectural monuments as the nation's cultural heritage throughout the 1940s and 1950s, the exigencies of socialist construction began to dominate debate at this time at the expense of preservationist questions. In Pskov, where local authorities had little sympathy for preservationist argu-ments, this cultural shift allowed local officials to ignore preservationist legisla-tion with impunity, implementing their own vision of a modern socialist town in which historic monuments were firmly subordinated to Soviet construction.

Pskov's 1945 General Plan was authored by "Lenproekt," a Leningrad-based group of architects and urban planners led by the architect A. I. Naumov. Lenproekt had in fact already designed two plans for Pskov in 1935 and 1938, though the outbreak of war and the region's occupation in 1941 had meant that neither scheme had been implemented in practice. The 1938 document had rec-ognized the preponderance of local architectural monuments, which it weakly noted "formed interesting ensembles" but expressed no clear commitment to the preservation of historic buildings or their integration into the town's modern development. It is remarkable, then, that the 1945 plan went to such lengths to safeguard the preservation of local monuments, referring to Pskov as a "city-mu-seum of unique monuments of ancient Russian architecture."[92]

Spegal'skii played a crucial role in ensuring the architectural "zoning" princi-ple was enshrined in the 1945 General Plan. The restorer had already developed the idea of zones of restricted construction while resident in Leningrad during the Blockade, and following his return to Pskov, he had lobbied the local Section of Architecture to implement his paper project.[93] After Lenproekt won the bid to create Pskov's General Plan, Spegal'skii provided the collective with detailed maps showing the location of Pskov's monuments and proposed boundaries for four zones of restricted construction.[94] The final draft of the plan revealed the influence of these ideas. An appendix entitled "Description of the Boundaries of Historical-Artistic Museum Reserves" provided details of three preservation zones in the town center, broadly corresponding to Spegal'skii's proposals.[95] The appendix likewise specified limitations on the height of any buildings constructed in the historic center: 40 percent were restricted to one story; 45 percent—to two stories; and just 15 percent—to three or four stories.[96]

The inclusion of Spegal'skii's zoning principle in Pskov's 1945 General Plan was revealing of the privileged status accorded to the region's historic architecture in the immediate postwar period. In the years that followed, however, local administrators gradually diluted and revised the zoning principle, resulting in a chaotic approach to construction that Spegal'skii, among other preservationsits, condemned in the strongest possible terms. On December 21, 1948, the Town Executive Committee introduced a number of amendments to the 1945 plan, including an increase to the percentage of two-story buildings whose construction was permitted within the historic center from 45 percent to 60 percent.[97] Population increases in the second half of the 1940s prompted further changes to official guidelines. On August 7, 1950, the Authorities for Architectural Affairs issued a special order, "On Shortcomings in the Project for the Planning of Pskov," which required the percentage of multi-story buildings constructed in the city center to be increased further to 50–60 percent.[98] The slow progress of this construction work over the next months resulted in Pskov's main architect, G. I. Salonnikov, being dressed down in front of the Regional Executive Committee at the Ninth Town Party Conference in Pskov, in February 1951. The First Secretary of the Executive Committee G. N. Shubin, an advocate of "progressive" urban modernization in Pskov, chastised the architect in terms that left no doubt where his priorities for postwar reconstruction lay:

> We need to build beautiful buildings, that are worthy of the Stalinist era. Main Architect, Comrade Salonnikov, presents himself as a passionate defender of Pskov's historic architecture. I am fully in favor of preserving historic buildings, but the dangerous thing is that Comrade Salonnikov with the permission of the Town Executive Committee approaches the ancient relics of our town like an archivist does

the preservation of documents, forgetting that his mission lies elsewhere. He must, while recognizing the value of ancient architecture and preserving the very best of it, construct majestic buildings, that are worthy of our time.[99]

In 1947, in the midst of these debates, Spegal'skii was removed from his position as head of the Pskov restoration workshop. The circumstances surrounding this event are contested in local restoration circles,[100] but Larry Cothren has provided perhaps the most comprehensive account of the conflict that resulted in the local architect's dismissal. Drawing on archival sources housed at the Pskov State Historical-Artistic Museum-Reserve,[101] Cothren has revealed the hostile relations between Spegal'skii and local administrators, in particular the town's main architect, Petr Tvardovskii, and the head of the Section for Architecture, I. Egorov.[102] Spegal'skii complained openly about the incompetence of these officials, writing of Tvardovskii in a letter to the Pskov Executive Committee in 1946 that "the Chief Architect of this city, the person responsible for fulfilling the conditions of the General Plan, is flouting these conditions and ignoring the project to resurrect the town's ancient streets."[103] In another letter to the local administration, he called for the dismissal of the local officials who were obstructing the implementation of central preservationist policy:

> If it is unrealistic to ask everyone to understand the value of culture and art, etc. in addition to the satisfaction of their most basic needs, that is, to ask that people realize the significance of monuments of the people's art and to try to preserve them, then at least we can ask that everyone, without exception, respect the decisions of the Soviet government. . . . I ask that you take measures against those who are not fulfilling the decisions of the Pskov ispolkom.[104]

Such vituperative criticism of Soviet officials had catastrophic consequences for the restorer. Regional officials regarded Spegal'skii with contempt and did not hesitate to lay the blame for the slow progress of local restoration work at his door.[105] The sympathy that preservationist authorities in Moscow had felt for the visionary architect gradually began to wane as Spegal'skii continued to take decisions about the restoration of Pskov's monuments without submitting the necessary paperwork.[106] With his reputation among the central restoration authorities compromised, and few political allies at the local level, it was easy to remove Spegal'skii from his position following accusations of misconduct. From 1947, he was forced into professional exile in Leningrad and other historic Soviet cities, only being permitted to return to work in Pskov two years before his death, in 1967.[107]

Spegal'skii's architectural publications in the years that followed revealed the restorer's frustrations with the choices made by Pskov's "Innovators" (*Novatory*), a sarcastic designation he used to refer to the Soviet planners, who were, in his opinion, causing irreparable damage to the town's architectural heritage. In *Pskov: Architectural Monuments* (1963), for example, he provided an overview of local architecture in which he lingered over the ruins of the medieval city, evoked the spirit of monuments past, and lamented the disintegration of heritage objects into historical curiosities. Pskov's monuments, Spegal'skii argued, were "stone chronicles" conveying information about the past to present and future generations. If, over time, the pages of these chronicles "get torn" (*vyryvaiut'sia*), "break off" (*razroznivaiut'sia*), and "get distorted" (*iskazhaiut'sia*), he argued, it was the government's responsibility to restore them, thus rendering them "legible" for the public once more.[108]

In his later writings, Spegal'skii argued not only for the preservation of heritage objects in their original aspect but also for the protection of the historic environment in which these monuments had been built. In *Pskov: Architectural Monuments*, he thus defended the idea of preserving Pskov's center as a zone of restricted construction, writing "it is pointless trying to understand or evaluate these buildings without having an accurate or clear idea what they looked like in the past. We have to see these buildings, not in isolation, but as objects embedded in their former surroundings."[109] Spegal'skii reiterated this point in pictorial terms in a book of sketches of Pskov's monuments, published posthumously in 1974. The pictures reflected what the restorer had been unable to achieve in reality: the conservation of Pskov's historic landscape, free from the creeping influence of Soviet modernity.[110]

In Spegal'skii's absence, Pskov's monuments nevertheless continued to benefit from the patriotic climate of late-Stalinism. Conservationist legislation continued to be issued from the center which the local authorities, despite their preservationist reservations, were unable to resist. The declaration of the Soviet Council of Ministers of October 14, 1948, "On Means to Improve the Preservation of Pskov's Cultural Monuments" thus instigated a new phase of restoration activity in the historic town. The intensification of local restoration work was reflected in the increases in annual expenditure: if, in 1946, the local authorities had spent only 18 percent (751,400 rubles) of the allocated budget for the preservation of local monuments, this figure had risen to 47.6 percent (521,500 rubles) by 1947, to 93 percent (1,217,500 rubles) by 1948, and to 98 percent (1,337,900 rubles) by 1949.[111] The high-profile restoration projects carried out at this time included Spegal'skii's childhood home, Pechenko House, the Archangel Michael Church, and several churches within the Mirozhk Monastery, as well as repairs to the roof of the St. John's Monastery Cathedral and the Nativity Cathedral on Sniataia Hill.[112] Given the cultural significance of these monuments, work was closely monitored and in some cases executed by the central restoration authorities: in September 1948, for example, a Special Commission of the Soviet Academy of Sciences carried out extensive repair work to thirteenth- and fourteenth-century frescoes in the churches of the Snetogorsk and Mirozhsk Monastery complexes.[113]

On August 22, 1952, the Council of Ministers of the RSFSR issued a historic declaration, "On Measures to Restore the Pskov Kremlin." This legislation assigned 250,000 rubles from state coffers for the "repair, reconstruction, and restoration of the entire complex of buildings within the Pskov Kremlin" and diverted a further 60,000 rubles to the project from the regional budget for major renovation work to architectural monuments.[114] A decision of the same name adopted by the Regional Executive Committee on September 10, 1952, detailed plans to transform the fortress ensemble into a "historical park," removing all temporary structures and employing the remaining buildings as museums. The document formed the blueprint for the transformation of the historic fortress from an overgrown and evocative ruin into a vertiable open-air attraction that could inspire feelings of patriotic pride and civic inspiration in visiting locals and domestic tourists.[115]

Between 1946 and 1950, restoration work, at a total cost of 6,120,000 rubles, was carried out to 76 of the 91 historic buildings in Pskov that had been damaged during the war.[116] This work undoubtedly saved the town's heritage landscape from imminent disaster: if, in January 1948, thirty-three buildings had been considered to be in a critical condition, by June 1, 1953, only two were accorded this status: the St. Sergei of Zaluzh'e Church (1322) and the Virgin Hodegetria Church (1537).[117] While some Moscow and Leningrad architects had contributed to the restoration effort, the lion's share of this work had been carried out by local restorers at the Pskov Workshop, and by Iurii Spegal'skii in particular. Despite adverse material conditions and the resistance of local administrators, Pskov's restorers were able to implement central legislation to preserve an impressive number of the town's ancient buildings. In the decades that followed, this restoration work would be exhibited to national audiences as evidence of Soviet strength and resilience, a symbolic rejection of the Nazi occupiers' efforts to "wipe Russian cultural heritage from the face of the earth."

FIGURE 4. Child playing on the ruins of Dovmontov Town, Pskov, June 2009.

Following the liberation of the occupied territories, the late Stalinist regime endorsed a categorically reconstructionist agenda that asserted a celebratory narrative of the war as a Soviet victory over foreign aggression. The ruins of historic buildings, which had formed the tools of wartime propaganda, were replaced by architectural reconstructions whose historical authenticity was endorsed in theory, if not always in practice. Heritage objects were no longer seen as the victims of external aggression, but rather as the symbols of wartime resistance and postwar renewal, phoenixes rising from the ashes of valiant conflict. In acknowledgment of their value, historic buildings were granted a privileged place in the postwar plans to reconstruct the historic periphery. While not always implemented by local officials, the ideals of heritage preservation enshrined in these official blueprints for the towns' urban development were a testament to Soviet patriotic politics of the postwar era.

A consequence of the state-sponsored drive to reconstruct the historic Northwest was the creation of influential lobbies for the protection of the towns' architectural monuments. Preservationist figures, such as Davydov, Spegal'skii, and Kushnir, emerged in the decades after the war as passionate defenders of historic architecture and vehement critics of the pitfalls of "socialist transformation." Such a stance made them vulnerable to the machinations of local officials, particularly following the shift in official politics from postwar reconstruction to urban modernization and crash industrialization at the end of the 1940s. The efforts of these individuals and the collectives of restoration experts that grew up around them nevertheless informed the shape of the architectural landscape, the content of local cultural life, and the appreciation of cultural heritage among local communities in decades to come.

The understanding of the role heritage should play in Soviet life shifted in the post-Stalin era. As the Khrushchev regime searched for new sources of political legitimacy after 1956, historic architecture was put to work for the purposes of the socialist state. In the more formal context of the museum-zapovednik, the principle vehicle for Soviet patriotic tourism in the Khrushchev and Brezhnev eras, heritage objects were made to signify ideas of military strength, cultural ingenuity, and collective solidarity that were associated with the Soviet people. Having been successfully reimagined as architectural monuments in the postwar period, churches and fortresses underwent another conceptual transformation in the late 1950s and 1960s: the region's historic buildings emerged at this time as exhibits of Soviet cultural identity, communicating to domestic audiences ideas of national unity and belonging.

2.

ZAPOVEDNIKS OR
TOURIST RESORTS?

Marketing Heritage to National Audiences

The decade after the war had seen extensive repairs to historical architecture across the Northwest, and this architecture had now gained a central place in the national imaginary as a symbol of rebirth after the repulsion of the foreign invaders. After 1956 this place was further enhanced as heritage began to play a strategic role in reimagining the Soviet nation and fostering solidarity and pride in a population shaken by the death of Stalin and Khrushchev's subsequent denunciation of him at the Twentieth Congress of the CPSU in 1956.[1] In the absence of a father figure who could guide and direct the nation, people were instructed to turn inward, to celebrate their own cultural history and achievements. A major new development at this time was the promotion of active engagement with historic monuments through face-to-face visits. Tourism in the Northwest started to be promoted on an unprecedented scale and became a central means of Soviet patriotic education, familiarizing citizens with a celebratory narrative of national history and culture stretching back to the Middle Ages.

This chapter examines the various stages of development that resulted in the towns of the Russian Northwest acquiring the status of national tourist destinations. It considers the ways that architectural heritage was put to work for the Soviet state, how it was packaged and presented to outsiders in order to affirm the political priorities of the time. Local residents were made to participate in the touristic exploitation of their regions, first as consumers of regional history and culture and then as distributors of this knowledge to outsiders. This chapter offers some reflections on the social consequences of this activity. The process of marketing the Northwest as an ideal of national heritage and culture created tensions in restoration circles and, more broadly, among the local population. Tourism raised people's awareness of the value of local architecture, creating a gap between expectations and reality in connection with the preservation of the heritage landscape.

From Restoration Miracles to Tourist Attractions

The understanding of domestic tourism as a form of patriotic stimulus was not new in the post-Stalin era. As Anne Gorsuch has pointed out, travel within the Soviet Union was promoted during the late 1940s as a means of limiting the influence of western culture on the communist territories and reinforcing Soviet identity.[2] In the first postwar decade, the focus of such patriotic tourism had been the symbolic center of socialist transformation, Moscow.[3] The advent of the Khrushchev era, however, saw Soviet "rituals of public self-admiration"[4] extend beyond the capital to the cradles of Russian civilization: the historic Northwest. Visitors to the heritage-rich localities were expected to admire the cultural genius of the Russian people, drawing associations between the craftsmanship of the medieval architectural masters and the achievements of the present-day "builders" of communism.

The most important vehicle for the organization of heritage tourism in the region was the architectural museum-reserve, or muzei-zapovednik, established by Order of the Council of Ministers of the RSFSR in 1956.[5] Prior to this, zapovedniks had comprised, almost exclusively, nature reserves, with their origins in the 1916 declaration "On Establishing a Hunting Zapovednik in the Zabaikal Region."[6] The creation of a network of open-air architectural museums was thus an entirely new departure for Soviet tourism and one intended to bolster pride in national achievements. Novgorod was among the first towns to be attributed zapovednik status, together with Vladimir-Suzdal', Kostroma, Nizhnii-Novgorod, and Yaroslavl-Rostov.[7] The local monuments comprising the Novgorod museum's exhibits were almost exclusively works of medieval fortress architecture and "Old Russian" churches, revealing the primacy placed by the Soviet state on ideas of antiquity and cultural authenticity in the attribution of historical and cultural value.[8]

In the late 1950s and early 1960s, the Soviet authorities organized a series of conferences in order to communicate to local elites the political function of these new museum-reserves. One such event, held in Novgorod in October 1960, was attended by over seventy delegates, including representatives of the Ministry of Culture of the RSFSR, members of Soviet and Communist Party organs, directors and vice-directors of national museums, as well as regional administrators and local museum workers. The panels at the conference focused on establishing the goals, methods, and principles of the architectural zapovedniks.[9] Discussions dealt with a broad range of questions, from matters of high ideological import, such as the way the museums should present the relationship between the medieval and Soviet past, to practical details, such as the best way to remove pigeons from monastery roofs.[10]

Minutes of conference discussions reveal the emphasis Soviet officials placed on the role of the zapovedniks in promoting socialist ideals and values. In a paper entitled "On the Goals and Tasks of Historical-Architectural Museum-Reserves," for example, V. N. Ignat'ieva, representing the Russian Ministry of Culture, underlined the museums' responsibility for disseminating anti-religious propaganda and enhancing people's understanding of Soviet history and culture. The exhibitions housed in the monuments, she pointed out, should include expositions of atheist culture, displays of Soviet science and technology, and retrospectives on the transformation of the Soviet urban realm. Rather than distracting visitors from the Soviet reality, architectural reserves should, on the contrary, draw attention to socialist achievements, inspiring collective pride and encouraging identification with the communist project.[11]

Following the conference, Novgorod's Executive Committee set about the task of transforming the historic province into a veritable Soviet tourist attraction. In response to a declaration of the Presidium of the All-Russian Council for Trade Union Councils of November 27, 1959, "On the Organization and Development of Tourism in the Novgorod Region," the regional authorities passed a series of measures to improve local tourist facilities. One of the first priorities was the creation of an infrastructure of tourist accommodation—hotels, dormitories, and campsites—in light of anticipated surges in visitor numbers. The matter was considered to be of particular importance given the state of local amenities: according to one report from 1959, because of a lack of properly equipped hotels, tourists were being accommodated in pioneer camps and makeshift dormitories at the edge of town.[12]

Another source of anxiety was the condition of the architectural monuments that were to function as museum exhibits in the newly established zapovedniks.

This matter had been discussed at length at the October conference, during which representatives of the Russian Council of Ministers had outlined requirements for further repair work to a number of the region's most important visitor attractions. In line with the ministry's recommendations, restoration work was carried out in 1961 to the Novgorod Kremlin's walls and towers, the Sophia Cathedral, the Church of the Transfiguration on Il'in Street, the Theodore Stratelates Church, and the St. Nicholas Church on Yaroslav's Yard.[13] The central authorities had also advised on the adaptation of the heritage objects for museum display. Accordingly, a number of buildings were fitted with facilities to help in their new roles as tourist attractions: stairwells were constructed to give visitors access to elevated wall decorations; floodlights were installed to create atmosphere around the buildings at night; and air conditioning systems were fitted to regulate internal temperatures and protect valuable frescoes.[14]

The Soviet authorities were not only interested in curating tourists' experiences of historical monuments. They were also keen to exhibit the town as a showcase of Soviet civilization with regard to its treatment of architectural relics. In order to demonstrate the local respect for heritage objects, local officials insisted on the removal of any signs of "uncultured" behavior in the vicinity of historical buildings. Along with other improvements to the Yaroslav's Yard complex outlined in 1961, for example, instructions were issued to take down a beer stand and to relocate a fruit and vegetable kiosk, both of which were considered out of keeping with the historic character of the site.[15] An article published in *Novgorod Pravda* in 1966 expressed similar concerns about littering near the St. George's Monastery complex, where macaroni containers, cigarette butts, rusty saucepans, and other objects "of a decidedly non-historical character" blocked the nearby paths.[16] The authors were particularly distressed about the fact that these paths, used during tourist excursions, were creating a distinctly negative impression of local attitudes toward heritage objects.

While Pskov was not included among the first towns to be awarded zapovednik status in 1956, it was nevertheless promoted to the rank of historical art museum (*istoriko-khudozhestvennyi muzei*) in 1958.[17] This status ensured that the town rated highly on Soviet tourist agendas, resulting in a rapid increase in the number of annual visitors to the historic locality.[18] The local authorities requested Pskov's promotion to the status of museum-zapovednik on several occasions throughout the 1960s, most formally in 1964, when they asked the Ministry of Culture to consider the improvements that had been made to local monuments with regard to adapting them as museum exhibits with entrance fees, along the lines of the museum complexes in Novgorod, Yaroslavl, and Vladimir.[19] Zapovednik status was finally conferred upon the town on April 12, 1968, by order of the Ministry of Culture of the RSFSR.[20] The architectural reserve, as it was recognized at this time, comprised the Pskov Kremlin and the Intercession Tower, the ensemble of the Mirozhsk Monastery, the Izborsk fortress, and the Assumption Church in Meletovo.[21]

As in Novgorod, Pskov's heritage objects were expected to function both as exhibits of Russian culture and showcases of Soviet civilization. This position was made clear in a letter from the RSFSR Ministry of Culture to the Pskov Executive Committee, in 1964, which requested that materials about the 22nd Party Congress of the KPSS (1961) and the forthcoming 50th anniversary of the October Revolution (1967) be included in the exhibitions housed in local monuments.[22] In their response to the ministry's instructions, local officials demonstrated ideological zeal, proposing not only to strengthen existing exhibitions but also to convert a number of other historic buildings into museums of Soviet history and culture. On the list of buildings for museum adaptation was the town's architectural centerpiece, the Trinity Cathedral, which, it was suggested, would be converted into a museum of atheism. Faced with such a high-profile initiative, the museum authorities reached out to experts in Moscow and Leningrad for advice about the structure and content of the exhibition. In 1964, the director of the Leningrad Museum of Religious History and Atheism advised on the most suitable objects for inclusion in the museum display. These ranged from relics of the Orthodox past, such as aluminum wearable crosses, confiscated from local residents, to symbols of the secular, socialist present, such as souvenir plastic picture frames gifted to newlyweds as part of Soviet wedding ceremonies.[23]

In May 1964, the Deputy Head of the Authorities for Museums and the Preservation of Architecture A. V. Seregin wrote the Pskov Executive Committee encouraging further innovation in work with local tourists and the presentation of architectural monuments. In response to the letter, the local authorities proposed a series of further measures that would put monuments to work for the purposes of the socialist state. Specifically, local officials promised the conversion of more historic buildings for touristic purposes, including the seventeenth-century Menshikov Palaces (Sutotsk House and Iakovlev House), which would be adapted as tourist accommodations, and a fourteenth-century bake house, which was deemed a suitable location for a locally themed tourist restaurant.[24] Monuments were also proposed as the subjects of tourist souvenirs. The report included a suggestion for a postcard set in which images of local churches were interspersed with iconic works of Soviet architecture, creating associations between the architectural achievements of the medieval past and the socialist present.[25]

The tourist sector expanded more gradually in northern Vologda. The town retained its less prestigious rank of "state integrated museum" throughout the 1960s and 1970s, and, despite repeated appeals to the Ministry of Culture, only attained zapovednik status in 1988.[26] This did not mean, however, that Vologda was overlooked as a Soviet tourist destination. Though it never achieved the same prominence as Novgorod and Pskov, the Soviet authorities enthusiastically marketed the town's heritage to national audiences, particularly following the opening of the Volga-Baltic Waterway in 1964. The revival of the historic canal system, which underwent major improvement works between 1960 and 1964, instigated a wave of restoration activity across the region. As the Vologda Executive Committee explained in a report on local restoration activity, in 1964, such improvements to the region's historic buildings had created the conditions for "the more effective exploitation of cultural monuments in work with foreign and Soviet tourists."[27]

A number of Vologda's most important historic buildings were already functioning as tourist attractions by the mid-1960s. Heritage objects had been adapted for cultural purposes in response to the 1960 declaration of the Soviet Council of Ministers "On Further Improvements to Matters of Preservation of Cultural Monuments in the RSFSR," which specified that federally protected monuments should be used only for purposes of museum exploitation. The objects adapted for museum display in 1960 had included the Vologda Kremlin complex, the St. John the Baptist in Roshchen'e Church, the Demetrius of Priluki on Navolok Church, and the Church of the Shroud on Kozlenskaia Street.[28] After 1961, following the eviction of its tenants, the Savior of Priluki Monastery complex was added to the list of local attractions; 25,000 rubles were subsequently spent on the monastery's adaptation for tourist purposes, including 5,000 rubles to relocate to the site a historic wooden church in the folk style from the Aleksandr Kushtsk Monastery in the Sokol' region.[29]

The expansion of Vologda's tourist profile generated concern about the condition of its remaining heritage objects. In 1966, the Russian Ministry of Culture issued recommendations for further restoration work to be carried out to local monuments, including historical-revolutionary monuments and monuments of military and labor glory. In its plan for restoration and reconstruction work for that year, the Vologda Executive Committee consequently dedicated 10,000 rubles to the restoration of local historical-revolutionary sites and memorial monuments, and 75,000 rubles to the restoration of historic architecture. The plan made specific mention of the Kirillo-Belozersk Monastery and the Feropontov Monastery, both of which contained valuable medieval fresco paintings.[30] These sites were to be adapted for museum display, the plan stated, creating a veritable network of visitor attractions that could provide the form and substance of tourist excursions in the historic region.

The number of tourists to the Northwest grew dramatically throughout the 1960s. From 82,000 in 1940, the number of visitors to the Novgorod Architectural Museum-Zapovednik grew to 139,827 in 1961. The number increased to 201,475 in 1965 and to 240,000 in 1966.[31] Similar patterns were in evidence in Pskov. Visitors to the Pskov Historical-Architectural Museum grew rapidly between 1962 and 1970, from 57,508 to 307,000.[32] While attendance at the Vologda Architectural Museum increased more slowly during these years, visitors still flocked to the town in growing numbers throughout the 1960s: the number of annual visitors to the town's sites of historical and architectural interest surged between 1961 and 1970 from 144,627 to 203,194.[33]

Another indicator of the towns' enhanced prominence as Soviet tourist destinations was the growing number of annual publications dedicated to the region's historical architecture and artistic culture throughout the 1960s and 1970s.[34] In the case of Novgorod, nineteen books were released in the first half of the 1960s on topics related to local heritage and culture, seven of which had high print runs (over 25,000 copies). This was a marked increase from the 1950 to 1959 period, when just one historical guide with a print run of over 25,000 had been published. Likewise, for Pskov, the total number of publications grew from five in the 1950s to eight in the first half of the 1960s and from one publication with a print run of over 25,000 between 1950 and 1959 to four in the following five years. While the number of books published about Vologda was smaller, the pattern was nevertheless the same: one work dedicated to local architecture was released in 1966 with a print run of over 15,000 copies compared to no such publications in the preceding decade.[35]

The Exploitation of Museum Objects

Speaking at the 1961 Party Congress, the First Secretary of the KPSS had made clear his reservations about the idea of preservation for preservation's sake. Khrushchev maintained that monuments, if they were to be preserved at all, should be made to work for the ideological purposes of the communist state.[36]

The influence of this authoritative position could be felt in discussions about the adaptation of historic architecture that took place in museums across the country in subsequent years. In the Northwest, it gave rise to proposals for museum exhibitions that ranged in their approach from slavish political conformism to outlandish displays of ideological zealotry.

One of the most remarkable projects to emerge at this time was the 1961 plan to convert the Novgorod Kremlin complex into an "open-air museum" (*muzei pod otkrytym vozdukhom*).[37] This plan took Khrushchev's instructions, that monuments should be made to work for their place on the urban landscape, quite literally by packing the fortress so full of attractions that it resembled more closely a Soviet theme park than a medieval ruin. The project's central concept was close to the hearts of Soviet administrators—the organic combination of old and new in an enlightened display of Soviet historical consciousness. As such, it formed an architectural analogy to the controversial initiative to modernize the Moscow Kremlin complex through the inclusion of the minimalist State Kremlin Palace within the fortress walls.[38]

The authors of the Novgorod Kremlin project proposed an architectural journey through Russia's history that began with the primitive origins of Slavic civilization and ended with the Soviet Union's victory in World War II. Each section of the complex was assigned a particular historical identity, while the paths weaving between the different sections were to form a metaphor for the cultural bonds joining together past and present. The journey began between the Savior and Kukui Towers, where an ancient stone cross, a boundary stone, and a stone marked by carvings of hands and feet were exhibited; visitors then moved forward in time toward the Savior Tower, where they could contemplate the ruins of the twelfth-century Boris and Gleb Church, as well as a number of wooden churches, all of which were to be relocated to the site from neighboring villages;[39] from here the time-traveling tourist proceeded to the nineteenth century, visiting a reconstructed provincial courtyard between the Intercession and Kukui Towers; the visitor concluded her tour in the Soviet twentieth century between the Zlatoust and Intercession Towers. Here she could admire a number of relics of World War II: a T-34 tank, a snow-plane, or a 5mm canon, for example.[40]

This ambitious (and expensive) project was, perhaps unsurprisingly, never realized. Another more modest plan to convert the interior of the St. Sophia Cathedral into a museum of local art and history, however, experienced more success. The authors of the St. Sophia project, who included the director of the Novgorod Museum-Zapovednik, Tamara Konstantinova, showed acute awareness of the political exigencies of the time. Their proposal played down the preservationist aims of the initiative, underlining instead the museum's ideological function as a vehicle for the political education and enlightenment of the masses:

> The plan we have developed for the exhibition of the St. Sophia Cathedral is intended to present the museum not just from a narrowly stylistic point of view, through the exhibition of Sophia as an architectural monument, but in a broader sense, that is, to show that the church has exceptional historical significance not only as a monument of Russian architecture, but as a monument of Novgorod's social-political history.[41]

Accordingly, the project's authors proposed a plan to create four departments within the church: "St. Sophia Cathedral—an exceptional monument of Russian architecture"; "St. Sophia Cathedral—a treasure trove of Russian art"; "St. Sophia Cathedral—a center of Old Russian literacy"; and "St. Sophia Cathedral—the history of the church."[42] Despite appearing ambitious on paper, the project in fact involved little change to the historic interior of the church; its religious contents were preserved in their former place, albeit with the important stipulation that these contents now constituted museum exhibits rather than sacred objects. It was perhaps this simplicity—not to mention the project's relative economy—that appealed to the committee of high-profile museum experts employed to assess the viability of the proposal. The project was approved and the museum opened to visitors in 1961.[43]

A third example from Novgorod completes the picture of museum exploitation in the late Khrushchev era. Following reconstruction work in the immediate postwar period, the twelfth-century St. Nicholas Cathedral on Yaroslav's Yard had reopened as a working church in 1946. The renewal of anti-religious sentiment under Khrushchev, however, brought a change in the church's fortunes, and in 1962, it was once more closed and converted into a planetarium and reading room for atheist propaganda.[44] In this function, the church performed hard labor for the socialist state: according to a report from March 1965, "On the Work of the Scientific Atheist Department of the Museum-Zapovednik," in 1964 the planetarium held 254 sessions attended by 7,741 people. It also hosted 34 lectures on anti-religious themes; held question-and-answer evenings on the topics of the cosmos, science, and religion; and hosted regular "Sunday readings" for both believers and non-believers.[45]

The report nevertheless contained some strong criticism of the ideological work underway at the church-museum. Not enough was being done to encourage

militant atheism, it was noted, and links between the museum and local schools
were weak. The political contents of the church were likewise deemed to be
"unacceptable": exhibitions were poorly structured and no links had been made
between the past and the present.[46] Finally, the report criticized the condition of
the church itself, noting that the glass in the roof of the cupola was smashed, the
iconostasis was covered in marks and stains, and alter decorations were broken.[47]
While working in the interests of the atheist regime, the report suggested, it was
still expected that the church and its contents be maintained in an acceptable condition and not fall into disrepair.

In the second half of the 1960s, the emphasis of local museum work shifted.
Rather than insisting that monuments be made to work for the socialist state, the
Soviet authorities began to stress the importance of adapting historic buildings for
purposes that were commensurate with their cultural status. This shift was linked
to the growing prominence of debates about the value of architectural heritage,
led by respected Russian preservationists, such as Dmitry Likhachev, on the pages
of the *Literary Gazette* and other Soviet "thick journals."[48] Medieval churches and
fortress architecture consequently began to be exhibited, unapologetically, from "a
narrowly stylistic point of view."[49] The celebration of architectural monuments as
museum exhibits in their own right was no longer considered politically suspect.
Indeed, by the mid-1970s, this had become the established model for architectural
adaptation.

A revealing illustration of the shift in museum priorities was the project to
convert the Transfiguration Church in Novgorod, whose valuable frescoes by
Theophanes the Greek had benefited from extensive restoration work in the postwar period.[50] The church's adaptation was the subject of lively debate within the
local preservationist community; at a meeting of restoration experts in 1968, which
included the restorers Liubov' Shuliak and Il'ia Kushnir, as well as the nationally
renowned archaeologist Valentin Ianin, the need to avoid overloading the church
with extraneous exhibits or information was underlined.[51] The exhibition that was
finally mounted in the church was consequently a masterclass in self-restraint:
exhibits were limited to the medieval frescoes and some photographic reproduc-
tions of the artwork in the church's cupola; a simple metal staircase led the visitor
to the paintings in the church's drum; and natural light was used wherever possible to show the frescoes in their best aspect.[52]

Similar debates surrounding the adaptation of the St. Paraskeva Church and
the St. George's Monastery Cathedral, also in Novgorod, indicate a general shift in
attitudes toward the exhibition of heritage objects at this time. In both instances,

the question of how the churches should be exhibited to tourists provoked controversy; proposals for exhibitions of political history or atheism were passed over in favor of more "appropriate" forms of display, and specifically the inclusion of exhibits of a "cultured" nature. In the case of the St. Paraskeva Church, this requirement translated into an exhibition of wooden engravings and ecclesiastical art from the era of the church's construction; in a similar vein, the St. George's Cathedral became the location for a retrospective of the monastery's history, including images and texts about the medieval origins and cultural identity of the architectural complex.[53]

Similar tendencies were in evidence in Pskov at this time. In a discussion about the adaptation of Intercession Tower, which took place in March 1968, the director of the Pskov Museum argued that the content of museum exhibitions hosted in heritage objects ought to complement, not contradict, the historic character of their location:

> There was an old excursion around the Intercession Tower, which dated from the prewar period, but we weren't happy with it. It's not right to bring modernity into old architecture [*nel'zia vnosit' sovremennost' v staruiu arkhitekturu*]. We can introduce models of restored monuments, but stands showing modern themes would just be inappropriate [*protivoestestvenno*].[54]

A proposal to exhibit cannonballs in the historic tower was consequently rejected on the basis that "these would not have existed at the time of the kremlin's construction." A more appropriate object for inclusion, the museum director argued, was the "Cross in Triumph" icon, which dated from the same period as the historic monument.[55] The selection of this conspicuously religious artifact in favor of more traditional military exhibits revealed a dramatic shift in exhibition practices. Monuments were no longer expected to contribute to the goals of socialist construction; they could instead form abstract focuses for reflection on the past, and its architectural and artistic output.

Framing the Tourist Experience

The Soviet authorities were keen to control the impression that tourists received of the historic region, and to this end, they provided mediating texts and individuals to direct and inform the tourist's "gaze."[56] Perhaps the most important of these interpretative aids was the Soviet excursion guide (*ekskursovod*), an individual whose strategic function was underlined by state officials in early discussions of museum exploitation. At the seminar of museum workers, hosted in Novgorod in October 1961, the question of "cadre formation" had been high on the agenda. Excursion guides had to be more than mere "talking machines," officials argued. They needed to possess a comprehensive knowledge of and love for their regions in order to inspire similar feelings in their listeners.[57] To this end, kraevedenie courses were established so that trainee guides could learn about the history, culture, art, and architecture of their regions.[58] In the Khrushchev period, these courses included classes on Marxist-Leninist theory, enabling guides to infuse their lectures with necessary political content and color.[59]

One gets a sense of the content of these lectures from the (at times quite substantial) commentaries left by visitors to the historic towns in museum response books throughout the 1960s and 1970s. A favorite topic among tourists at this time was the guides themselves, many of whom received high praise for their erudition, rhetorical fluency, and accessibility. One memorable example of this kind of commentary was provided by a tourist from Leningrad, who attended an excursion around Novgorod's architectural zapovednik in 1968. The tourist, who claimed to have good knowledge of local history and architecture, explained that he had "seen Novgorod with new eyes" thanks to the scholarship and local knowledge of his guide:

> [Anatolii] Otsurov has at his disposal a huge wealth of knowledge, but doesn't try to blind you with his erudition, to make you dizzy with figures, facts and dates, thus highlighting your ignorance. On the contrary, you have the feeling that he's only drawing on a tiny part of his knowledge. But this tiny part is extremely sound and well selected.[60]

Of particular note, this visitor thought, was the intellectual substance of Otsurov's lectures; the guide's explanations revealed his extensive knowledge of local art, history, and culture, as well as his flair for engaging cultural commentary:

> Otsurov is particularly adept at layering his presentation with different materials, with the result that the established theme of his lectures is presented with lots of so-called secondary details, "non-obligatory information," fresh associations, unexpected references, prompted by the logic of the story he is telling, and allusions to

historical literature, art, and music. All this imparts to his narrative volume, significance, and depth. And the things Otsurov says aren't ready prepared or learned by heart. The guide is a master of improvised speech. His answers to the most unexpected and, in some cases, awkward questions are miniature, interesting novellas, which are nevertheless always pertinent to the theme of the excursion.[61]

In addition to their erudition, guides were often complimented on the "patriotic" content and delivery of their lectures. A group of visitors from Moscow, for example, praised their local escort for the "great love and patriotism" with which he presented his lectures on local architecture.[62] Visitors from Leningrad echoed these words, congratulating another member of the museum staff on the patriotic tone of her presentation: "you get the sense from her speeches that she is a patriot of her town."[63] In a particularly laudatory entry, another group of tourists from Moscow demanded institutional recognition for the "knowledge and genuine Novgorodian patriotism" of their guide.[64] From these entries it was apparent that local patriotism was not merely an institutional requirement of tourist guides, but one that was enthusiastically implemented in practice and positively received by consumers of local culture.

Another way in which the Soviet authorities mediated visitors' impressions of the local landscape was through the provision of architectural and tourist guidebooks. Authored, for the most part, by regional historians and restorers, these directories of the towns' most important historical sites doubled up as in-depth study manuals and informative traveling companions. Of particular note within this corpus were the prestigious "Art" Press guidebooks, first published in the 1960s, that were similar in tone and content to the erudite "Pevsner Guides" to British architecture or the meticulously researched "Blue Guides" to European heritage towns. The way that these guides were ordered, the textual space that they dedicated to individual monuments, and their strategic use of images revealed much about the political values associated with heritage objects. The "atmosphere of intellectual rigor" communicated through the form and production of the guides, moreover, reinforced the idea of Soviet tourism as a formative rather than frivolous act.[65]

The "Art" Press guides were structured according to a particular formula: an essay on the architectural development of the towns was followed by descriptions of individual heritage objects grouped according to region. The ordering of these monuments was instructive. Guides to the medieval towns of the Northwest began with excursions around the local kremlins, reinforcing the region's associations with ideas of military strength and wartime resilience. Indeed, the kremlins were not as obvious a starting point for architectural guidebooks as might be thought; guides published at other moments in history began their tours in very different locations. The reader of V. P Laskovskii's 1910 *Guide to Novgorod*, for example, arrived in the town via the River Volkhov, her attention directed toward the Khutyn Monastery and the Savior of the Transfiguration Church, perched picturesquely on the river bank.[66] The reader of A. I. Sazonov and E. A. Starikov's *My Vologda* (2007), by contrast, began her tour at the town's eighteenth-century Resurrection Church on Cathedral Hill, the place the authors considered to be the spiritual heart of the medieval city.[67]

The authors of the "Art" Press guides led their readers on tours of the towns via the region's most emblematic monuments, both in terms of Russian architectural history and Soviet restoration work. Mikhail Karger's textual excursion around Novgorod's "Sophia Side" in *Novgorod the Great* (1961), for example, began at the St. Blaise the Martyr Church, while its tour of the "Trade Side" ended with the St. Nicholas on Lipno Island Church, both of which had been reconstructed from ruins in the first decade after the war.[68] The guides can thus be seen to have formed props in the performance of Soviet patriotic tourism. The ideal reader would benefit intellectually and physically from touring architectural monuments in the open air but would also develop a sense of pride in the work of the Russian medieval masters and Soviet postwar restorers, fusing Russian and Soviet achievements in the popular imagination.

One of the difficulties facing the authors of tourist materials was the negotiation of politically problematic associations with local architecture. Particularly thorny was the case of Novgorod's Sophia Cathedral, which, as the historic location of the town's medieval public assemblies, or "veche" parliament, was associated in popular consciousness with the "Novgorod Democratic Republic." The legend of the freedom-loving Republic had to be packaged carefully by those writing about the Cathedral since it had the potential to undermine the "democratic" credentials of the Soviet government. In their descriptions of the site, local historians thus tended to emphasize the protocommunist character of the veche and the role of the "common people" (*chernye liudi*) in its governance. In his guide to the Novgorod Kremlin published in 1964, for example, A. I. Semenov painted a picture of medieval politics on the site that bore striking resemblance to descriptions of the October Revolution: "Here, in feudal times, the town's lower classes [*nizy*] would rise up against the governing boyar class.

[In the veche] local craftsmen and serfs would take part in politics together with the privileged sectors of the population."[69]

Another architectural object that presented difficulties to Soviet historians was the sculptural centerpiece of the Novgorod Kremlin, the Millennium of Russia Monument. A multi-layered composition whose bell-like shape referenced Novgorod's democratic past, the monument was an unapologetic celebration of tsarist power. The composition contained a total of 129 individual sculptures, a large number of which were renderings of Lithuanian dynasts and Muscovite princes (though Ivan the Terrible, the notorious author of the "Novgorod Massacre," was notably absent). Reading Soviet political values into this monument required a feat of interpretative dexterity. One local writer took up the task in an introduction to a photograph album dedicated to the sculpture by drawing the reader's attention to the almost imperceptible figure of a Russian peasant, who bore the weight of a gigantic globe at the monument's center. This Atlasesque symbol, the author argued, conveyed the essentially proletarian message of the sculpture: "We are reminded that the real essence of the work is him, the simple Russian peasant, worker, or soldier, who for a thousand years has supported and defended the great Russian state."[70]

Local historians also had to negotiate the politically fraught subject of the Northwest's annexation by the State of Muscovy in the late fifteenth to early sixteenth centuries. In line with Stalinist historiography, this event was interpreted as an act of "progressive centralism," desired and, indeed, helped along by the "common people."[71] The architectural consequences of the region's inclusion within the Muscovite sphere of influence were, moreover, presented in terms that could cause no offense to the capital. Discussing Pskov's annexation, in an edited collection of kraevedenie materials, S. I. Kolotilova thus reasoned that "unification" had brought about the economic and political conditions necessary for the town's artistic advancement.[72] This interpretation remained dominant into the 1980s. According to Lagunin's 1984 architectural guide, *Pskov. Izborsk*, unification with the centralizing Muscovite state had provided the impetus for economic and cultural growth, resulting in a boom in architectural innovation and an intensification of building work.[73]

Tourist guides to Vologda revealed a similar tendency to read socialist values into the architectural landscape. Vologda's architecture, local authors explained, reflected the "democratic" character of the local people. On the one hand, it was characterized by "laconicism" and "severity," the architectural equivalent of the noble "reserve" that was said to distinguish the northern population.[74] On the other, local monuments, and particularly churches, were described as "full-blooded" and "authentic," free from any lofty pretensions or obscurantist "mysticism."[75] By insisting on the "democratic" quality of local culture, the authors of the guides were able to align their interpretations with the artistic values of the time, which, during the Khrushchev period in particular, rejected "decorative extravagances" (izlishestva) in favor of more popular architectural forms.[76] As G. Bocharov and V. Vygodov have underlined, there was nothing ostentatious or snobbish about Vologda's architectural heritage; on the contrary, its "simple and, at times, primitive forms are so concrete and democratic that they can be understood as a living folk fantasy."[77]

In the late 1960s and 1970s, the tone of architectural guides to the Northwest became more eulogistic. In line with the shifts in popular perceptions of architectural heritage, medieval monuments began to be praised not only as historical relics but as objects of sublime and transcendental beauty. Taking inspiration from the romantic writers of the eighteenth century, authors identified certain "natural" elements in objects of local cultural heritage: the organically undulating walls of the St. Sophia Cathedral; the upward surging form of Theodore Stratelates Church; or the laconic purity of decoration in the case of Savior on Nereditsa Church in Novgorod.[78] Architectural monuments, like the awe-inspiring mountainscapes of the romantic poets, were described as having a transcendental effect on the observer. The fictional flâneur passing through the medieval Russian province could thus find herself contemplating the mythical town of Kitezh as she approached the Savior of Priluki Monastery on the outskirts of Vologda.[79] Upon beholding the disintegrating walls of the Pskov Kremlin, she might be whisked back in time to the arrival of the Slavs of the banks of the River Velikii.[80]

Consumers of Heritage Culture: Soviet Tourists

The zapovedniks and architectural museums of the Russian Northwest were primarily sites of domestic tourism. Among the 3,359 excursions conducted in Novgorod in 1961, for example, just 141 were with foreign tourists.[81] The large part of this foreign tourism, moreover, issued from the "friendly" countries of the communist East Bloc and other socialist-leaning nations. This trend was confirmed by the statistics for foreign language publications. In Novgorod, which was by far the most popular of the three tourist destinations for foreign

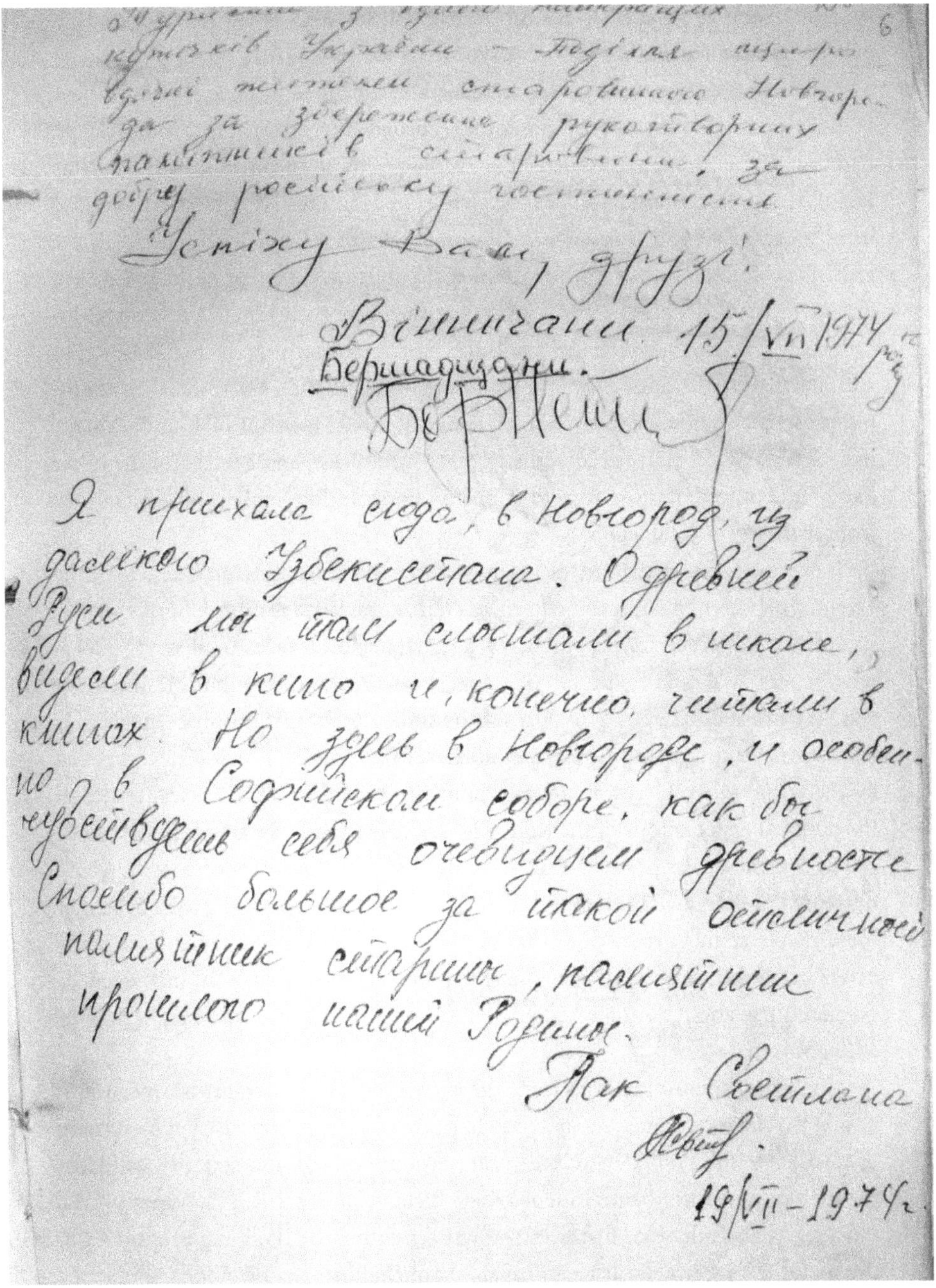

…куточків України — Поділля щиро вдячні жителям старовинного Новгорода за збереження рукотворних пам'ятників старовини, за добру російську гостинність.
Успіху Вам, друзі!
Вінничани 15/VII 1974 р.
Бершадчани.

Я приехала сюда, в Новгород, из далекого Узбекистана. О древней Руси мы так слышали в школе, видели в кино и, конечно, читали в книгах. Но здесь в Новгороде, и особенно в Софийском соборе, как бы чувствуешь себя очевидцем древности. Спасибо большое за такой отличной памятник старины, памятник прошлого нашей Родины.
Пак Светлана
19/VII-1974 г.

FIGURE 5. Example commentaries about excursions around the St. Sophia Cathedral in Novgorod from a response book at the Novgorod Museum for 1967–1979.

tourists in the 1960s and 1970s, no tourist guidebooks or historical materials existed in languages other than Russian until the late 1970s.

Tourists nevertheless flocked to the Northwest from all over the Soviet Union. Visitor response books at local museums recorded entries of groups from Belarus, Ukraine, Uzbekistan, Azerbaijan, and Moldova, among other Soviet Socialist Republics. Within Russia, visitors traveled from Moscow and Leningrad, but also from more distant regions such as Perm, Cheliabinsk, and Vladivostok. These tourists visited the towns on individual excursions or as part of package tours of different historic locations. The selection of places for inclusion in these multi-location excursions often revealed a political agenda concerning the presentation of national history: tours of Kiev and the towns of the Russian Northwest, for example, presented tourists with a vision of medieval Rus' as the cultural foundation for the modern Soviet state; excursions to Novgorod, Brest, and Minsk, on the other hand, encouraged visitors to reflect on the phoenix-like rebirth of the country from the ashes of total war.[82]

The impression that tourists received from the historic towns can, to some extent, be discerned from the comments left in museum response books, correspondence preserved in local archives, and letters and articles published in local newspapers. It should be noted, of course, that this kind of public commentary was far from spontaneous. Not only was it moderated by institutional gatekeepers (museum authorities and newspaper editors, for example), it was also controlled by the writers themselves, many of whom demonstrated an acute awareness of the political expectations of the time.[83] Nevertheless, and in spite of these factors, public commentaries provide some indication of the degree of success with which museums and zapovedniks were able to achieve their political goals. Whether monuments actually roused feelings of pride in Soviet achievements is, to some extent, irrelevant; Soviet citizens' ability to reproduce elements of the official patriotic discourse about heritage and its political relevance is indication enough of its social impact.

A number of commentaries from the early 1960s demonstrate visitors' awareness of the political values attributed to heritage objects. A response left by a group of students to the Vologda Architectural Museum in 1961, for example, validated the idea of a historical monument as a vehicle of political enlightenment: "The museum is an archive of history!" the writers enthused. "Walking around all of the museum's rooms, we learned much about the history of Vologda, about the advances of industry, and toilers of the land. We wish the museum the very best of luck for the future!"[84] Numerous other commentaries pointed out the value of heritage in understanding developments in the Soviet present: "Thinking about the past, you see the present more clearly," one visitor to the Vologda Kremlin mused before thanking the staff for preserving the relics of the past for Soviet audiences.[85] This feedback, compiled by museum workers in reports to the central authorities, provided evidence of heritage tourism's role in stimulating patriotic identification with the Soviet state.

During the Brezhnev era, in line with a shift in the norms of museum exploitation, a more nationalistic tone crept into some visitors' commentaries. One tourist to Novgorod's architectural zapovednik in 1970, for example, gushed: "Thank you, Mighty Rus', for leaving us this inheritance. Thank you, Russian people of Novgorod, for preserving it for us. I achieved complete spiritual harmony contemplating all of this true Russianness—Our heritage [*gladia na vse eto istinnoe russkoe—Nashe*]."[86] While such overtly ethno-centric commentaries were unusual, acknowledgments of the cultural value of architectural monuments became more common at this time. An Uzbek visitor to the St. Sophia Cathedral in 1974, for example, commented on the emotional impact of her visit to the great monument of Russian history and culture:

> I visited Novgorod from faraway Uzbekistan. There we'd learnt about Ancient Rus' at school, seen it in the cinema, and, of course, read about it in books. But here in Novgorod, and particularly in the Sophia Cathedral, you feel like an eyewitness to the past. Many thanks to this wonderful ancient monument, which has preserved the past of our Motherland.[87]

Comments such as these revealed the all-Soviet impact of the idea that the towns of the Northwest captured the essence of Russian culture. This culture—as the emphatic "our" in both commentaries suggested—was not perceived as something remote or foreign, but rather an integral part of the Soviet collective self.

Consumers of Heritage Culture: Local Tourists

The second most important group of visitors to the architectural zapovedniks of the Russian Northwest were the residents of the historic towns themselves. The promotion of tourism within one's own locality was linked to the revival of the repressed discipline of kraevedenie in the late Khrushchev era, which involved a series of measures designed to stimulate Soviet patriotic consciousness through the promotion of local knowledge.[88] As the authors of the political pamphlet "Kraevedenie and Tourism" explained, tourism within one's local area could help generate feelings of loyalty and pride toward the Soviet Motherland: "whatever its goal (recreation, sport, curiosity, etc.) tourism will inevitably attract travelers to kraevedenie; some to a lesser degree, others to such an extent that many will become inveterate kraevedy, diligently studying their beloved regions."[89]

Promoting engagement with the historic landscape was also a means of ensuring residents made the correct impression on national audiences. In an extension of the debate about "civilized" forms of interaction with heritage objects, critics underlined the need to improve local knowledge of architectural monuments and for locals to perform this knowledge to visiting outsiders. This was the gist of an article published in *Novgorod Pravda* in October 1966 that described the travails of a visiting tourist who had wandered around the town for half a day asking ignorant locals for directions to the St. Demetrius of Thessaloniki Church. The fact that no one had been able to direct the visitor to the historic monument was a disgrace, the author maintained: "All Novgorodians should take an interest in the attractions of their town so that they never have to say, on meeting a visiting tourist, 'I don't know.'"[90]

Throughout the 1960s, various measures were taken to improve residents' knowledge of local history, culture, and architecture. A report on the work of the Novgorod zapovednik in 1961, for example, noted that excursions around the monuments of the Novgorod Kremlin had been carried out with workers at the local knitting and sewing factories, the building trust, the porcelain factory, and the state-owned farms—along with residents of neighboring villages.[91] Further measures to improve local awareness of heritage matters were outlined in another report on museum activity in 1970. The document contained details of plans to create a tourist base in St. George's Monastery and a summer camp at the Peryn Monastery complex, while also establishing excursions for local residents to Staraia Rus', Mikhailovskoe, and other historic destinations.[92]

Residents began to learn about their region's cultural heritage not only through local tourism but also in schools and museums. In an order of the Ministry of Enlightenment of the RSFSR of May 1961, "On the Strengthening of Kraevedenie Work in Schools and the Publication of Kraevedenie Materials for Schoolchildren," schools were instructed to incorporate materials about local heritage into their teaching in order to stimulate Soviet patriotic consciousness among the next generation of communist citizens:

The existing links between study and life need to be significantly strengthened through kraevedenie work in schools. The use of kraevedenie materials in geography, biology, history, literature, and other lessons will allow pupils to acquire knowledge more consciously and to see evidence of the patterns they are studying in the world around them. The engagement of pupils in extracurricular kraevedenie work will create more opportunities for them to apply the knowledge they have acquired to real life.[93]

In addition to the abstract logic behind the promotion of kraevedenie work in the classroom, the order provided a number of practical instructions to school directors and teachers about how to strengthen local study in their institutions. These included the construction of kraevedenie rooms or corners in every school, the involvement of school pupils in the creation of local "chronicles" detailing the history of their villages or towns, and the promotion of architectural preservation among school-age children through their active involvement in the upkeep of local monuments.[94]

Schools were likewise encouraged to work actively with museums and zapovedniks to improve pupils' knowledge of local cultural heritage. A report on the work of the Vologda kraevedenie museum for 1961 demonstrated the ways in which this requirement was implemented in practice. In a section on "work with schoolchildren," the report detailed plans to create heritage-themed study aids for pupils to be used during school trips.[95] In a way that was similar to guides and museum exhibitions, which presented Soviet citizens with an officially endorsed interpretation of local history and culture, these exercises were designed to inculcate in schoolchildren an appreciation of local architecture that corresponded to the political agenda of the time.

What is an "Architectural Monument"?

The promotion of local knowledge among the towns' populations resulted in a discernable growth in historical consciousness. In the 1960s and 1970s, every town, village, school, and club became a prospective site of scholarly research, every local building a potential museum exhibit, and every piece of information a possible historical fact. By the mid-Brezhnev era, many local factories, collective farms, and institutes had established their own community (*narodnye*) museums. A list of museums in the Vologda region compiled in 1974, for example, included the museums of the "The Glory of Work" sewing factory, the Vologda car equipment plant, and the Vologda sheepskin and fur factory.[96] Locals were engaging in micro-historical analysis, studying their cultural environments and creating archives of materials about local heritage objects.[97] The process of "historicizing" the lived environment stimulated curiosity about the local past but also raised questions about Soviet preservation and, specifically, the definition of an "architectural monument."

Throughout the 1960s, residents began to write to their local authorities with questions about the status of historic buildings. Many of these letters questioned the privileged status of museum objects and asked for the category of architectural monuments to be expanded to include other buildings that were perceived to hold artistic or historical value. In one such letter, published in *Novgorod Pravda* in 1967, a local electrician expressed concerns about the preservation of buildings from the late Imperial period, none of which had been included among the zapovednik's exhibits: "Maybe these old houses don't have particular architectural value and can't compete as masterpieces of architecture. But they are monuments all the same," he reasoned. "And if it is far from necessary to put up a memorial plaque on each and every one of them, it is still our duty to preserve them."[98]

A letter on a related topic was sent to the Vologda Society for the Preservation of Historical and Cultural Monuments in 1971. In this correspondence, the writer showed awareness of the role of heritage tourism in stimulating pride in the country's history and culture. Cautious of appearing too critical of local politics, the author was at pains to demonstrate her commitment to the Soviet project:

> I'm sorry to disturb you. Firstly, about the St. Andrew the Apostle Church from the middle of the seventeenth century, which is situated in front of our house on the bank of the river. We're pretty sure that the church is a historic monument. But do you know what kind of state it's in? Well, it just stands there like a shelled egg. It's shameful to look at! Tourists go past on the river and in their coaches and look at that ancient monument. And it's all filled with rubbish. They're using it as a dump. On the radio and television they talk about the need to reconstruct and restore monuments, so why not make it into some kind of museum? Then it will be nice for the tourists to look at. And the church would be in a proper state too. Secondly, Happy Day of Workers Solidarity! And Happy Victory Day![99]

Letters such as this revealed the impact of heritage tourism on local historical consciousness. Participating in tourist excursions and learning about local architecture had heightened people's awareness of heritage matters and made them more appreciative of the historic landscape. Moreover, this knowledge and the language in which it was imparted provided them with a means of extracting concessions from the political authorities. By making use of the vocabulary of Soviet preservation, residents could try to control developments in their localities and to defend objects of perceived cultural value from state-inflicted damage and destruction.

A third letter and its response, penned ten years later, in 1981, show how this form of cultural lobbying persisted and evolved over time. The writer, in this instance, was a resident of a rural settlement in the Vologda region, and the subject of her letter was the fate of a local church: "My name is Galina Ivanova and I am the head of a family residing in the village of Gliadkovo in the Sheksninsk region," the writer explained. "We are very interested in the church located in our village. Does it represent any interest as a monument? If so, will its restoration be considered?"[100] On this occasion, the attempt to solicit state patronage was unsuccessful, though the tone of the response penned by the local preservation authorities suggested that the enquiry could be useful in mounting a case for the church's restoration in the future:

> Respected Galina Ivanova!
>
> In answer to your letter I am writing to inform you that the ecclesiastical building near to the Gliadkovo settlement in the Sheksninsk region has no real value and cannot be considered either a historically or architecturally important monument. It is a run-of-the-mill [*riadovoe*] cultic building, an architectural monument of the eighteenth century. It would be wonderful to restore all buildings like this, despite their cultic character, so that they were a pleasure to look at and could be used in the work of cultural institutions. But, at the present time, there are simply no means to do this.[101]

Preservationist Resistance to Heritage Tourism

One might assume that local architectural restorers, many of whom had lobbied energetically for the preservation of the historic landscape, would have been gratified by the touristic interest the northwest region. Evidence suggests, however, that the development of the towns as Soviet tourist destinations gave rise to tensions between local restoration workshops and the political authorities, particularly with regard to the allocation of precious restoration resources. For example, a report on the work of the Novgorod Restoration Workshop, compiled in 1961, revealed a conflict of opinions regarding the most appropriate focus for restoration activity in the historic town. While restorers continued to divide their efforts between buildings of different styles and periods, the local authorities argued that zapovednik "monuments," the state-sponsored focus of touristic attention, should be privileged over "less prestigious" historical buildings:

> Some shortcomings in the present arrangement should be noted. More than half of the plan of the Novgorod Restoration Workshop is currently taken up with work that has nothing to do with museum objects. As a result, there are too many objects to deal with and the Workshop is unable to concentrate its attention on the monuments [*pamiatniki*]. The Workshop only works on museum objects in the winter, rather than summer period, and this arrangement is reflected in the duration and quality of the work carried out.[102]

Local budgets for restoration work underlined the bias in favor of museum attractions. In Vologda, state funding was allocated almost exclusively for the restoration of zapovednik exhibits: the Vologda Kremlin complex and the Savior of Priluki Monastery together absorbed 202,000 of a total 281,000 rubles earmarked for restoration in 1961 and 252,000 of a total 400,000 rubles in 1964.[103] Figures for repair work in Pskov demonstrated similar emphasis on museum buildings. Spending on zapovednik objects thus rose from 213,000 rubles in 1967, to 230,000 in 1976, and 364,000 in 1979.[104] At the same time, funding for repairs to buildings outside of the museum zone, such as Pskov's seventeenth-century merchant palaces or Vologda's historic wooden mansions, for example, remained minimal throughout this period.[105]

This was not the only source of frustration for local preservationists. Many also regretted the physical changes to the historic landscape that the growth in Soviet tourism had engendered. A particular source of vexation in Pskov, for example, was the development of a tourist base at Pushkin's historic estate, Mikhailovskoe, near the town of Pushkin Hills, which had begun in the early 1960s.[106] The destination had proven remarkably popular—in 1963, about 200,000 visitors were reported to have visited the site. Accordingly, a number of additional tourist services had been established at the estate throughout the 1960s. In 1964, these had included, aside from the tourist base itself, a ticket booth, photographers, chemists, a post office, and a café—all of which had been built just meters away from the poet's historic eighteenth-century residence.[107]

The perceived disfigurement of the historic landscape prompted an outcry from the highest reaches of the Soviet cultural intelligentsia. In 1965, a collective of Russian writers, including Anna Akhmatova, Mikhail Dudin, and Viktor Shklovskii, penned a letter to the *Literary Journal*, complaining that the historic view over the Kuchane Lake, a source of inspiration for Pushkin's romantic verse, was being ruined by the sight of souvenir stalls, heavy goods vehicles, and thousands of milling Soviet tourists. The development of the site had to be carried out "sensitively and tactfully," the literary collective argued. The planned construction of a five-story tourist hotel complex in close proximity to the estate, for example, would be better situated in a nearby forest, where it would not distract from the romantic panorama.[108]

The writers' appeal, however, fell on deaf ears. Between 1971 and 1975, a further 13,538 square meters of tourist accommodation was built at the site, including a 105-room tourist hotel, a tourist base that could accommodate 500 visitors, a car park, and a playground.[109] Continued tourist interest in the estate prompted a declaration by the RSFSR Council of Ministers in 1978 titled "On Measures to Further Develop the A. S. Pushkin State Museum-Zapovednik." Additional "improvements" to the complex consequently included the construction of a 2,000-seat concert hall, newly asphalted roads between Novgorod and Pushkin Hills, and (most ambitiously) plans for the construction of an orangery.[110] In this, as in other cases of architectural conversion for cultural purposes, the tug of tourist rubles ultimately proved more persuasive than the arguments of the country's revered preservationist elite.

Preservationist commentators continued to note the damaging impact of tourist activity on the historic landscape throughout the Soviet period. In 1971, an employee at the Vologda Architectural Museum thus complained that visiting tourists had been vandalizing the town's valuable folk monuments: "[They] are dismantling our town: they pull off platbands, decorations, and engravings. It's simply unacceptable!"[111] When the propagators of such uncivilized behavior were foreigners, local outrage was redoubled. The (possibly fictionalized) story of an American tourist who had slipped away from her excursion group to photograph overflowing rubbish bins in a nearby courtyard was, for example, relayed with particular relish by a journalist writing in *Novgorod Pravda* in 1961. Disrespecting the historic landscape in such a way was unacceptable, the article's author scolded: "When we invite you to our homes, we don't expect you to put your feet on our tables. If you forget who is the guest and who is the host we will politely but firmly remind you."[112]

• • •

In the post-Stalin period, the towns of the historic Northwest were marketed to national audiences as museums of Russian heritage and culture, but also as showcases of the Soviet state's enlightened treatment of historic ruins. The careful ideological work of local actors and institutions linked the town's architectural exhibits to the project of building communism, asserting an understanding of heritage as the cultural foundation upon which Soviet civilization had been built. Making this connection was sometimes difficult, involving feats of counterintuitive reasoning that might appear in retrospect disingenuous and contrived. Nevertheless, evidence suggests that efforts to market historic Russia as a symbol of Soviet cultural identity produced results. The public commentaries about heritage objects recorded at this time reveal Soviet citizens' familiarity with the official patriotic discourse and, more intriguingly, their ability to deploy this discourse to strategic effect in state-mediated forums.

In the Brezhnev era, the touristic idea of the Russian Northwest began to change. Less emphasis was placed on linking heritage to the goal of socialist construction and, accordingly, visitors' appreciation of the landscape shifted. More nationalistic tones crept into public commentaries about architectural monuments: historic kremlins and medieval churches began to be perceived, first and foremost, as objects of Russian cultural heritage. The public's more ethnocentric understanding of northwestern architecture was aligned with shifts in cultural politics more generally at this time. The permissive political climate of the Brezhnev years, which some critics have referred to as an era of "inclusionary politics," had specific consequences for preservationist matters in the Northwest. These consequences were felt in particular in the field of folk heritage preservation and tourism, which, as discussed in the following chapter, experienced a state-sponsored growth in popularity across the 1970s and 1980s.

The promotion of the Northwest as a center of Soviet heritage tourism had a number of other, more specifically local consequences. The exposure of residents to politically inspired arguments about the value of the heritage landscape had the result of stimulating pride in local culture and achievements, but also of creating critical awareness of the shortcomings of Soviet preservationist policy. Rather than strengthening the legitimacy of the post-Stalin regime and fostering social solidarity, the promotion of local knowledge had the inverse effect. Residents of the historic region began to question preservationist decisions and to challenge the authority of the political center to resolve and arbitrate matters pertaining to local culture.

The regional boom in heritage tourism likewise aggravated relations between local preservationist communities and the political authorities. While restorers and museum workers had wielded some influence over restoration agendas in the early postwar period, the growth in the town's cultural profiles in the 1960s and 1970s saw authority for preservationist matters pass to higher echelons of government. The centralization of control over heritage matters was a source of frustration for local cultural elites. As preservationist questions became increasingly politicized in the decades that followed, these frustrations heightened, consolidating into forms of regional lobbying and political opposition in the perestroika and post-Soviet periods.

3.

LANDSCAPES OF LIVING HISTORY

Folk Architecture in the National Imaginary

In the mid-1960s, the focus of preservationist interest in the Northwest expanded to include the region's abundant wooden folk architecture. Tourists continued to visit historic towns to contemplate "Old Russian" monasteries and onion-domed churches, but an interest also arose in wandering around open-air museums of izbas, barns, and windmills to participate in reconstructed scenes of Russian village life. As Russian themes began to be strategically promoted by the Brezhnev regime, heritage tourism became part of a patriotic spectacle, the emphasis of which was placed firmly on ethnic Russian heritage and traditions.[1] An exoticized idea of Russian folk culture was established at this time: the region's ornate wooden churches and elaborately carved peasant huts formed props in a state-sponsored performance of Russian cultural identity.

This chapter begins with an outline of the fate of folk architecture in the first half of the twentieth century followed by an account of the shifts in cultural politics that led to a reappraisal of the genre in the mid-1960s. It links the revival of interest in folk themes and aesthetics to the work of the culturally conservative "Village Prose" writers, whose literature focused on the fate of Russian rural traditions and material culture in the Brezhnev era. A detailed look at the state-sponsored promotion of folk heritage through the creation of museums of folk architecture, displays of ethnic Russian arts and crafts, and performances of folk song and dance supports the chapter's argument that the endorsement of this heritage was part of a strategy to contain rising ethno-nationalism in the late Soviet era that gave rise to an aestheticized vision of northwestern folk culture as the epitome of the "national style."

The Status of Folk Architecture after 1917

Like other cultural relics of late Imperial Russian life, the status of folk architecture following the Revolution was precarious. The combined factors of Bolshevik hostility to peasant culture, the militant drive against religion, political tumult and economic crisis meant that many wooden buildings in the folk style, a large part of which were village churches, chapels, and belfries, were abandoned or demolished in the first decades after 1917. Matters worsened still further following the outbreak of war in Russia in 1941. During the years of wartime occupation and fighting, wooden churches and houses were converted for utilitarian purposes— as storehouses for grain, vegetables, or salt, for example—with the result that, by the mid-1940s, many found themselves in a state of extreme dilapidation or on the brink of total collapse.[2]

Two additional factors informed early Soviet attitudes to folk architecture. The first was the limited resources of the Central Restoration Authorities (TsRGM) in the 1920s and 1930s, which were unable to finance excursions to the difficult-to-reach northwestern periphery of the country, where many folk buildings were located; the second was the prejudicial attitude toward wooden architecture, which was seen as an expression of Slavic folk culture and, as such, as artistically and aesthetically inferior to stone architecture.[3] There were, nevertheless, some important exceptions to the general rule of disinterest in and neglect of the country's folk heritage. Most notable was the project led by the architect and restorer Petr Baranovskii to relocate three wooden folk buildings from the Preobrazhenskii settlement, in the Moscow region, to the city's Kolomenskoe Park at the end of the 1920s.[4] This project resulted in the creation of the Soviet Union's first open-air museum of folk architecture, an outlier in a cultural landscape that otherwise excluded folk themes.

In the mid-1940s, in line with the general rise in Russian national consciousness, opinions about wooden folk architecture began to change.[5] The publication of *Russian Wooden Architecture* by the prestigious USSR Academy of Architecture Press in 1942 was the first indication of a growth in academic interest in this style.[6] Following the war, studies of the condition of the country's wooden heritage began to take place, particularly in the regions most affected by wartime occupation and fighting. Many of these studies were carried out by Moscow-based architects and restorers, including A. N. Buinov, B. V. Gnedovskii, L. M. Lisenko, I. K. Rybchenko, and, most famously, A. V. Opolovnikov.[7] The attention of this restoration elite focused primarily on the church ensembles of the North and Northwest: the complex of churches on Kizhi Island (18–19 c.); the Dormition Cathedral in Kondopoga (1774); the Assumption Cathedral in Kem' (1711–1777); and the St. Barbara the Martyr Church (1656) in Yandomozero, among others.[8]

As Alexey Golubev has noted, the restoration of wooden architecture in the late 1940s and early 1950s was governed by similar principles to those governing the reconstruction of stone buildings at this time.[9] Like the postwar architects discussed in chapter 1, Opolovnikov and colleagues were interested in restoring wooden buildings back to an "optimum date." In the case of the Kizhi Pogost complex, this date was located in the precapitalist period, before late tsarist restorers had introduced their "eclectic" and "ahistorical" interpolations. Restoration thus involved the removal of planking and domes sheathed with iron, which according to restoration theorists hid the authentic fabric of the buildings. This process was understood in romantic-patriotic terms, as means of liberating the eighteenth-century "song of wood" that was muffled beneath the layers of bourgeois accretions.[10]

Golubev has noted the ideological charge of some theoretical arguments relating to the restoration of folk architecture in the postwar period. Theorists connected the precapitalist folk style with the perceived cultural purity of the Russian North, a region that was argued to have survived the "tsunami of the Mongol invasion" culturally intact. Restorers such as Opolovnikov consequently prioritized "antiquity and authenticity (real or imagined) of old wooden buildings over the meanings, and contexts, of their use in local communities."[11] Folk churches and houses were invested with value on the condition that they "performed authenticity and traditionalism, thus objectifying the much-sought-for historical depth of modern Soviet society."[12]

A more fundamental shift in attitudes toward folk architecture took place in the 1960s. At this time, the preservation of Russian folk heritage shifted from being a niche concern of a metropolitan elite to become a national cause célèbre, endorsed by practitioners and amateurs from across the country. This shift was linked to the rise of the Russian patriotic intelligentsia, including medieval historian and conservative critic Dmitry Likhachev and the outspokenly nationalist writer Vladimir Soloukhin, who lobbied for the preservation of "authentic" Russian traditions and ways of life. The widely circulated literature of the Russian Village Prose writers likewise proved influential at this time, informing the thinking of architectural practitioners at the center of the drive to preserve Russia's folk landscape and the attitudes of readers and preservationist enthusiasts more generally.

"Derevenshchiki" and "Derevianshchiki"

The writer and poet Vladimir Soloukhin was a formative figure within the literary intelligentsia and played a significant role in highlighting the plight of Russian village heritage in the Brezhnev era. Soloukhin's writing focused in particular on his native region of Vladimir, which he explored in his travelogue of the local countryside, *Vladimir Back Roads* (1957), and in his most famous publication on the joys of icon collection, *Black Boards* (1967).[13] By contrast with the contemporaneous writings of Likhachev, which dealt, for the most part, with the preservation of urban heritage, Soloukhin explored the artistic and architectural traditions of rural Vladimir. His writings thus formed a bridge between the thematic concerns of preservationist critics in the Brezhnev years and the preoccupations of the Russian Village Prose writers, whose works I discuss in more detail below.

Black Boards is perhaps the best example of Soloukhin's literary treatment of rural heritage. In this semi-autobiographical novel, the writer describes his early experiences collecting Russian icons, a pursuit he took up after witnessing the seemingly miraculous restoration of a discolored old icon at a friend's workshop. Like *Vladimir Back Roads*, which describes a forty-day hike through the Vladimir countryside, *Black Boards* relates the writer's encounters with the people and places of his native region as he searches for Russian icons. Soloukhin positions himself as a zealous amateur whose lust for the objects of his desire contrasts with local peasants' more familial and selfless love of Russian icons. Over the course of his travels the author-narrator slowly realizes that the value of these objects lies not in their aesthetic merit but in their folkloric meaning, as expressions of authentic Russian culture and spirituality. As he reasons, following an encounter with a seasoned Russian icon collector, "When you collect stones, you collect just stones, and when you collect butterflies, you collect just butterflies. But when you collect ancient Russian paintings, you collect the people's soul [*dusha naroda*]."[14]

Soloukhin's writings highlight the shift in preservationist concerns in the Brezhnev years. From the architectural heritage of the country's medieval center, the attention of the preservationist elite broadened in the late 1960s to encompass Russia's rural art, architecture, and traditions. Village Prose, which Kathleen

Parthé has described as "the most aesthetically coherent and ideologically important body of published writings to appear in the Soviet Union between Stalin's death and Gorbachev's ascendancy," serves to illustrate this change.[15] The writers formed a cultural lobby for rural heritage from the 1960s to 1980s. Among the many authors that might be grouped within this genre, I limit my focus in the following section to the "Vologda School," whose works explore questions of preservation that are particularly pertinent to the Russian Northwest.

In the 1960s and 1970s, Vologda became a hub of activity for a Russian patriotic literary elite, the ranks of which included migrant writers, such as Viktor Astaf'ev, and natives of the Vologda region, Vasilii Belov, Ol'ga Fokina, Nikolai Rubtsov, Vladimir Tendriakov, and Aleksandr Iashin. This development was the result of a confluence of factors. As Geoffrey Hosking and Vasilii Belov have pointed out, writers were attracted to the region because of its strong oral folk culture, which survived relatively intact as a result of Vologda's remote location and the fact that it had been spared the worst effects of serfdom in the tsarist period.[16] Another important factor, however, was Vologda's historical status as a center of political exile in the late Imperial period. This experience bestowed upon the town an intellectual capital that enhanced the quality of local cultural life. Moreover, Vologda's reputation as the place of exile for prominent cultural figures such as Petr Lavrov, Anatoly Lunacharsky, and Nikolai Berdiaev encouraged local writers to perceive themselves as descendants of the nation's finest intellectual talents.[17]

Perhaps the best known among the "Vologda School" writers were Aleksandr Iashin and Vasilii Belov. While it should be noted that Belov never associated himself explicitly with the Village Prose movement, the author's preoccupation with rural themes and preservationist questions justifies his inclusion in the genre. Both writers dedicated works to the local countryside and its heritage and traditions, and they wrote with patriotism and pride about their native region. Both writers can also be described as literary ethnographers who embarked on imaginative expeditions to their surrounding villages and settlements with the intention of chronicling and preserving for posterity various aspects of the local culture. In this way, the works of Iashin and Belov constitute acts of preservation that, like the work of local restorers and historians of the same period, influenced the cultures in which they were produced.

Aleksandr Iashin was born to a peasant family in the village of Bludnovo in the Nikolsk region of the Vologda oblast in 1913 and worked as a teacher and journalist in Vologda during his youth.[18] Writing poetry from an early age, he quickly rose to literary prominence in his native region, becoming head of the

Vologda Section of the Council of Soviet Writers in 1934. In the late 1930s, Iashin left Vologda to study at the Maxim Gorky Literary Institute in Moscow, where he continued to write and work as a journalist. With the outbreak of the war, he volunteered to serve as a front-line correspondent and reported from such fulcrums of military activity as Leningrad during the Siege, Stalingrad, and Crimea. After the war ended, he traveled widely throughout the Soviet Union, visiting hydroelectric plants in the Far North and the Altai region before settling back in Moscow. While never returning to live in Vologda, he continued to pen literary dedications to the landscapes and communities of his "little motherland" (*malaia rodina*) throughout his life. Arguably the most famous and important of these was the short story "Vologda Wedding," published in the literary "thick journal" *New World* in December 1961.[19]

The author-narrator of "Vologda Wedding," Aleksandr, is an urban migrant who returns from Moscow to his native village to attend a wedding "in the traditional style [*po-starinnomu*]." Noting the incongruous sight of villagers who file through the capital's airport with their jars of gherkins and baskets of berries, he boards a plane for his homeland. On arrival, Aleksandr encounters a scene that is at once inherently traditional—it features a cast of folkloric characters, from the matchmaker (*svakha*) to the groomsman (*druzhka*)—and strangely modern—the bride and groom travel by truck and not *troika*, for example, and art by the local zoo technician adorns the walls of the peasant izba. Aleksandr observes with ethnographic restraint the unfolding performance of the wedding rituals and the exchanges between his fellow guests. It is only following his return to Moscow, in the closing paragraphs of the story, that he engages critically with his experience. The village traditions he has observed, he notes, are the fleeting phenomena of a disappearing way of life, the heritage of a culture on the verge of extinction.

The ethnographic tradition that marked the writing of Aleksandr Iashin, among other Village Prose authors, was embraced and developed by Vasilii Belov in the many works that he dedicated to the rural culture of the Vologda region. Like Iashin, Belov employed the vehicle of the "insider-outsider" narrator as a means of documenting the rural experience. In his novel *The Carpenter Tales* (1968), for example, an urbanized narrator returns to his native village and bears witness to the life stories of two feuding villagers who have lived through the experience of collectivization.[20] However, Belov did not limit himself to chronicling the folk traditions and culture of his native region: he strove in his later works to incorporate folklore and legends directly into his prose.

The influence of oral tradition is obvious in Belov's dialogue, which is alive with dialectical quirks and syntactical surprises.[21]

Belov's prose can likewise be understood as an act of cultural preservation. By inscribing the folkloric modes of the village in his writing, Belov conserved and perpetuated local traditions that he perceived to be threatened by the standardizing effects of Soviet modernity. This tendency can be perceived most clearly in his novel *Business as Usual* (1966).[22] While the subject matter of this work is fairly conventional within the Village Prose genre—a peasant family disintegrates under the pressures of agricultural reform—the fragmented nature and constantly shifting register of the narrative voice are more remarkable. Belov succeeds in commemorating the animistic beliefs of the peasant world through the egalitarian attribution of narrative voice to different characters, human and non-human alike. The narrative probes the inner workings of the minds of Ivan's nine children, including his newborn baby, whose simplicity and naivety recalls Ivan's own state of mind. Belov even offers the reader privileged access to the inner world of the family cow, Rogulia, highlighting the symbiotic relationship that exists between man and the natural world in peasant Russia.

In the acclaimed opening section of *Business as Usual*, Ivan drunkenly addresses his horse, Parmen, in an intimate and jovial fashion that draws attention to the relationship of equality that exits between humans and their natural environment in the village context. The passage is also a striking example of Belov's reproduction of folk speech, the decorative embellishments and idiosyncratic texture of which brings to mind the ornate folk architecture of the region:

—Parme-en? Wherezat Parmenko got to, eh? Aah, there 'e is, there's Parmenko. You freezin'? You are, aren't you lad, freezin'. Silly boy, Parmenko. What, cat got your tongue, eh? Well, hop to it, lad, let's get us home. Don't fancy it, eh? Parmen', what'm I goin' to do with you, eh?

[—Парме-ен? Это где у меня Парменко-то? А вот он, Парменко. Замерз? Замерз, парень, замерз. Дурачок ты, Парменко. Молчит у меня Парменко. Вот, ну-ко мы домой поедем. Хошь домой-то? Пармен ты, Пармен . . .][23]

Belov's interest in linguistic innovation was motivated, as Geoffrey Hosking has noted, by a desire "to clear away the weary bureaucratic patina which had accumulated over so many words and phrases."[24] Yet it can also be understood as part of the author's preservationist enterprise. Like Iashin's work, Belov's prose was part literary innovation, part ethnographic document. As such, it formed a constituent part of a broader corpus of preservationist thinking that bound together literature, criticism, and cultural practice in the context of Brezhnev-era politics.

The rise of the Russian Village Prose movement in the 1960s and 1970s was directly aligned with the contemporaneous growth in academic interest in rural folk architecture. Both movements were motivated by the perceived threat that Soviet modernization and, specifically, the "rationalization" of the rural sphere, posed to village traditions.[25] Both movements, moreover, were populated by first- and second-generation urban migrants, whose nostalgia for the rural traditions of their childhood spurred interest in and enthusiasm for the preservation of Russian folk heritage.[26] The coincidence of motivating factors and cultural values explains the similarity of the terms that have been used to refer to the adherents of both movements. The literary chroniclers of the Russian village became "derevenshchiki" in the writings of the Soviet critics published in literary thick journals, while scholars of folk architecture have more recently been labeled "derevianshchiki" by cultural commentators.[27]

The biography of one prominent folk preservationist, Leonid Krasnorech'ev, illustrates the coincidence of backgrounds and cultural interests between the two groups.[28] Krasnorech'ev grew up in a peasant family in the Novgorod region and moved away, in his case to Leningrad, to pursue his studies in the 1940s. The restorer's early exposure to rural crafts and traditions (his great-grandfather had been a master craftsman, constructing wooden barrages and windmills) appears to have fostered his passion for the folk aesthetic. Following his appointment at the Novgorod Restoration Workshop in 1952, Krasnorech'ev studied the techniques of folk architectural preservation at weekends and during his holidays, gaining the expertise necessary to assume the position of director at Novgorod's folk architectural museum "Vitoslavlitsy" in 1964. Like Aleksandr Iashin, Krasnorech'ev held an "insider-outsider" status with regard to Russian folk culture that sparked interest in, while still allowing, critical distance from the heritage and traditions at the center of his practice.

"High Artistic Value, Chasteness, Purity"

In the more patriotically permissive conditions of Brezhnev-era society, individuals such as Krasnorech'ev received state patronage to pursue their nostalgic ambitions of preserving an architectural record of Russian folk culture. In January

1964, the Ministry of Culture of the RSFSR issued the order "On the Means to Improve the Preservation of Wooden Architecture," which underlined not only the need to preserve folk architecture but also the important role that this heritage should play in the political education of Soviet citizens.[29] The legislation foresaw the creation of a number of open-air architectural museums in Russia, including museums of folk heritage in Novgorod, Kizhi, Myshkin, and a number of other locations.[30] The Novgorod Museum of Wooden Folk Architecture, Vitoslavlitsy, located on the former Orlov country estate, was one of the first to open its doors to visitors in June 1964. Vitoslavlitsy was heralded as a sanctuary for endangered folk architecture and a major tourist attraction in the region, drawing visitors from across the country.[31]

The creation of an architectural record of Russian folk culture involved the relocation of buildings in the folk style from their original village settings to a preordained museum space for their preservation and touristic exploitation. This process of cultural transplantation was in obvious contradiction with some restoration theory of the 1950s and 1960s, which maintained that heritage objects should not only be restored to their original form but also preserved in their historic surroundings.[32] Restorers of folk architecture such as Krasnorech'ev negotiated this contradiction with reference to the crisis facing Russian folk architecture as a result of Soviet policies that aimed to rationalize the rural sphere. As a result of the depopulation of thousands of "unviable" villages, they argued, many objects of wooden architecture had been abandoned, and without immediate intervention these buildings would soon disintegrate into ruins.[33]

The first object of folk architecture to be relocated to Vitoslavlitsy was the sixteenth-century Church of the Assumption from the village of Kuritsko in the Novgorod region. Immediately following the museum's foundation in 1964, the church was dismantled and relocated to the site, where urgent restoration work, led by Krasnorech'ev, was carried out.[34] The Assumption Church was followed by the sixteenth-century Church of the Nativity, which was transported to the museum in 1967 from the settlement of Peredki, seventeenth- and eighteenth-century chapels from the villages of Gar' and Kashira, which arrived in 1972, and the seventeenth-century St. Nicholas Church from Miakishchevo, which was also relocated to the museum in 1972.[35] An average of 70,000 rubles a year was spent on restoring these folk monuments, a sum that was roughly equivalent the annual budget for restoration work on the prestigious Khutyn (1192) and the St. Nicholas of Viazhishchi Monastery (1411) complexes, in the Novgorod region, during the same period.[36]

FIGURE 6. The Nativity of the Virgin Cathedral (1539), Vitoslavlitsy Folk Architecture Museum, Novgorod, November 2008.

As was true in the case of the zapovedniks of stone architecture discussed in chapter 2, norms of museum exploitation at these sites shifted over time. By contrast with the Khrushchev era, when museum collectives had striven to highlight the ideological significance of heritage objects, the exhibitions constructed in the 1960s and 1970s aimed to preserve the buildings as works of art in their own right. Museum collectives reconstructed folk churches and chapels as they imagined them to have existed in their traditional village context, recreating the buildings' interiors and furnishings in their historically authentic entireties. For objects of religious folk architecture, this process sometimes included the recreation of iconostases, religious icons, and imagery.[37] Unlike the exhibitions of the 1950s, in which interpretations of religious art and culture were mediated through the inclusion of politically correct explanatory notes, displays of folk religion at Vitoslavlitsy were allowed to speak for themselves. Such exhibitive strategies bore similarities to the approach of the Village Prose writers, whose depictions of rural *byt* (everyday life) demonstrated a similar preference for ethnographic distance over didactic ideologization.

Toward the middle of the 1970s, the ideal of Russian folk culture showcased at Vitoslavlitsy began to change. Rather than focusing exclusively on the most visually impressive examples of folk architecture, the museum began to collect pieces of residential and utilitarian architecture in the folk style. The museum's ornately decorated and meticulously carved wooden churches were joined at this time by peasant izbas, threshing barns, wells, and windmills, which were arranged in accordance with the structure of a traditional Russian village.[38] This more inclusive approach to the preservation of folk architecture was prompted by a growing concern that further restructuring of Soviet agriculture would critically endanger the architectural heritage of the Russian village. Faced with the complete eradication of rural traditions, museum collectives felt compelled to preserve a representative sample of Russian folk architecture, preserving this heritage for posterity in a historical reconstruction of village life.

Anxieties about the fate of the region's folk architecture were at the center of a conference on heritage preservation held at the Novgorod State Museum in 1978. The scholars and heritage practitioners present at the event discussed in particular the impact of the 1974 declaration "On the Future Development of Agriculture in the Non-Black Earth Region." The declaration, it was speculated, would result in a reduction in the number of agricultural settlements in the Novgorod oblast from 4,302 to just 380.[39] Such a radical decline in rural communities meant an uncertain future for buildings in the folk style that would be abandoned in decommissioned villages:

> In the not too distant future, not just hundreds, but thousands of settlements in the Novgorod region are going to disappear completely. And yet, many of these sites contain numerous monuments and memorial places. What are we going to do with them? How should we preserve monuments that are situated outside of their natural environments?[40]

The answer to these questions was provided by Krasnorech'ev, who had, by the late 1970s, established himself as one of the most influential figures in the field of folk architectural preservation.[41] In his keynote address, the restorer delivered an impassioned defense of Novgorod's folk heritage, stating that the "high artistic value, chasteness, and purity" of the folk style rendered it a *primus inter pares* among architectural traditions and a priority for preservation.[42] Many neglected objects of folk architecture were languishing in the dying villages of the Soviet Union, he explained, awaiting expert intervention. Responsibility for this heritage, the value of which was not acknowledged by the state, lay with the Soviet people themselves:

> We need to preserve not only the monuments that have been placed under state, oblast, and local protection, but also the monuments that have been discovered but are not yet officially protected. This is a task, not only for the organs of architectural preservation and the local soviets, but also for socialist farms, collective farms, and for other community organizations in the local area.[43]

Krasnorech'ev's appeal to preserve an accurate record of the vernacular landscape revealed a tension between the Soviet authorities and local preservationist lobbies. The Brezhnev regime endorsed an exoticized ideal of Russian folk culture that laid emphasis on highly ornamental and structurally complex examples of wooden architecture. Local restorers, by contrast, were committed to the preservation of a more inclusive record of the folk landscape, which included aesthetically banal, everyday structures, such as barns and farm sheds, as well as ornate churches and belfries. The promotion of objects of folk heritage to the status of symbols of national identity thus contradicted the ambitions of local actors, who sought to assert through preservation the distinctiveness of regional traditions. It was only in the perestroika era that the ethnographic understanding of folk heritage gained precedence, as restorers were able to assert with greater authority their interpretations of the Russian folk landscape.

"The Living Spiritual Culture of Our People"

Interest in northern folk culture, and the folk traditions of Vologda in particular, grew exponentially throughout the 1960s and 1970s. In 1977, for example, the Russian musicologist Iurii Marchenko led an expedition of students from the Rimskii-Korsakov Conservatory in Leningrad to the region with the stated intention of collecting local folk songs. The songs recorded during the trip were made available to Soviet composers, who were encouraged to draw inspiration

from the folk motifs for their contemporary compositions.[44] The political significance of this preservationist work was underlined in Soviet propaganda, including
the Vologda weekly *Red North*, which published an article praising the songs as
"expressions of the living spiritual culture [*aktivnaia dukhovnaia kul'tura*] of our
people" in March 1977.[45]

National institutions likewise played an important role in stimulating interest
in the region's folk culture. In 1965, the Vologda museum was invited to participate at a major international conference at the Russian Museum in Leningrad on
the theme of "Folk Art of the Russian North."[46] The official affirmation of local folk
culture gave rise to a flurry of expeditions within the Vologda region in search of
ethnographic objects for inclusion in museum displays. In 1966, museum expeditions were carried out in the Tarnog, Nikolsk, and Verkhovazh'e regions, resulting
in the collection of over 550 ethnographic objects. The contents of these ethnographic hauls were proudly listed in the annual report on the museum's activities.
Among them were engraved and decorated wooden distaffs, wooden crockery,
objects made from birch bark, women's sarafans, embroidered men's shirts, and
plaited belts, all of which were integrated into the museum's exhibition work in
subsequent years.[47]

The growing preoccupation with folk themes was reflected in the focus of
museum work throughout the 1970s. Exhibitions at this time included "Northern
Distaffs" in 1970, featuring examples of the eponymous tool, as well as wood carvings, folk sculptures, and other objects of applied art;[48] "Folk Crafts" in 1973, which
included an entire section on the art of Vologda lace;[49] and "Vologda Folk Dress"
in 1979, an exhibition of ethnic Russian clothing from the Vologda region.[50] The
regional folk revival was bolstered by national legislation; for example, the 1977
declaration of the Central Committee of the KPSS "On Folk Artistic Crafts" provided the impetus for a major conference on "The Evolution of Vologda Lace."[51]
The conference included papers by over sixty participants, including scholars
from local and national museums as well as heritage practitioners from the local
region.[52]

These years also saw the state-sponsored promotion of Vologda as a center of
Russian folk performance art. A report on the organization of mass festivities in
1970 was replete with folk-inspired activities, both in the regional capital and the
surrounding towns and villages.[53] Perhaps the most striking of these events was
the "Russian Souvenir" festival organized by the Vologda Museum in 1970. The
festival featured a host of folkloric characters, from "jokers" (*zateiniki*) who welcomed visitors at the entrance and urged them to join in a Russian round dance,

to "buffoons" (*skomorokhi*) whose task it was to spout jokes, humorous one-liners (*pribautki*), proverbs and sayings (*poslovitsy i pogovorki*), while advertising the festival's program. The festival featured folk choirs, dance ensembles, and competitions, such as stilt racing and flax pulling. Visitors were even invited to participate in mock debates on pseudo-folk themes such as "Does a beard adorn a man or a man adorn a beard?"[54]

Given the state's endorsement of folk culture, it is perhaps surprising that Vologda's folk architecture was not granted a similarly privileged status at this time. Throughout the 1960s, restorers had to fight to ensure the preservation of folk monuments, many of which were regularly destroyed by fire or damaged through collective neglect.[55] The case of the wooden Elijah the Prophet church (1690) in the Kirillov region of the Vologda oblast illustrates the precarious status of folk monuments in the 1960s. This remarkable tiered structure, comprising three octagonal wooden domes mounted one on top of the other, was registered on the list of federally protected monuments. Yet, despite its protected status, the church was regularly threatened by destruction. In 1960, for example, the local authorities wrote to the Ministry of Culture to request permission to demolish the church.[56] After permission was denied, a decision was made in 1963 to remove the building from the list of state protected monuments altogether in response to cuts to the federal budget for the preservation of architectural heritage.[57]

Attitudes to wooden folk monuments began to change with the growth in tourist interest that accompanied the construction of the Volga-Baltic Waterway in 1964. A list of historic buildings whose restoration was to be prioritized in 1964 thus included the wooden Assumption church in the village of Deviatina, whose restoration was allocated 10,000 rubles, and the aforementioned Elijah the Prophet church and its surrounding territory.[58] Further plans for restoration, which were submitted to the Ministry of Culture in 1966, included wooden churches in the Deviatina, Paltoga, and Saminsk Pogost villages in the Vytegra region and a wooden church in the Potsk Pogost village in the Tarnogsk region of the Vologda oblast. Further funding was allocated for the conversion of these buildings, all of which were located close to the tourist waterway, into museum exhibits for touristic exploitation.[59]

In 1979, following a decision by the Regional Council of People's Deputies, a museum of folk architecture, "Semenkovo," was created.[60] Plans for the museum's design were drafted by the Vologda Restoration Workshop and local museum and approved by the Ministry of Culture in 1983. In accordance with these plans, seven architectural sectors were created, dedicated to different regions of the Vologda oblast: the Sukhonsk sector, Verkhovazhsk sector, Western sector, Central sector, Nikol'sk sector, Veliki Utiug sector, and Town sector. Throughout the 1980s, the museum conducted expeditions within the Vologda region with the aim of identifying the most valuable monuments of folk heritage to relocate to the museum. Among the first objects to be transported to the site were the wooden Bolotova House (late 19 c.), the Parygina Barn (late 19 c.), and the Chadromtsev Barn (late 19 c.), all from the village of Korolevskaia Nizhneuftiuskogo in the Niusensk region.[61] These were followed by nine residential houses and eight household buildings over the next ten years. By 1991, the museum comprised several dozen buildings in the local folk style.[62]

The state-sponsored promotion of regional folklore and folk architecture throughout the 1970s and 1980s was undoubtedly connected with the activities of Russian Village Prose writers and the Vologda branch of the movement in particular. The most obvious illustration of this fact came in 1982, when the first secretary of the Vologda KPSS, Vladimir Parmenov, met with a delegation of Village Prose writers, including Valentin Rasputin, Viktor Astaf'ev, and Vladimir Soloukhin, on the occasion of Vasilii Belov's fiftieth birthday, to discuss the question of architectural restoration in the Vologda region.[63] At this meeting, Parmenov officially requested the writers' input into the design of a cultural program for the preservation of regional heritage, which had been developed by the local government in collaboration with the town's Principal Architect.[64] This notable instance of cooperation between the local authorities and the literary elite revealed the influence of preservationist criticism on the formation of Soviet urban policy, as well as the importance attributed to the Russian patriotic intelligentsia in generating popular support for such work.

Folk Monuments vs. "Old Wooden Houses"

The distinction drawn by Soviet architects between "folk architecture" and the "derivative" (*podrazhatel'nye*) wooden buildings of the exploiting classes was an important one for preservation in Vologda. As Golubev notes, the category of folk architecture included churches and village houses that were considered to encapsulate the essence of the national character; the second category, by contrast, included wooden merchant architecture and other "capitalist" constructions, which were seen as lacking any artistic or historical value.[65] At the end of the 1960s, Vologda was replete with buildings of the second category, the inheritance of the city's vibrant merchant culture in the eighteenth and nineteenth centuries.[66] Furthermore, many of these building had served as people's homes, schools, and workplaces in the first decades after the war, forming part of the everyday fabric of town life in the 1950s and 1960s.

Residents had fond memories of growing up in wooden houses. Natal'ia (b. 1934) remembered life in her family's wooden mansion on "Annunciation" Street, a name that stuck stubbornly in local vocabulary despite Soviet efforts to rechristen the road "Clara Zetkin." Natal'ia's father had received their grand apartment thanks to his influential position at the local linen factory. The house had been the setting for many formative moments in Natal'ia's life, from the endurance of hunger and cold during wartime to the happier experiences of postwar Soviet festivals, celebrated on the house's wide wooden balcony:

> NATAL'IA: Our flat was very cozy. Three rooms, two entranceways, from the front entrance you went into a large hallway. There was a big balcony too. That balcony— Masha already showed you the photos—well, we used to dance on that balcony. After the war, that was. It was that big! My mother's sister and her husband used to come round, and my mother's brother's family too.
>
> VSD: Was that during the holidays?
>
> NATAL'IA: Yes, that's right. Back then we used to celebrate October and the first of May. We didn't used to dance out there at New Year's though. It was too cold for dancing at New Year's!

Wooden houses were a ubiquitous feature of everyday life in Soviet Vologda, but they were also relics of the capitalist past and, as such, an ideological embarrassment. The former identities of these buildings were sometimes underlined by the presence of their former proprietors, the descendants of the merchant families who had owned the houses in the prerevolutionary period. Rimma (b. 1934), who lived in a listed wooden building on Zasodimskii Street, had, for example, paid rent directly to the prerevolutionary owner, who lived on the floor above. Her daughter, Irina (b. 1957), mirthfully recalled an incident from childhood when she and fellow Pioneers had launched a campaign against this "lady of the manor" (*pomeshchitsa*), whose treatment of a fellow resident the children considered to be exploitative:

> People lived there too, but at the top, well, that was where this "lady of the manor" lived. She lived on the top floor. I can't remember what she was called now . . .

FIGURE 7. Women sitting on the porch of a historic wooden house, Vologda, July 2010.

Kutitska or something ... but us Octobrists, us Pioneers, well, for us, that "lady of
the manor" was an enemy of the people! It was that generation, you see. Imagine, a
"lady of the manor!" And she was mean too! You know, a commanding woman. And
she had a servant [*sluga*]! This old man with a stick who'd hobble back and forth to
the shops for her. Well, we were outraged! It was exploitation! ... But it would be
him who'd lay into us most of the time. It wasn't her. It was him who used to chase
us away. We wanted to save him from that "lady of the manor," but he'd just chase
us away! (laughs)

In the 1960s and 1970s, many of Vologda's wooden houses began to be demolished. The waves of urban migration that accompanied the opening of new manufacturing plants, such as the Poultry Factory and the State Ball Bearing Factory,
resulted in the mass construction of new residential housing.[67] New concrete

suburbs—or *spal'nye raiony*—replaced whole districts of wooden houses, often assuming the names of the regions they supplanted—Byvalovo or Teplichnyi, for example—at the town's periphery.[68] The transformation of the urban landscape was rapid and dramatic: according to figures published at the time, 150,000 square meters of residential housing was built in Vologda between 1965 and 1967, followed by a further 145,000 square meters in 1967 and 1968 and 143,000 square meters in 1971.[69] Cobbled streets and wooden pavements, whose inconveniences were remembered by older residents, were also replaced by asphalted roads and pavement at this time.

While the preservation of "Old Russian" architecture and folk architecture was prioritized in postwar legislation, wooden buildings from the nineteenth century fell into a legislative gray area of civic and cultic architecture, creating the need to resolve the ambiguity about their eligibility for preservation.[70] The first list of state-protected architectural monuments in Vologda, compiled in 1960, included just three of Vologda's historic merchant mansions: the Volkhov House and Zasetskii House on Leningrad Street and the Levashov House on Hertzen Street.[71] The large majority of the town's wooden buildings were consequently left vulnerable to the whims of Soviet planners, who ostensibly had no sympathy for the architectural style. The General Plan for Vologda's development, approved by the RSFSR Council of Ministers in 1962, thus advocated the mass demolition of the town's wooden buildings and their replacement by modern urban housing.[72]

The disappearance of the historic wooden landscape was heralded in the local press as a victory for Soviet civilization. "Vologda is getting a facelift!" exclaimed the author of a 1968 article published in *Red North*. "On Vetoshkin Street, where, not long ago there were just lines of old wooden houses, there are now these five-story beauties!"[73] Another article, published in *Red North* a year later, remarked that, where once cramped wooden houses had spoiled the view of the city center, there now existed the promise of a "wide construction site."[74] Vologda's "rejuvenation" was even picked up on by local writers and historians, who honored the theme in publications dedicated to the town. A photograph album of Vologda's historic and natural landscapes published in 1964 thus opened with the celebratory ditty "For you fate was flush with glory/ Russian city, my Vologda/ Restored to youth, you stand sublimely/ Your wealth of strength for all to see."[75]

Some locals welcomed the mass construction of residential housing, a process that transformed Vologda's wooden periphery into sprawling micro-districts of shops and flats. Valentina (b. 1958) remembered how happy her parents had been to exchange their wooden house on "Annunciation" Street for a new, two-roomed apartment in a building that had been built to celebrate the 60th anniversary of Soviet rule in 1977: "my parents were delighted they'd been given such a nice apartment. . . . The old house was falling apart by then." Irina (b. 1957), who still lived in a wooden house on Priluki Street in 2008, remembered pining for a new apartment herself in the 1970s:

> Because you wanted things to be better, you see. If you see someone living in a brick house with nice straight walls, while in your house the walls are all warped and it's freezing, you've got to heat the stove with logs, and there's mud everywhere, you also start to think: why am I worse than them? I want that too.

For other, more preservation-minded residents, the mass demolition of the town's nineteenth-century wooden buildings was a grave concern. Aleksandr Rybakov, the head of the Vologda Restoration Workshop from 1970 to 1985, was one of the most outspoken critics of the town's urban transformation. Throughout the 1970s, Rybakov campaigned relentlessly for the promotion of the town's merchant mansions to the status of federally protected architectural monuments.[76] These efforts eventually bore fruit in the mid-1970s. Following numerous letters to the Central Council of the All-Russian Society for the Preservation of Historical and Cultural Monuments in Moscow complaining about plans to demolish wooden buildings on the historic Hertzen and October Streets, the chairman of the Russian Council of Ministers, Viacheslav Kochemasov, wrote to the Vologda executive committee to demand corrections be made to the town's General Plan.[77] As a consequence, in 1977, thirty-three wooden monuments were "uncovered" by the local authorities and added to the list of federally protected monuments.[78]

The promotion of a building to the status of federally protected monument, however, did not always guarantee its preservation and maintenance. This much was clear from a letter by the residents of the Volkhov House to the chairman of the Vologda executive committee in 1966. The letter described the substandard living conditions that the communal apartment residents had been forced to endure in the preceding years, but it also gestured at the decrepit state of the wooden monument, at this time one of only three state-protected wooden mansions in the region:

> It's become completely impossible to live in these conditions. The ceilings of many of the apartments are falling to bits and there's a terrible draft from the cellar. The

stoves need a complete overhaul and the chimneys need replacing. The window sills and transoms are rotting away, it all needs changing. . . . In the wintertime, the walls freeze over in the communal kitchen, which is shared by six families, and it feels just like being outside.[79]

The incremental disintegration of the town's wooden architecture continued to worry local preservationists throughout the 1980s. A 1986 report by Vologda's Principal Architect, N. N. Smirnov, thus drew attention to the plight of the town's historic wooden buildings. "All interested parties must resolve, once and for all, the question of how to preserve our town's wooden architecture," he wrote, addressing the local administration. As part of the Soviet establishment that often found itself at loggerheads with local conservationists, Smirnov strove to underline his sympathy for the preservationist agenda: "I am on the side of the Society [for the Preservation of Historic and Cultural Monuments]," he wrote. "And I consider it a good thing that we have found and continue find on this issue a common language."[80]

The logic of Soviet preservation meant that the wooden heritage of the nineteenth century never achieved the same cultural standing as monuments of folk architecture. While the latter exemplified an ideal of Russian cultural authenticity endorsed by the Brezhnev regime, the heritage of the prerevolutionary period remained ideologically problematic throughout the late Soviet period. Moreover, nineteenth-century wooden architecture, unlike the architectural exhibits at local folk museums, was unable to generate its own income in the form of tourist rubles. Local authorities consequently felt little incentive to ensure the survival of these buildings, and during the last decades of Soviet rule, many perished as a result of neglect or purposeful demolition.[81] The position of Vologda's merchant mansions became especially precarious during the years of political and economic restructuring in the 1990s. The mood of popular resentment and frustration with preservationist politics at this time was captured in a poem, published an architectural guide to Vologda in 1993:

> "Our town has become unrecognizable"
> The old boast rings out once again.
> Oh, sad thought! We're changing so
> That, yes, we're hard to recognize.
> Houses with verandas, balconies,
> And mezzanines—alas!

It's hard to say that you're not doomed
When you face a fate like this![82]

This chapter has viewed the state-sponsored drive to promote Russian folk traditions through the lens of the Brezhnev-era "Russian revival." From this perspective it is clear that the creation of museums of folk architecture, the collection and exhibition of objects of folk heritage, and the performance of folk traditions were measures intended to placate an increasingly vocal cultural intelligentsia and to the stem the rise of nationalist sentiment in late Soviet-era Russia. The folk architecture of the Russian Northwest was a direct beneficiary of these self-preservationist politics. Over the course of the 1970s and 1980s, this heritage, dismissed as artistically worthless in the decades before the war, was reappraised as the pinnacle of the country's architectural achievements. The region, already a symbol of wartime resistance and postwar renewal, was established at this time as a center of authentic national culture, a landscape that encapsulated the indigenous traditions of the Russian people.

The strategic endorsement of folk themes, like the promotion of medieval heritage after the war, nevertheless had unintended consequences. Most obviously, it resulted in the creation of local lobbies for the promotion of folk culture whose agendas were decidedly more ambitious than those of Soviet policymakers. Individuals such as Leonid Krasnorech'ev, who dedicated his professional life to the preservation of folk heritage and traditions, advocated a form of preservation that differed dramatically from the romantic idea of Russian folk commemorated in official institutions. Rather than exoticizing folk culture in exhibitions of ornate wooden churches and colorful sarafans, local lobbyists campaigned for the preservation of run-of-the-mill folk objects that constituted a record of everyday village culture. The Brezhnev regime, whose interest in Russian folk traditions was rooted in their potential for political mobilization, had little interest in endorsing this ethnographic notion of cultural authenticity.

The fate of nineteenth-century wooden architecture, the focus of the second part of this chapter, underlines some important nuances of preservationist politics in the late Soviet era. While the Brezhnev regime was prepared to endorse a romantic ideal of Russian folk culture, it was unwilling to promote urban folk heritage in the same way, despite its significance for residents of provincial towns. Nineteenth-century merchant mansions, such as the Volkhov and Levashov Houses in Vologda, were considered too distant from the romantic ideal of

Russian cultural authenticity promoted by the socialist state to merit concerted preservation. Yet many of these buildings had greater sentimental value for the average Soviet citizen than the village churches preserved in museums of folk architecture. The outpouring of popular anger in connection with the disintegration and destruction of these buildings in the 1990s, discussed in more detail in the following chapter, underlines this contradictory reality.

Part 2

THE NORTHWEST AS LIVED MEMORY

4.

BURNT-OUT FAIRY TALES

Preservation as a Metaphor for Loss After Socialism

By the time the Soviet Union collapsed in 1991, the historic Northwest was well established at the center of the national imaginary. The region's heritage had acquired associations with postwar renewal and Soviet urban transformation, but also, in the Brezhnev era, with ideas of Russian cultural authenticity. Citizens from across the Soviet Union had studied the region in school, admired its historic landscapes in films, and even contemplated its monuments face to face during tourist excursions. The work of local institutions and actors had succeeded in cementing an idea of northwestern heritage as the people's property—indeed, as a reflection of the all-Soviet values of heroism and resilience, simplicity and strength. For residents of the historic region, moreover, years of participating in the upkeep of local monuments, learning about them at school and in museums, and performing this knowledge to outsiders had helped to establish architectural heritage as an integral part of local identity.

For these reasons, the years of political transition under Russia's first President, Boris Yeltsin, had dramatic consequences for the Northwest. As the government struggled to redefine Russian cultural identity, fierce competition emerged for ownership over the country's most valuable heritage resources. One of the major factors contributing to the cultural instability of these years was the resurgence of influence of the Russian Orthodox Church (ROC), which entailed the recon-secration of buildings and artworks that had, in the Soviet period, been considered public property or state-owned monuments. The introduction of liberalizing market reforms in the early post-Soviet period contributed further to reshaping the country's cultural economy. As legislation was passed permitting the privatization of heritage objects, historic churches, monasteries, and mansions were transferred from public institutions into private hands and began to be developed for diverse and, to the minds of some commentators, inappropriate purposes.

In the increasingly complex sphere of Yeltsin-era cultural relations, debates about heritage began to emerge that employed the contemporary notions of historical justice, atonement, and retribution. This chapter considers the positions of local actors who participated in these debates on the pages of local and national newspapers, in radio and television interviews, and even in courts of law. The arguments that emerged at this time reveal a bitter struggle for control between cultural elites in the Northwest, who had traditionally acted as guardians of heritage objects, and influential new actors, from clergymen to supermarket barons. The privatization of the heritage economy, which resulted in the commodification of many heritage objects as sites of elite entertainment and recreation, struck a particularly dissonant chord with local preservationists. The criticisms advanced by these lobbies with regard to developments in the heritage sphere revealed a profound sense of displacement and disillusion with the new conditions of post-socialist life.

From Preservation to Protest

The drive to "restructure" (*perestroit'*) Soviet society in the second half of the 1980s impacted on the work of architectural preservation, as it did on all areas of cultural life. In particular, the policy of "restoring social justice," which constituted an assault on the corruption and elite privileges of the Brezhnev era,[1] brought with it a crackdown on violations of preservationist regulations. Toward the end of the decade, local preservationist organizations began to document offenses against monuments in their localities and to finger culprits, even when these were members of privileged local lobbies. For example, following an instruction from the Ministry of Culture titled "On the Organization of Preservation Zones in Novgorod," the Novgorod VOOPIiK enumerated dozens of cases in which building work in the town had contravened preservationist legislation. Among the violations recorded in 1989 and 1990 was the unauthorized construction of high-rise blocks of flats next to the federally protected Nativity of Our Lady Church and the Church of St. Michael Maleinos (1199); another was the installation of a weed-killer plant in the corpus of St. George's Monastery, the vibrations from which were undermining the complex's foundations.[2]

In 1990, another, more flagrant case of elite corruption was uncovered by the preservationist society. Following reports of illicit construction work filed by local residents, the Novgorod VOOPIiK discovered plans for the creation of an elite dacha settlement just a hundred meters from the celebrated Savior Church on Nereditsa. The choice of location in this instance was particularly controversial given the special status of the church, which had been destroyed during World War II and rebuilt entirely from ruins in the early 1950s.[3] The assault on the monument by a group of self-serving local bureaucrats, which included the head of the Novgorod police force and the vice-chairman of the Novgorod district executive committee, thus appeared to some indicative of the rotten state of Soviet politics. In their report on the case, local preservationists condemned the plans in the strongest terms possible, making use of the perestroika-era vocabulary of legality and social responsibility to attack the conspirators for their "increasingly slack regard for the rule of law [*oslableniie vnimaniia k sobliudeniiu zakonodatel'stva*]."[4]

The association of architectural preservation with the pursuit of social justice transformed the cultural cause into a political rallying point for disillusioned elements in late Soviet society. Exploiting a perestroika-era initiative on the foundation of unofficial societies, individuals began to form their own preservationist groups across the country for the advancement of their reformist agendas. Invested with a new sense of relevance and boasting a sizable support base, a number of these groups evolved into veritable movements for social change at the end of the 1980s. In an interview conducted in 2008, Aleksandr Margolis, a St. Petersburg-based architect and restorer, described the transformation of his local preservationist group in Leningrad into a force for political transformation in the perestroika era:

> There emerged this arc, you see, drawing together people from virtually all generations. They really did feel empowered to lead people out into the streets and the squares, and in large numbers too. And these club meetings that we'd all attended in the '60s and the early '70s, when we'd all got together and talked about our problems, given papers to each other and looked at slides and so on, all that suddenly turned into a civic movement, even a popular movement, perhaps.[5]

Not all preservationist groups were enlightened movements for the advancement of the social good, however. One of the most high-profile civic movements for the preservation of heritage to emerge at this time was the radical antisemitic organization "Memory" (*Pamiat*). These "primitive patriots," as members of the society were dubbed, developed conspiratorial theories about the destruction of Russian civilization, holding "Judeo-Masonic groups" responsible for the country's social and economic problems, including the destruction of national heritage.[6] Yet, despite claims by the movement's leaders that membership had reached 5,000 in Leningrad and 20,000 in Moscow by 1990, with sections of the organization existing in thirty Russian towns, the popularity of "Memory" appears to have been grossly exaggerated. There is no evidence of branches of the movement having existed in the towns of the Russian Northwest, despite the fact that established associations of the heritage landscape with ideas of Russian cultural authenticity would, one would assume, have made them a prime target for the group.[7]

Despite the resurgence of popular interest in cultural conservation, the All-Russian Society for the Preservation of Historical and Cultural Monuments began to flounder at the end of the 1980s. The Society's decline was hastened by the foundation of the Soviet Cultural Fund (SKF) in November 1986, at whose helm could be found a troika of cultural preservation: the medievalist and cultural commentator Dmitry Likhachev; the Soviet statesman and historian Georg Miasnikov; and the wife of the CPSU First Secretary, Raisa Gorbacheva. The SKF became the preferred site for investment in cultural matters of the flagging Soviet state, attracting an alleged 100 million US dollars in the years before the USSR's collapse.[8] After 1991, the SKF, reconfigured as the Russian Cultural Fund, continued to attract the patronage of high-profile cultural figures, including the filmmaker and self-declared Russian patriot Nikita Mikhalkov, who assumed the fund's presidency in 1993. Throughout the 1990s, it drew support from some of the most powerful actors in post-Soviet Russian society, counting the Moscow Patriarch, federal and regional state bodies, and a number of influential foundations and public institutions among its benefactors.[9]

Church or Monument?

The rehabilitation of the Russian Orthodox Church and its emergence as a powerful lobby in Russian society engendered a shift in the politics of architectural preservation. The cause of the ROC had featured prominently in the power struggle between Gorbachev and Yeltsin during the years of perestroika and political transition.[10] In his bid to wrest legitimacy from the hands of his communist counterpart, Yeltsin had actively courted the ROC and its followers, painting himself, in the late 1980s, as a defender of civic freedoms, including the freedom of religion.[11] Once he had secured the leadership of the post-Soviet Russian state, Yeltsin continued to play the Russian Orthodox "card" to consolidate his power in the new conditions of democratic politics. During the 1995 elections and again in the presidential campaign of 1996, Yeltsin fell back on his patriotic and religious credentials to secure the support of the Russian electorate. By the late 1990s, following Yeltsin's second, less obvious, victory at the polls, the ROC had become a hugely influential lobby within Russian politics.[12]

The growing influence of the ROC was reflected in its increasingly assertive demands for material and symbolic compensation for the church's treatment at the hands of the Soviet Communist Party. This compensation frequently took the form of the transference of ownership rights of objects of religious architecture from local authorities to local dioceses.[13] In Novgorod, Pskov, and Vologda, where many local churches had been designated "architectural monuments" and exhibited to the public in museum-zapovedniks, this process raised a whole series of difficult and controversial questions. Who were the rightful owners of artistic and architectural masterpieces such as the St. Sophia Cathedral in Novgorod and the Savior of Priluki Monastery in Vologda—the ROC or the authorities for cultural preservation? Who was liable for the cost of the restoration of such monuments—the local diocese or the state responsible for their disintegration? And who were the rightful beneficiaries of these historical sites—Orthodox believers or the Russian nation as a whole?

The case of the St. Sophia Cathedral in Novgorod, a symbol of local and national identity, was one of the first to be raised following the collapse of the socialist state. The cathedral had been recognized as an architectural monument of federal significance during the first survey of Russian heritage conducted in 1960 and had served as a prominent site of local cultural activity for the thirty years of socialist rule that followed.[14] As the centerpiece of the Novgorod architectural zapovednik, the cathedral had been visited by hundreds of thousands of tourists and had hosted a series of high-profile exhibitions. The church had also benefited from thoroughgoing restoration work funded by both the federal and local authorities.[15] By 1991, the cathedral was consequently one of the town's best-equipped exhibitive spaces and an asset that was highly valued by the local museum.

The decision of June 1991 to transfer the cathedral to the Novgorod diocese, together with the nearby St. George's and Khutyn Monasteries, consequently met with a tepid reception from the Novgorod Museum collective.[16] Employees worried in particular that the use of the cathedral as a place of worship would endanger certain valuable works of art that were located within the building. The focus of controversy was the Our Lady of the Sign icon (1170), one of Russia's oldest icons and an object that was historically revered as the palladium of the medieval Republic. Yet, despite protests by local preservationists, the Novgorod authorities maintained that the proper context for this object was a sacred rather than exhibitive one. "In reality there exists no risk of damage to the icon from 'ecclesiastical exploitation,'" the local authorities insisted. "The only issue is to make sure that the correct conditions are in place for its preservation in the St. Sophia Cathedral. This is a run-of-the-mill museum matter."[17]

The museum's reaction to the local authorities' decision to allow the icon to revert to its original religious function is revealing of the reality of Yeltsin-era cultural politics. Rather than appeal to the central preservationist authorities with their concerns, the museum solicited the support of their most powerful patron, Likhachev. In response to the museum's appeals, Likhachev addressed a letter to the head of the St. Sophia Cultural and Philosophical Society in 1991. The letter reinforced the museum's position as the rightful owners of the historic church:

> I do not consider the return of the St. Sophia Cathedral to the faithful a realistic possibility. Today the church has the status of a legal entity and, thus, the question must be resolved conjointly by the secular and spiritual authorities.
>
> My personal opinion on the matter is the following:
>
> 1. Religious services may be held at the St. Sophia Cathedral two or three times a year with the permission of the museum;
>
> 2. The Our Lady of the Sign icon (like many particularly valuable and ancient icons) must be left in the museum, where it can be preserved in the appropriate conditions. A copy can be made for the church;
>
> 3. Photography must be prohibited, as is the case in many museums.[18]

The solicitation of celebrity sponsorship for local cultural causes was a tried and tested mechanism for influencing political decision making in the undemocratic conditions of Soviet politics. And, indeed, as this interaction reveals, it was one that continued to be deployed by local elites in the post-Soviet 1990s. But while the patronage of Likhachev had been enough to force the hand of the local authorities on such matters in the past, the status of the ROC had grown so significantly by 1991 that the historian's intervention was no longer sufficient to sway the decision of the administration. The church was duly transferred to the local diocese and reconsecrated by Patriarch Aleksei II in August 1991; the Our Lady of the Sign icon was, moreover, incorporated as the centerpiece of the church's impressive iconostasis, contrary to the advice of the esteemed medieval historian.[19]

Many such conflicts surfaced in the years that followed the collapse of the socialist state. In an almost identical scenario that emerged five years later in 1996, the head of the Committee for Culture and Tourism in Pskov, A. I. Golyshev, wrote to the head of Pskov's regional administration, V. N. Tumanov, to oppose the transfer of the fourteenth-century Nativity of the Virgin Church (1311) within the Snetogorsk Monastery to the local diocese.[20] In this case, the sticking point was a series of fourteenth-century frescoes—unique examples of the Pskov School of fresco painting, according to Golyshev—that were located within the building. The frescoes had been carefully restored in the postwar period thanks to extensive funding from the central preservation authorities.[21] Moreover, the installation of expensive dehumidifying and air-conditioning equipment in the 1980s had established a delicate microclimate, which, Golyshev argued, would be compromised if the church began to be used for religious services.[22]

Like the plea of the Novgorod Museum collective, Golyshev's request that the church be preserved as an object of museum exploitation was never communicated to the Russian Ministry of Culture. Yet, if the church remained in the hands of the Pskov diocese, the appeals of the preservationist lobby did not fall entirely on deaf ears. In 1998, services were discontinued in the Nativity Church and moved to the refectory of the nearby St. Nicholas Church.[23] While the reasons for this decision are unclear from archival sources, one may speculate that these were connected to the preservationist concerns raised by local actors, such as Golyshev. While relatively powerless in administrative terms, local preservationist authorities, it would seem, retained a stock of cultural capital that lent weight to their recommendations in the postsocialist period.

These cases from the early post-Soviet period can be compared to a related conflict that emerged in Vologda two decades after socialism's collapse in 2000. At this time, controversy emerged around the declared intention to repurpose the Resurrection Church on Cathedral Hill—serving at that time as the museum's art gallery—as the Cathedral Church of the local diocese. In a strategic maneuver, the Father Superior of the Vologda diocese had raised the question of the church's transfer at a ceremony celebrating 2000 years of Christianity in Vologda. The idea immediately met with strong resistance on the part of the museum collective, however, who argued that the building was a crucial component of the Vologda museum complex and one that had been adapted at some cost to the local authorities for the exhibition of valuable works of art.[24]

By contrast with the decision to return the St. Sophia Cathedral to the Novgorod diocese in 1991, the question of the rightful ownership of the Resurrection Cathedral generated fierce debate. The fact that the Vologda diocese had reappropriated twenty-seven other local churches since the collapse of socialism threw the legitimacy of its claim to this particular building into doubt. One local journalist, Liudmilia Martova, writing in the year 2000 in the Vologda weekly *Premier*, emerged as a central voice in the discussion, expressing concerns that the diocese might not limit its demands to the Resurrection Church but might instead attempt to colonize the whole of the Cathedral Hill complex, as it had during the transfer of the Priluki Monastery complex several years earlier.[25] Martova objected to this idea on the grounds that the cathedral was more than just a sacred space and had broader cultural relevance for the local community:

> In my opinion, the cultural significance of Cathedral Hill and the Vologda Kremlin is much greater than its religious significance. It is hardly possible to measure accurately the number of the faithful among the inhabitants of Vologda today (real faith is incompatible with mathematics, after all), but those who live in a secular way, not according to the laws of the church, surely comprise the majority and are just as entitled to consider Cathedral Hill their sanctuary as the faithful.[26]

The decision to refuse the diocese's demands in this instance was indicative of a shift in attitudes toward church politics at the end of the decade. If the Church's claim to religious objects had been almost impossible to resist in the early 1990s, when pressure for political atonement was as its height, the situation had changed notably by 2000.[27] A decade after the collapse of Soviet power, Russian officials exhibited greater sympathy for the cause of the cultural institutions that had been resident in repurposed churches and had, in many cases, been instrumental in the preservation and restoration of these heritage objects. While some notable cases of reconsecration took place at this time, the resolution of heritage conflicts in favor of the church was no longer a foregone conclusion.[28] In the case of Vologda's Resurrection Cathedral demonstrated, recourse to the language of historical restitution—Maximilian's insistence on the need for "historical justice" and reference to the "lamentable historical circumstances" that had led to the building's desecration—no longer resonated with the political authorities and could no longer be relied upon to produce the desired result.[29]

FIGURE 8. The Resurrection Cathedral (1772) and St. Sophia Cathedral (1568–1570) on Cathedral Hill, Vologda, June 2010.

The Sacralization of Public Space

Adrian Forty and Susanne Küchler have described the paradox of memorials in *The Art of Forgetting*. The creation of a material presence in place of an absence, they argue, forecloses the possibility of semantic abundance, making memorialization an exercise in forgetting rather than remembering.[30] The desire to replace symbolic ambivalence with cultural definition can be remarked in the commemorative practices of the early post-Soviet period. One of the most obvious manifestations of this tendency was the erection of crosses or monuments in the empty spaces where Orthodox churches had stood before their destruction by the communist regime. The act of attributing to the empty spaces a strictly spiritual significance marginalized alternative readings of the churches' destruction—for example, as acts of violence against the local community for whom these buildings were focuses of cultural life.

One notable case of the symbolic appropriation of public space took place in Vologda in the late 1990s. The central Revolution Square (formerly Haymarket Square) had been the site of a cluster of seventeenth- and eighteenth-century churches until the mid-1920s. In line with the Stalinist drive against religion, the St. Athanasius of Alexandria church (late 17 c.) and the St. Nicholas on Haymarket Square Church (1713–1777) were demolished in 1924 and 1928, respectively.[31] The neighboring Savior of All the Town Cathedral (1654) was, however, left in place, quite possibly as result of its status in local folklore (legend had it that the church had been built in one day to fend off an incoming epidemic of the Bubonic Plague).[32] In 1924, the cathedral was closed and adapted as a Soviet Palace of Culture; in the postwar period, it was refashioned again as the popular Maxim Gorky Cinema, a multi-purpose venue for playing chess, reading newspapers, and socializing with friends.[33]

In 1972, in a rare decision for the time, the head of Vologda's executive committee, Vladimir Parmenov, ordered that the church be demolished. The reasons for this decision are unclear from archival sources; it would appear that they were linked to the drive for urban modernization underway at this time and a generally held opinion that the church contradicted the "organizational logic" of the historic center.[34] The church's destruction was a dramatic affair; decommissioned tanks were deployed to raze the thick seventeenth-century walls and soldiers surrounded the demolition site to ward off local spectators. The military violence of the scene was nevertheless etched into many local residents' memories. In interviews conducted in the mid-2000s, a number of locals recalled the episode, drawing on images displayed at local museums and folk knowledge to narrate a collective memory of the destructive event.[35]

During the last two decades of Soviet power, the site where the church had stood formed part of the Revolution Square complex, which hosted demonstrations, performances, and other Soviet festivities. With the reversal of the fortunes of the Orthodox Church in the post-Soviet period, however, the sacred identity of empty space was restored. In 1997, on the initiative of the Vologda diocese and the local hierarch, Maximilian, a seven-meter high steel "Wayside Cross" was erected, in accordance with archeological studies, on the site of the former church's altar.[36] In the media coverage of the event, the grassroots nature of the initiative was emphasized. An article published in *Red North*, for example, pointed out that steelworkers at the local "Northern Steel" works had manufactured the cross and that its thoughtful design had been the result of the efforts of the local community.[37]

At the monument's opening ceremony in 1997, the mayor of Vologda, A. S. Iakunichev, declared that the cross's construction had altered the symbolic meaning of the square, transforming it from a "Square of Revolution" into a "Square of Harmony."[38] This statement obliquely referenced the presidential decree of November 7, 1996, to rename the "Anniversary of the Great October Socialist Revolution" the "Day of Harmony and Reconciliation," part of a national initiative to replace the symbolic vocabulary of state socialism with language more fitting with the postcommunist reality.[39] The administration's efforts to present the cross as a symbol of post-Soviet democracy, however, were quickly challenged by the Orthodox Church. In 1998, the local diocese inaugurated an annual religious procession between the Shroud on the Marketplace Church (c. 1486) and the "Wayside Cross," which, it claimed, reanimated a seventeenth-century tradition, establishing continuity between Orthodox believers, past and present. This ritual,

FIGURE 9. The Wayside Cross on Revolution Square in Vologda, July 2010.

quickly established as a staple of the local festive calendar, asserted the symbolic exclusivity of the site, the primacy of its spiritual value over its social or cultural functions.[40]

The "Wayside Cross" thus emerged in the post-Soviet period as a site of contested local memory. On the one hand, the post-Soviet administration strove to associate it with the values of the Yeltsin era, linking the monument's construction in the 1990s to the processes of political transformation underway in the fledgling Russian state. On the other hand, the local diocese sought to assert the symbolic exclusivity of the space as a site of reflection on and mourning for the treatment of the Orthodox Church by the communist regime. Intriguingly, however, the identity of the space that proved most resilient in the 2000s turned out to be its everyday Soviet one. Every summer, and despite repeated complaints from the local diocese, a complex of children's attractions, including a colorful bouncy castle, was located on the square in close proximity to the cross. This more spontaneous use of the site as a shared social space appeared to reference—albeit unwittingly— the postwar identity of the square as a place for socialization and entertainment rather than politics or pious reflection.

Heritage "In Private Hands"

One of the most controversial post-Soviet reforms in the domain of cultural preservation was the privatization of heritage objects. This process began with the 1994 presidential decree "On the Privatization of Historical and Cultural Monuments of Local Significance in the Russian Federation," which stated that "objects acknowledged as immovable historical or cultural monuments of local significance [could] be privatized on the condition that they [were] maintained by their new owners in the necessary conditions in accordance with the requirements of the preservationist authorities."[41] The policy was ostensibly intended to "activate economic transition" and to attract much needed investment into the sphere of heritage restoration. The reality of procuring ownership of heritage objects was, however, far from straightforward. The bureaucratic hurdles presented to potential investors initially discouraged many Russian citizens from entering into negotiations. According to one article published in the *Russian Journal* in 2008, only 1000 interested parties presented themselves in Russia in the fifteen years that followed the decree. By the end of the 2000s, most local monuments consequently remained unoccupied or the subject of unsuitable exploitation by rental tenants, further contributing to their structural disintegration and decline.[42]

The financial burden of this heritage weighed heavily on local governments during the years of economic downturn and crisis. A report on local spending in Pskov from 2004 revealed the sums allocated to heritage preservation at this time: in 2002 a total of 14,693,000 rubles had been spent on restoration and repair work, of which 10,800,000 issued from the federal budget, 1,063,000 from the oblast budget, and 2,830,000 from extra-budgetary sources. By 2003, these amounts had risen dramatically to a total of 40,289,0000 rubles, of which 35,950,000 came from the federal budget, 1,988,000 from the oblast budget, and 2,351,000 from extra-budgetary sources.[43] Despite increased spending, however, the condition of local heritage objects remained precarious. In 2004, about one thousand monuments, or 30 percent of the total number of historical buildings in the town, were reported to be in "an unsatisfactory condition." Furthermore, four hundred of these, it was reported, urgently needed private investment, although it was estimated that only two hundred had the capacity to attract potential investors.[44]

As the decree's title suggests, federal monuments were excluded from this first wave of privatization. In order to avoid the concentration of the country's most prestigious buildings in the hands of a privileged few, a moratorium was placed on the sale of federally protected architecture in the immediate post-Soviet period. The removal of this embargo in 2008 caused considerable anxiety among local preservationists. As one journalist ominously explained in an article published the same year, it meant that "for each unit of cultural heritage there could emerge a concrete proprietor, with their own priorities and philosophy."[45] There nevertheless remained strict regulations governing the purchase of federal heritage sites that precluded such nightmarish scenarios as the conversion of the St. Sophia Cathedral into an elite casino or the adaptation of the Pskov Kremlin as a local heliport. Specifically, the law stipulated that churches, monasteries, and other sacred buildings could only be acquired by religious communities or cultural institutions, while buildings housing state organizations (such as museums, archives, and schools) were excluded from sale altogether.[46]

As a consequence of these conditions, much of the privatization activity in the late 2000s concentrated on the civic architecture of the eighteenth and nineteenth centuries. In particular, investors were drawn to the many noble mansions and estates that populated the outskirts of provincial Russian towns. Denis Bezrukov, the head of the authorities for the state preservation of cultural heritage in Novgorod, remarked upon the upsurge in sales of noble estates in the region: "Right now estate properties are selling like hotcakes," he commented, in an article that appeared in the *Russian Journal* in 2010. "Not long back one of the estates of the Chudovsk region, the 'Piney Refuge,' passed into private hands. That building was in dire straits a while ago, and now it's been transformed into an elegant hotel complex."[47]

This type of development, however, was not straightforward. The legal restrictions on internal reconstruction meant that nineteenth-century noble estates could be converted into hotels with a maximum of around twenty rooms. One journalist speculated that this limited potential for exploitation meant that—after incurring expenses on repairs and restoration work—a developer would only break even on such properties after approximately ten years.[48] Many provincial noble mansions were consequently acquired not as business ventures by developers but as prestige purchases by local politicians and businessmen. While staying in Vologda in 2008, I visited with friends one such estate that had been bought and renovated by the owner of a chain of local supermarkets. Residents of the town were invited to view the premises in the hope that this sort of lifestyle tourism would create business in the form of conferences or hunting parties.[49] The exterior of the estate left much to be desired in terms of preservationist ideals (a pitched roof extension had been added to the property and a satellite dish protruded from beneath the balcony), while inside original fittings had been replaced by mock historical features: imitation parquet flooring, faux structural columns, and a baroque-style staircase. Yet, despite its failure to adhere to strict preservationist norms, the restored estate was admired by my fellow visitors, who thought it appropriate that it had been retuned to its former grandeur, albeit of a different post-Soviet kind. "Better that than it disintegrate into ruins," commented Valentina, the landlady of my flat in Vologda, echoing the opinions of many residents in the historic northern province.

"Decrepit Half-Ruined Buildings"

A tourist to the northern Russian city of Vologda in the late 1990s could have been forgiven for thinking that the town had recently been caught in the middle of a violent military campaign. Along the quiet, tree-lined streets of the provincial capital, one regularly encountered the ruins of a burnt-out wooden house, or an empty space between houses where a wooden building had once stood. According to Vologda's head architect, Leonid Ragutsky, quoted in 2001 in the local newspaper *Russian North*, 41 listed wooden buildings had been destroyed by fire following the collapse of the Soviet Union in 1991, of which 17 had been federally protected and 24 regionally protected monuments.[50] This was to say nothing of the unprotected wooden buildings that burned down as a matter of course on a weekly basis in the town. In a shocking tally of the damage wrought to local architecture, the same journal reported that 60 fires had taken place in the town in the preceding week alone, causing six deaths and two serious injuries, along with material damage at a cost of 590,000 rubles.[51]

According to public commentators, the destruction of local heritage was linked to the emergence of a super-affluent local elite, who had benefited from the redistribution of public wealth after socialism. The efforts of these "New Russians" to assert their status through the construction of prestige projects in the historic center of the city had brought them into conflict with local architects and preservationists. Encountering obstacles to their plans in the form of preservation zones and state-protected buildings, Vologda's business class had ignored regulations, bribed officials, and engaged in violent tactics to get their way. One journalist, writing in the Vologda weekly *Chronometer* in 1999, described the shady deals and criminal acts that had become commonplace in dealings with architectural heritage by the end of the 1990s:

> Just look around you—filth, decrepit half-ruined buildings here and there. Dozens of these "places of local interest" burn down every year, and it's no surprise to anyone when yet another "monument" goes up in smoke, and a few months down the line a nice little "New Russian" mansion pops up in its place. And this is rarely down to a drunken tramp who has burned his own house down, or if it is, then it's not on his own initiative or as a result of getting soused, but because he's received a "social commission" [*sotszakaz*][52] from some anonymous party or another.[53]

For a number of heritage-aware journalists, the destruction of architectural monuments by a wealthy and unaccountable elite was emblematic of a deeper malaise afflicting Russian society. These writers understood heritage to be the material manifestation of national identity, and as such, its destruction was presented as a symbolic act of violence against the Russian people. Writing about architectural preservation, journalists thus played on the trope of war, making use of military vocabulary in their descriptions of damaged wooden houses and populating their stories with humiliated veterans and war widows. For example, the center of the Vologda province Ustiuzhna was compared to the Chechen capital of Grozny in an article published in *Vologda Weekly* in March 2001.[54] Another journalist writing in *Our Region* in the same year ruefully stated, "you have the impression that the town has come under enemy attack."[55] Yet another commentator compared a ruined monument in Vologda to an "enemy pillbox" (*vrazheskii dot*).[56] Vologda, according to these writers, was caught in the midst of a de facto state of war, the origins of which lay in the country's failed transition to market capitalism.

FIGURE 10. A burned-out wooden house in Vologda, April 2009.

The narrative that perhaps best illustrates this tendency relates to the head of the Vologda state inspectorate for the preservation of monuments, Mikhail Karachev. Karachev, a native of the Vologda region, born in 1953, was a notable figure in Yeltsin-era local politics, attracting attention from the local press for his fundamentalist line on architectural preservation and his fearless interactions with local politicians and businessmen. His resistance to the construction of new buildings in the city center from materials other than the traditional wood had brought him into conflict with the local governor, Nikolai Podgornov, who publicly condemned Karachev in 1995 with the words, "this man does not understand the damage he's inflicting on the history, culture and architecture of our nation."[57] Such open clashes with the administration did not deter the local preservationist, however. Throughout the 1990s he continued to lock horns with the political and commercial elite in the town in his battle to preserve the architectural integrity of historic Vologda.

In 1995, Karachev found himself embroiled in a scandal that culminated in violent conflict. In his role as head of the state inspectorate for historic monuments, he became aware of a suspect deal to build a number of elite "cottages" within the town's central preservation zone brokered by a local bureaucrat, Boris Uladyshev (later, deputy governor of Vologda), and a number of other officials and businessmen. By the time Karachev had brought the issue to the attention of the local authorities, Uladyshev and his partners had already succeeded in demolishing and incinerating several federally protected wooden monuments. Despite the obvious criminality of the group's actions, however, Podgornov refused to pursue the matter. Instead of punishing the perpetrators or seizing the land from the developers, Podgornov passed a temporary measure that contradicted the Constitution of Russia by granting rights to the developers to build in the preservation zone.[58]

Demonstrating characteristic tenacity, Karachev refused to let the matter rest with the decision of the Vologda governor. Instead he pursued the case at the Office of the Public Prosecutor and succeeded in having the ruling overturned and halting construction work in the preservation zone. Yet, if Karachev's actions had brought an end to the violation of monuments in the preservation zone, the security of his own state-protected home was now in question. In the months that followed the public prosecutor's intervention, two arson attacks were made on Karachev's federally protected house on Zasodimskii Street, and in a more dramatic turn of events, a hand grenade was thrown through the preservationist's bedroom window.[59]

Karachev's determination and his treatment at the hands of corrupt elements in Vologda society appealed to local commentators, who returned to his story repeatedly throughout the 1990s. Within the discursive framework of "a state of war," Karachev was portrayed as a freedom fighter battling for the rights and principles of a dispossessed and marginalized majority. The local weekly *Premier*, for example, described him in 1998 as "a Robin Hood kind of figure, who battles fearlessly for the preservation of Vologda's historic façade."[60] The episode with the grenade, while undoubtedly shocking in any context, was fetishized in the local press as the ultimate expression of the conditions of violence that had accompanied the introduction of capitalism since 1991.

Revealingly, Karachev was also described as possessing authentically Russian credentials, which were juxtaposed in this writing with the alien culture of the "New Russians." When discussing the brave preservationist in an article published in *Russian North* in 1995, the local journalist Robert Balakshin thus explained, "he's not one of the 'new' ones [*on ne iz 'novykh'*]—he's a real Russian, and acting like a prostitute just isn't in his nature [*moral' prostitutki emu ne privita*]."[61] Karachev's selflessness and commitment to the common good (as well as his sexual propriety, it was intimated) were contrasted here with the exploitative and mercenary character of the "New Russian" class in a caricature worthy of the best of Soviet anti-capitalist propaganda. In this case, however, the threatening foreign culture was not located beyond the national boundaries, but within the Russian state itself; authentic Russian culture, it was suggested, had been besieged by degenerate, westernized forces, and it was up to the likes of Karachev to secure its ultimate liberation.

Gilded Heritage and "Golden Embankments"

It is tempting to view the violence and conflict that characterized heritage preservation at this time as unique to the "wild capitalist" conditions of the post-Soviet 1990s and 2000s. Yet, in many ways, the character of the debate about architectural conservation demonstrated continuity rather than rupture with the past. From the late Khrushchev era, commentators writing about preservation in the Northwest had fallen broadly into two camps: those who privileged the preservation of the towns' architectural legacy above all other developmental concerns, and those who, by contrast, saw the conservation of local monuments as a hindrance to urban transformation and modernization. In the postsocialist period, one can trace the evolution of these two perspectives, albeit in radically changed political and economic conditions. Instead of Soviet architects arguing for the erection of social housing in conservation zones, preservationists found themselves locking horns with private investors who maintained that local economies would benefit from the construction of elite housing complexes, hotels, and tourist facilities.

In one of the most high-profile conflicts of this sort, which emerged in the early 2000s, local preservationists in Pskov clashed with developers over a project to reconstruct a historic quarter of the town opposite the Pskov Kremlin that was quickly dubbed the "Golden Embankment." This project envisioned the recreation of a number of nineteenth-century merchant houses along the Soviet (formerly American) Embankment that had been partially destroyed during World War II and had grown even more dilapidated as a consequence of neglect by the local authorities. The project was financed by a local businessman, Iurii Brokhman, who presided over the Pskov-based development company "Pskovinkomstroi." As *Pskov Province* reported in 2002, the investor's intention was to create an "architectural refuge" from contemporary life in Pskov by constructing the district "in the style of a provincial town, completely free of any distracting contemporary features."[62]

Brokhman's project was marketed to local communities in a language of progress and improvement that was familiar from the heritage debates of the Soviet period. The quarter would "rejuvenate" (*pomolodet'*) the central district of the town, locals were told, enhancing the regional economy through the attraction of private investment from Moscow and St. Petersburg.[63] According to one local journalist, Svetlana Prokop'eva, these arguments were warmly received by the town's principal architects, who acknowledged a certain responsibility for the deterioration of the original embankment.[64] Preservationist elements in Pskov nevertheless expressed reservations about the project. Mikhail Menikov, the head of the Pskov Society of Kraevedy, pointed out that the buildings Brokhman proposed to reconstruct were far from masterpieces of nineteenth-century architecture and would be better left to fade out of local cultural memory. Moreover, the director of the Pskov Museum-Zapovednik, Ol'ga Volochkova, noted that the construction of the new region would obscure the view of the Pskov Kremlin that had only recently opened up as a result of the demolition of House No. 2 on the Leon Pozemskii Street.[65]

These objections may well have been dismissed as the habitual grumblings of a recalcitrant preservationist minority had it not been for an unexpected development. In 2002, Brokhman and company were informed that, in accordance with the newly adopted presidential decree "On Objects of Cultural Heritage,"[66] they would have to carry out archaeological excavation work on the federally protected cultural layer beneath the embankment before they began building. Such a requirement, which had a precedent in the 1976 law "On Objects of Cultural Heritage," was commonplace in medieval towns such as Pskov, where the discovery of ruins on a building site frequently brought construction work to a standstill. Nevertheless, Brokhman interpreted the imposition of the law in this instance as an underhanded maneuver and a scurrilous attempt to thwart the proposed construction plans. Speaking with *Pskov Province* in 2002, the developer accused local archaeologists of "cunning" (*lukavstvo*) and "bandwagon jumping" (*shapkozakidatel'stvo*), and suggested that their actions were driven by a desire to enhance their own dusty collections of relics and exhibits rather than to see their town thriving and prosperous.[67]

It is instructive to note how closely aligned this dispute was with discussions about heritage preservation of the Soviet 1960s. As indicated in chapter 2, public commentators in the postwar period were apt to criticize preservationist lobbies for wanting to museicize their cities and make them unsuitable for habitation.[68] In his interview with *Pskov Province*, Brokhman reproduced this Soviet line of reasoning in its unreconstructed entirety. Responding to a question about whether he would carry out the excavation work, he cast the town's cultural elite into the role of recalcitrant stick-in-the-muds, more concerned with their esoteric academic enterprises than the community as a whole:

> In theory, we will do everything that we can, but how much is it going to cost? We're not prepared to finance the research and dissertations of archaeologists. It's the state that should finance that. Archaeology in any case will benefit from the project. We are prepared to finance the excavation work, but only within reasonable limits. I'm from Pskov too, and I value very highly everything that's going on here.[69]

Statements such as this suggest the existence of two opposed models of patriotic identity in the post-Soviet Russian regions. On the one hand, figures such as Brokhman espoused a "pragmatic patriotic" approach to local heritage, claiming to perceive an opportunity to invigorate the local economy through the exploitation of the towns' principle resource—its historic architecture. On the other hand, preservationists who dominated branches of the local media and cultural institutions endorsed a "romantic patriotic" vision of cultural heritage. For this group, the preservation of the historic integrity of the towns was paramount and, indeed, a necessary condition for the spiritual and cultural survival of the region. This point of view, invested as it was in the idea of a culturally coherent local identity, presented an attractive paradigm to Russian nationalists. As demonstrated above, romantic patriotic approaches to preservation could easily degenerate into overt chauvinism and anti-western commentary as critics launched into vitriolic attacks on "liberal" tendencies that threatened the cultural integrity of the region or locality.

FIGURE 11. The "Golden Embankment" in Pskov, August 2009.

Monuments to a Failed Transition

The culture of corruption surrounding architectural preservation in the 1990s and 2000s cultivated a mood of deep cynicism and distrust in local politics. Burnt-out houses and ruined monuments became symbols of public disillusionment with government rather than focuses of local pride and social solidarity. One local history publication that illustrates this atmosphere is *My Vologda: The Town in Our Memory*, published in 2007, which catalogued the destruction of the town's historic buildings and condemned the contemptuous attitude of local authorities to the preservation of the region's architectural heritage.[70] A similarly plaintive account of architectural preservation could be found in A. I. Sazanov's earlier publication *In Russia There Is But One Such City* (1993), which lamented the disappearance of Vologda's traditional wooden landscape.[71]

Local residents echoed these concerns in interviews in the late 2000s. In conversation at his home in a federally protected monument on Vorovskii Street, Leonid (1946) shared his anxieties about the preservation of local heritage objects. He had been battling for years to secure funding for the restoration of his historic building, which had been severely damaged by fire in the early 2000s. Leonid was convinced that the local authorities were responsible for many of the acts of arson in the region and explained that, without fundamental changes to planning regulations, the destruction would persist until the town's traditional landscape had been completely destroyed:

> I'm absolutely sure that officials burned down a lot of these houses. There's no doubt in my mind. They free the land up, and then they . . . well, they sell it on to someone or another. And it all comes down to bribes then, at the end of the day. That way they get rid of these unique houses, houses that were monuments back in the day, and put up new houses in their place. You know, I wrote to our governor telling him to pass an order saying that on the spot where a burnt-out monument had stood—and I'm talking about monuments here, not just ordinary houses, because, you know, far from all wooden houses are monuments—on the spot where these monuments had stood, that they ought to have to build the exact same monument or not build anything at all for thirty odd years, if they don't have the money. And in thirty years they'll find the money from somewhere probably . . . and that way, they'd stop burning them down. But, you'd have to stop the land being transferred to the municipality. Because officials wouldn't be able to make any money from it then, you see.

Leonid's sentiments accorded with those of many local journalists and public commentators,[72] yet he was perhaps more tenacious than most in his defense of local heritage. In his efforts to secure funding for his building's restoration, he had petitioned local and national authorities and even approached the descendants of the merchant who had originally owned the house, all without success. Many in the town nevertheless shared his sense of frustration and anger in connection with local preservationist failures. For those brought up in the Brezhnev era, when cultural preservation had been high on the social agenda, the contemptuous attitude of the local authorities to the town's historical architecture appeared particularly objectionable. The fact that officials failed to recognize their civic duty to defend and preserve the material heritage of the nation was, for many, indicative of the self-interested and fundamentally undemocratic character of post-Soviet politics.

Conversely, official efforts to preserve and restore heritage objects were viewed by locals with skepticism, as acts of political opportunism at best and elite corruption at worst. A popular anecdote concerning a visit by President Vladimir Putin to Vologda in 2001 captures the air of disenchantment that pervaded the Russian regions at this time. According to locals, the route the President would follow through the town—which local authorities had attempted conceal from the community—was made obvious when buildings on particular streets began to be restored and repainted.[73] Vologda, it seemed to many, had become a modern-day Potemkin (or perhaps "Putinkin") village, whose political elite was more concerned with appearances than the welfare and material culture of the local community.

The collapse of socialism in 1991 saw Soviet society fragment into a myriad of competing allegiances and identities. The façade of national unity, which the regime had struggled to maintain since Stalin's death, disintegrated into a multitude of territorial, religious, and social affiliations. New elites who came to prominence at this time attempted to assert their authority by invoking the symbols of national and local identity, which, they claimed, had been misappropriated by the Soviet regime. The Orthodox Church thus laid claim to its "rightful property" in the form of listed churches and religious artwork, while regional authorities asserted their ownership of heritage objects that had been purloined by the atheist Soviet state. While the post-Soviet scramble for heritage objects was predictable enough in the conditions of cultural flux that marked Yeltsin's presidency, the position adopted by local preservationists in the debate is more interesting. As this chapter has demonstrated, preservationist elites argued vehemently against the transfer of monuments from the state into ecclesiastic or private hands after the collapse of socialism. As such, the critics of the modernizing Soviet regime found themselves in the unexpected position of defending the Soviet status quo, rejecting the essentialist arguments of the ROC, and asserting instead an understanding of heritage as a public resource.

The Northwest's status as a state-sponsored center of Russian heritage and culture created a particular set of circumstances after 1991. Cultural elites were quick to mobilize in response to the perceived betrayal of Soviet-era norms of heritage preservation, and their arguments were reinforced by a sympathetic local press, which helped to generate public consensus over the idea of the inviolability of heritage and outrage at its mismanagement. Public commentators writing about heritage in this period drew on preservationist discourses that were already well established from the postwar period. The military imagery used to describe Vologda's burnt-out architecture can thus be compared to the presentation of Novgorod's monuments after the war as victims of Nazi barbarity and violence. Notably, however, the discourse of military aggression was used introspectively to condemn part of post-Soviet Russian society rather than to demonize an external aggressor. By casting "New Russian" developers and elites as enemies of the Russian people and their traditions, commentators were able to galvanize public opinion against these cultural "fifth columnists" who threatened to undermine the foundation stones of local and national identity.

5.

GUARDIANS OF OUR HERITAGE

Rebranding the Northwest in the Putin Era

The political instability that marked the early post-Soviet period created confusion over the status of cultural heritage in the historic Northwest. As Yeltsin struggled to establish a clearly defined national idea, the position of local heritage objects, the state-sponsored symbols of Russified Soviet identity, was thrown into question. In the Putin era, this situation changed. The Russian patriotic resurgence of the late 2000s, which intensified during Putin's third presidential term (2012–2018),[1] saw the Northwest reemerge at the center of the Russian national imaginary. This process involved the reaffirmation of the region's architectural monuments as the expression of authentically Russian cultural values. Spirituality, strength, military prowess, and simplicity were once more reasserted as qualities inherent to the historic region.

Putinist state patriotism nevertheless differed qualitatively from the Soviet patriotic politics of the late twentieth century. As Peter Pomerantsev, Mark Lipovetsky, and others have pointed out, Putin-era patriotic culture showed a preference for "spectacles of power," that is, stunts and theatrical performances, over ideological discourse and rational argument.[2] In the increasingly authoritarian conditions of managed democracy, the Russian state reverted to the propagandist methods of the early Soviet period, designed to win the political affections of a disengaged Russian citizenry.[3] These tendencies influenced new forms of engagement with cultural heritage in the Russian Northwest. Heritage objects became stages on which to play out reimaginings of the past and theatrical performances of Putin-era politics and culture.

This chapter presents the ways that northwestern heritage objects were used as props in patriotic performances of Russian identity in the 2000s and 2010s. The particular focus is on forms of engagement with local architecture at anniversary celebrations and town festivities, events that were used to rebrand the region as a distinct cultural entity with a dynamic and vital relationship to the political center. The chapter builds on the discussion of rebranding to examine several initiatives that emerged in the 2010s, creating new heritage objects that could function as focal points for patriotic reflection and performance. Specifically, two projects in Pskov are considered—one to create a site of national pilgrimage and the other to establish a saint cult in the region. Both projects aimed to market Pskov, a region facing grave social and economic difficulties in the mid-2010s, as a center of Orthodox spirituality and Russian culture.

Patriotic Rebranding and the Russian Regional Renaissance

Before discussing heritage objects as sites of patriotic performance, it is neces-sary to say a few words about territorial "rebranding" in the twenty-first-cen-tury Russian regions. Lyudmila Parts has noted a shift in cultural commentary about the Russian provinces in the 2000s and 2010s. From places whose pri-mary characteristics were deemed to be "backwardness" and "sameness" in the literature of the nineteenth and twentieth centuries, the provinces, according to Parts, have reemerged in the twenty-first century as "the locale where true Russianness resides and from where the new Russia will emerge."[4] This eval-uation is consistent with a number of recent studies of provincialism led by Russian anthropologists and sociologists. Maria Spivak, writing in Liudmila Zaionts's edited collection on provincial identities, notes, for example, that the term "provincial" has undergone a semiotic reinvention in the post-Soviet period, acquiring connotations of sophistication and even eroticism in connec-tion with shifts in the cultural representation of life outside the capital in the mass media.[5]

One of the reasons for the renaissance of provincial culture, Parts argues, is ter-ritorial "rebranding." In the absence of viable sources of local funding, rebranding, or the communication of a place to potential target markets through a plethora of images, ideas, and representations, has formed a means for local authorities to enhance their region's commercial and investment attractiveness.[6] Ekaterina Melnikova confirms this tendency, noting, however, a distinction between, on the one hand, the territorial branding that emerged as a managing practice in the United States and Europe in the 1990s and, on the other hand, the kinds of activity underway in the twenty-first-century Russian regions. While a number of prominent educational establishments have offered university courses on territorial marketing, she notes, the production of regional brands in Russia has on the whole been realized by local and regional authorities, with no assistance from professional marketing agencies.[7]

One of the greatest challenges of territorial rebranding has been to market as culturally unique regions whose primary characteristic has traditionally been seen as their indistinguishableness from other places.[8] A distinction must drawn here, however, between "true provinces," which Parts defines as places that are "not exotic or exceptional in any way," such as Voronezh, and regions that have a particular claim to cultural specificity.[9] The Russian Northwest presents a specific case in this regard, not only as a consequence of its rich cultural heritage, but also in connection with the privileged status it achieved in the Soviet period as a symbol of Russian cultural identity.[10] The efforts of local administrations to "sell" the region in the twenty-first century have thus been shaped by the legacy of Soviet "branding" *avant la lettre*. Like Soviet attempts to market the region as a national center, they demonstrate a fixation on heritage as a means to signify territorial specificity and cultural uniqueness.

Heritage as a Stage: Historical Precedents

The use of heritage objects as a stage on which to perform patriotic identity was not a new invention of the twenty-first century. The practice had an important precedent in the artistic propaganda of the early Soviet period, and, specifically, the anniversary celebrations of the October Revolution between 1918 and 1920. During the first anniversary celebrations in Petrograd, for example, artists had been commissioned to decorate the city's most prominent squares with revolutionary art, demonstrating through the juxtaposition of old and new aesthetics the inauguration of a new epoch in politics and culture. A notable commission for this anniversary was Natan Altman's abstract decorations adorning Palace Square (at that time Uritskii Square). The bold geometric forms, which the artist positioned around the imperial vertical of the Alexander Column in the square's center, exemplified the way that heritage objects were infused with new political meaning in the postrevolutionary era.[11]

Another heritage-related commission that deserves mention in this context was Nikolai Evreinov's *Storming of the Winter Palace*, a historical reenactment of the October Revolution that was staged, again on Palace Square, during the third anniversary celebrations in 1920. Evreinov's drama of the revolution played out on three stages simultaneously: two conventional stages erected in front of the general staff headquarters opposite the Winter Palace and the historical stage of Palace Square itself, which was reimagined as the fulcrum of revolutionary activity.[12] The historical setting was a crucial component in achieving the public impact that Evreinov—motivated by the Commissar for Enlightenment Anatoly Lunacharsky's writings on Bolshevik popular festivals[13]—aspired to in his performance. Inspired by the events playing out on the historic square, audience members, Evreinov hoped, would spontaneously join the storming of the palace scene, embodying the revolutionary experience and transforming it into cultural memory.

The performances of patriotic identity that formed part of the twenty-first century anniversary and town celebrations in the Russian Northwest were unlikely to have been influenced directly by these postrevolutionary recreations. Nevertheless, some striking similarities can be noted in the thinking about heritage objects and their role in inculcating in audiences ideas about the past that informed both sets of events. In Novgorod, for example, architectural complexes such as the Novgorod Kremlin and Yaroslav's Yard became the settings for immersive recreations of historic battles and performances of medieval life in much the same way as Palace Square had functioned in Evreinov's historical drama. In Pskov, architectural heritage was incorporated into festive imagery and art in a way that recalled the treatment of historic space in propaganda for the revolutionary anniversaries. In both cases, monuments were exploited for political ends by the local authorities. Kremlins and churches, transformed into stages for dramatic reimaginings of the past, were used to reinforce an understanding of the Northwest as a center of Russian history and culture.

"Novgorod the Great—Birthplace of Russia"

In 2009, I attended Novgorod's much-lauded 1150th anniversary celebrations, organized to commemorate the city's first mention in the medieval chronicles in 859. Preparations for the festivities had been underway for over a year and the celebratory days were hotly anticipated. Alongside controversial restoration work to the Novgorod Kremlin, "improvements" to the town had included the unveiling of monuments of Sergei Rakhmaninov and Peter the Great, the opening of new restaurants, including a restaurant-nightclub aboard a nineteenth-century ship, moored outside the kremlin walls, and the construction of an Olympic-sized indoor ice-skating rink. According to the festival website, 1.8 million rubles had been spent on repair work to roads between Novgorod, Moscow, and St. Petersburg, and the town had been "gifted" a new arterial highway at a quoted cost of 328.2 million rubles.[14]

In the summer of 2009, the town was decked out in full festive paraphernalia: stages had been erected both inside the Kremlin complex and in Yaroslav's Yard; dozens of stalls selling regional food, drink, and crafts lined the banks of the River Velikii; and Russian flags hung from lampposts and balloons lined the streets. The anniversary slogan—the local authorities' bold attempt to relaunch the Novgorod brand—was emblazoned on stages, posters, and flyers all around the town: "Novgorod the Great—Birthplace of Russia" (*Velikii Novgorod—rodina Rossii*).

As Melnikova has noted, the title of "birthplace of Russia" was fiercely contested in the 2000s. Staraia Ladoga, a small village in the Volkhov district of the Leningrad region, had also laid claim to the accolade on the basis of a well-known record of one of the editions of the Primary Chronicle, and local officials had been working hard since the village's 1250th anniversary, in 2003, to consolidate the local brand.[15] Novgorod, however, had several advantages over the Leningrad province. For one thing, the region's preponderance of architectural monuments and established tourist infrastructure facilitated attempts to market the town as a center of Russian history and culture. At the 1150th anniversary celebrations, the efforts of the local authorities to assert the validity of their historical claim were obvious. Historical monuments were put to work for the purposes of local politicians, signifying antiquity and authenticity in a way that supported the town's claims to historical primacy.

The "conceptual program" for the festival, launched several months before the anniversary date, revealed much about the local authorities' intentions regarding the rebranding of the northwestern region.[16] The quotation by Likhachev that opened this document was indication enough of the ambitious scope of local claims. Extracted from the historian's 1983 school textbook *Motherland* (*Zemlia rodnaia*), it dodged references to the multicultural origins of the Novgorod Republic, instead opting for the more ethnocentric assertion that: "At the dawn of Russian history, we have the Novgorodians to thank for the fact that we are the way we are, the fact that we are Russians."[17] Ignoring the fact that Likhachev nuanced this statement in his next sentence, noting that Russian statehood had two territorial origins—Novgorod and Kiev—the festival's organizers made the idea of Novgorod's primacy in Russian history and culture the central motif of the program.

Each day of the three-day festival was dedicated to a particular theme, and all of them together formed the conceptual foundation of the celebrations. Day One was thus committed to the idea of "The Origins of Russia," described in the program as "the genesis and evolution of the Russian state [*gosudarstvo*], the centuries-long history of which is reflected in the 'Millennium of Russia' Monument." This sculpture, whose associations with the town's postwar reconstruction are discussed in more detail in chapter 1, formed a focus for the day's activities. The highlight of these was the official opening ceremony, which took place around the monument, and at which a telegram from President Putin praising Novgorod's history and heritage was read aloud:

> One of Russia's most ancient towns, Novgorod the Great is rightly praised for the bright pages of its history, for the important role that it played in the creation of the Russian statehood [*gosudarstvennost'*]. It was here that the traditions of civic-mindedness [*grazhdanstvennost'*] were born, that the rich cultural, spiritual and moral heritage of our people was formed, that its military glory was forged, and that its genuine masterpieces of architecture were raised.[18]

Putin's statement lent official endorsement to local claims about the origins of Russian statehood while carefully sidestepping the thorny question of the town's historical primacy. More intriguingly, it observed the well-established tradition of binding together national values (spirituality, morality, and military strength) with local heritage and architecture. The rest of the day's events, which included the opening of a market of local foods and crafts among the medieval churches of Yaroslav's Yard, an exhibition on the theme "The Origins of Russian Statehood" inside the Novgorod Kremlin, and the performance of folk ensembles outside the St. Sophia Cathedral, reinforced the link between national traditions and local monuments. The association was perhaps most explicitly referenced in the symbolism of the main stage: in a visual rendering of the fusion of local and national cultures, the stage's central frame—flames in the colors of the Russian flag—was bordered by sepia wings featuring excerpts from the Novgorod Chronicle. The primacy of heritage in this symbolic imagining was indicated by the presence of the festival crest—a gold and silver cupola, a reference to the St. Sophia Cathedral—which appeared three times, at the center of each wing and at the very pinnacle of the stage's main frame.

Day Two was dedicated to the theme of "Russia's Treasure Trove [*sokrovish-chinitsa*]" and commemorated Novgorod's status as a historic center of trade and commerce. While the concept offered potential to celebrate Novgorod's multi-ethnic origins and foreign links, the overarching idea of the city as the birthplace of Russian statehood continued to dominate the proceedings. Activities scheduled for the day consequently included an archaeological exhibition "The Town beneath the Town" at the Monastery of the Tithe and a festival of sand sculptures of folkloric figures from the Novgorod byliny. The only ostensible nod in the direction of the region's multi-cultural heritage and international connections was the festival of traditional games held on Yaroslav's Yard, which claimed to include both medieval Russian and European folk pastimes.[19]

An important component of this second day of festivities was historical reenactment. The organizers made special mention of this feature in the conceptual program, stating that: "Over the course of the day, interactive spaces [*interaktivnye ploshchadki*] will be in use all around the historic center. Novgorodians and visitors to the town can enjoy dramatized representations of the life and times of the ancient town and also get involved themselves in the preparation of traditional crafts, folk games, and fun."[20] In a similar way to the spectators of Evreinov's *Storming of the Winter Palace*, visitors to the festival were encouraged to immerse themselves in the imagined history of the town and embody the medieval experience, including interactions with historic monuments. These could include activities, such as storming the gates of the kremlin fortress as part of the "Convocation of the Druzhina Warriors" recreation or engaging in medieval sack fights in the shadow of the Arcade of the Trade Yard.

Another noteworthy event at the celebration was the performance of folk festivities on a second stage located in the Yaroslav's Yard complex. It was not so much the performances themselves, however, as the scenery that was worthy of particular attention in this instance. The stage was designed to resemble the interior of Novgorod's St. Sophia Cathedral; the decorative vaulted ceilings and multi-tiered chandelier immediately signified to the spectator the historic location. Yet through the windows depicted at the back of the stage another St. Sophia Cathedral, identifiable from its iconic gold and silver cupolas, was visible. The performances, so the scenery suggested, were taking place simultaneously inside and outside of the iconic monument. The way space had been collapsed in the scene had an interesting analogy with the way the organizers of the festival had collapsed local and national space more generally: in the festive imagination, Novgorod likewise took on a composite identity, as both nation and region, progenitor and product of Russian national culture.

A Festival of "Military Glory"

Pskov's "Days of the Town"—an annual celebration that I also attended in 2009—were a much more low-key affair. Funded entirely by local sources and commercial sponsors, the proposed agenda was notably more modest than the federally supported anniversary celebrations in neighboring Novgorod. Efforts to assert Pskov's cultural uniqueness were nevertheless evident from both the content and symbolism of the festival program and, as in Novgorod, heritage objects played an important part in efforts to rebrand the region as a distinct cultural entity. While in Novgorod architectural heritage had been deployed to assert the region's historical role as the birthplace of Russian nationhood, Pskov's monuments, in line with Soviet tradition, were incorporated into performances of military triumphalism, in which ideas of strength, defense, and heroic self-sacrifice were paramount.

The structure of the festival was revealing of the order of value attributed to local cultural life.[21] Day One was designated "The Day of Military Glory" and involved the laying of flowers on the mass graves of soldiers; excursions around sites of military note; the laying of flowers at the "Grave of the Unknown Soldier" memorial; and an evening of festive song and dance by the Russian paratroop regiment. Day Two, by contrast, was dedicated "The Day of St. Ol'ga" and included liturgies in the town's cathedrals; a "Procession of the Cross" around Pskov's historic churches; and a solemn prayer outside the Trinity Cathedral. Days Three and Four were more thematically amorphous and comprised a variety of sporting events, including a parachuting competition in honor of the 65th anniversary of the "Liberation of Pskov" and a festival of historical reconstructions. The festival ended in true Soviet tradition with an expression of gratitude to the authorities who had arranged the celebrations.[22] An exhibition of flowers on the theme "With Love to the Town" and a concert of song and dance by local children's collectives formed the grand finale to the festivities.

Particularly remarkable in the festive imagery was the association of historic architecture, and particularly Orthodox churches, with the ideas of military strength and glory. The poster advertising the festival of historical recreations, for

FIGURE 12. Actors performing heritage during a dramatization of the St. Ol'ga myth at the "Days of the Town" celebrations, Pskov, July 2009.

example, combined an image of a medieval archer with a panorama of the Pskov Kremlin complex, drawing links between historic monuments and the city's military defense. The main festival poster likewise paired symbols of military might—the upturned machine guns that formed the striking "Grave of the Unknown Soldier" memorial, for example—and objects of Orthodox heritage, such as the reconstructed St. Ol'ga's chapel.[23] These associations were reinforced during the festive events themselves: at the laying of flowers at the "Grave of the Unknown Soldier," Orthodox clergy and local military regiments combined ritualistic forces to bind together in the minds of spectators the military and religious identities of the town.

As in Novgorod, architectural monuments formed the stages for performances of local identity. Historical reconstructions of medieval battles were mounted in the shadow of the kremlin walls, while market stalls manned by residents in historic dress snaked between the St. Vasilii the Great Cathedral (1413–1415) and the New Resurrection Church (1373–1375). Heritage objects were also "performed" by local residents in a literal embodiment of the historic landscape. During a dramatization of the St. Ol'ga myth that concluded "The Day of St. Ol'ga,"[24] five performers dressed as Orthodox churches descended the steps of the stage and approached the audience. This climactic moment in the performance, which was staged against a panoramic backdrop depicting modern-day Pskov, affirmed the place of historic architecture in the town's mythology and contemporary identity. Restored as the symbols of Orthodox identity in the post-Soviet period, historic churches, together with military heritage, were presented as the essence of Pskov's reconstituted local brand.

Staging Traditionalism on the Folk Landscape

Like the region's medieval architecture, folk monuments formed the stages for performances of cultural identity in the Putin era. Indeed, the deployment of folk heritage had been identified early in the post-Soviet period as a means to stimulate popular engagement with Russian culture and traditions. In 1993, a regionally targeted initiative to improve the quality of cultural and artistic life in the Russian Northwest, entitled "The Russian Province," had identified young people's sense of alienation from the country's folk traditions as one of the major social challenges facing the region. The initiative had received funding of two million rubles from the Russian Ministry of Culture and a further 300,000 rubles from other charitable sources in 1993.[25] "Connections between generations are being severed, cultural traditions are dying out with the people who performed them," the program's organizers pointed out. "The constant striving towards violent change, the negation of age-old principles, which have been in place for seventy years or more, has destroyed the 'old' culture and disturbed the natural laws of cultural evolution."[26]

One of the means of correcting this "unnatural" situation, the program coordinators argued, was through more sustained forms of popular engagement with the folk landscape: "The assimilation of the historical-philosophical and cultural heritage of the past will form the start of a process of renewal and enrichment of the spiritual life of our contemporaries. It will create the conditions for the rigorous intellectual life of the provincial intelligentsia."[27] Specifically, assimilation meant learning the traditional arts and crafts of the region in the traditional setting of the Russian village. Folk architecture, either *in situ* in rural settlements or in the artificial context of folk museums, such as Vitoslavlitsy in Novgorod or Semenkovo in Vologda, was to form the context for a symbolic transferal of cultural traditions between generations.

Accounts of the events organized in the villages of the Pskov oblast in the mid-1990s give a sense of the ways folk heritage was incorporated into such rituals of cultural transmission. At the "Il'ya Day" festival in 1993, for example, visitors to a village in the Pskov region were invited to join in traditional forms of Russian carousing, such as the appointment of a festival king and queen (the oldest inhabitants of the village), the performance of folk songs and circle dances, and preparation of traditional gingerbread, all in the vicinity of historic wooden izbas, churches, and other objects of folk architecture.[28] At the village of Myza festival in the same year, folk revels included competitions between "milkmaid-mothers" on topics such as how best to feed your family, the inner world of your husband, and the definition of the word "love." Here, too, heritage formed an important part of the celebrations. The festival ended with awards for the village's most beautiful houses, indicating the importance of folk architecture in performances of traditional Russian life.[29]

Folk heritage continued to provide the setting for stagings of Russian traditional culture into the twenty-first century. At museums of folk architecture, annual festivities were designed to include activities that engaged residents with the folk landscape in a number of ritualistic ways. In February 2009, I attended one of these celebrations at the Semenkovo museum in Vologda—the Maslenitsa festival, commemorating the imminent end of winter. The impressive folk izbas that formed the village high street performed a variety of functions at the festival, from stages for Russian folk puppet shows to venues for birch bark plaiting and straw doll-making workshops. Locals wandered between the houses, dropping in, as one would on a neighbor, on scenes of traditional village life. As in Novgorod and Pskov, historic reenactment played an important part in transforming the heritage landscape: Cossacks, peasants, and gypsies were among the theatrical figures wandering among the crowds. Despite the thick snow and searing wind, visitors participated enthusiastically in these activities, embodying the reimagined past and reinforcing local identity through performance, play, and the observance of folk tradition.

Rebranding Pskov: St. Ol'ga of Kiev

In the post-Soviet period, Pskov faced grave difficulties adapting to the new conditions of market capitalism. Partly as a result of its peripheral location, many of
the factories that had provided work for the population, including a radio parts
factory and telecommunications plant, closed after 1991, leading to mass unem-
ployment and poverty.[30] The demographic consequences of these developments
were dire. In the 1990s and early 2000s death rates in Pskov rose stratospherically
relative to birth rates, with the average age of death in 2005 plummeting to record
lows of 53 for men and 63 for women.[31] At the same time, the ratio of pensioners
to those of working age and the young rose dramatically in the region, reflecting
the mass exodus of young people to St. Petersburg and other, more economically
viable Russian towns.[32] These developments generated anxiety among the local
community, prompting some inhabitants to revile their region as a "godforsaken
province," a place broken by post-Soviet restructuring and abandoned by national
politicians.

In the midst of the crises of the 2000s and 2010s, a number of cultural initiatives emerged in and around Pskov with the apparent goal of lifting the region
from the economic and social doldrums and establishing it as a center of national
spirituality and culture. In 2003, to mark the 1100th anniversary of the first mention of Pskov in the Primary Chronicle, Vladimir Putin penned a letter to the
local townspeople celebrating their historic heroism and spiritual strength. "No
one major historical event has taken place in this country without in some way
implicating the Pskov lands," Putin effused. "Your town has since time immemo-
rial defended the Russian state and has steadily secured glory as the Russian outpost of the Northwest."[33] In a gesture suggesting an intrinsic connection between
Pskov's military might and spiritual faith, Putin evoked the figure of St. Ol'ga of
Kiev: "It is deeply symbolic that it was here, in the Pskov lands, that St. Ol'ga of
Russia, the wise leader of Rus', was born. Her descendants preserve her blessed
memory."[34]

The mention of Princess Ol'ga in the president's letter was far from fortuitous.
The warrior-princess was a handy embodiment of the fusion of military and
spiritual values that formed the core of the Russian national idea in the Putin
era. Ol'ga, wife of Prince Igor', son of the Novgorod Prince Riurik, was famed
for having avenged her husband's death at the hands of the Drevlians, a tribe of
early Eastern Slavs, in a variety of gruesome ways. Upon assuming the Kievan
reign, legend had it that she ordered twenty Drevlian matchmakers, dispatched to

Kiev to win her hand, be buried alive. Other acts of vengeance included burning Drevlian ambassadors in a bathhouse, slaughtering Drevlians at a funeral feast for her husband, and razing Drevlian lands by tying burning paper to the legs of doves and letting them fly back to their homes. The warmongering princess was reputed to have left thousands of corpses in her wake and never to have yielded to the constant courtship by power-hungry suitors, preserving the throne for her infant son Sviatoslav.[35]

Coexisting with this narrative of bellicose loyalty was the legend of Ol'ga as the first convert to Christianity among the rulers of Kievan Rus'. While the conversion of the Kievan state to Christianity is usually attributed to her grandson Vladimir I, Ol'ga, it was claimed, was the first ruler to be baptized in Constantinople and played an important role spreading Christianity throughout the country. As a result of her proselytizing influence over the country, Ol'ga was canonized by the Orthodox Church and declared "Equal-to-the-Apostles" in 1547. Her romantic image, conventionally shown with the Orthodox Cross and the instruments of her baptism, became a favorite among artists in the nineteenth and early twentieth centuries, inspiring the likes of Vasilii Surikov and Mikhail Nesterov, among others.[36]

Ol'ga's "descendants," in Putin's words, had formed several local lobbies in Pskov in the early 1990s for the rehabilitation of the saint's memory and the preservation of her cultural legacy. The most influential of these was the "Society of Saint Ol'ga of Russia," founded in May 1991 by Nina Petrovna Osipova, who was, at that time, director of the Pskov Museum-Reserve Archives. Osipova had played an important role in determining the society's agenda, the main items of which were the restoration of Ol'ga-related commemorative sites in Pskov and Vybuty (Ol'ga's birthplace); the reconstruction of the razed Chapel of Saint Ol'ga in Pskov; and the erection of a monument to the town's patron saint in Pskov's city center. In the climate of collective self-recrimination that marked the collapse of state communism in 1991, the society had been able to advance its agenda with relative ease: a commemorative cross had been erected on the site of the destroyed chapel in July 1991, and restoration of the church in Vybuty had begun in 1993.[37]

In 1995, in response to an initiative proposed by the society, the Pskov Regional Administration adopted the declaration "On the Memorialization of the Memory of Princess Saint Ol'ga of Russia," which included plans to create a preservation zone restricting construction around the historic church in Vybuty.[38] The regulations, which were intended to stay the incremental creep of dachas into the surrounding countryside, facilitated the transformation of the church into a site of national pilgrimage.[39] In the years that followed, ever-larger numbers of the Orthodox faithful joined the annual procession along the River Velikii to pay tribute to the town's patron saint. Orthodox celebrities, including the Soviet literary critic and philologist Aleksandr Panchenko, and the poets Larisa Fedotova and Sergei Vikulov, also paid high-profile visits to the site, giving speeches and readings.[40]

In 1994, the society launched its most far-reaching campaign to reconstruct Pskov's Chapel of Saint Ol'ga (early 19 c.), which had been bulldozed to the ground during the development of the Velikii embankment in the 1960s.[41] The initiative won the support of the local administration and a national competition was announced for the best design project to reconstruct the historic church. The four competition finalists were exhibited to the general public at the Pskov Museum and advertised in the local newspaper *Pskov News*.[42] The jury, comprising local architects, art historians, and members of the municipal and regional administration, was instructed to take into account feedback from residents when making its decision. The winning project was authored by a Pskov-based architect, Aleksei Krasil'nikov, and proposed to reconstruct the chapel on a stone podium in close proximity to the building's original site. Notably, federal funding for the project was provided by the Ministry of Culture, indicating support for the initiative at the highest echelons of national government.[43]

The reconstructed chapel nevertheless provoked controversy among the local preservationist community. Certain architectural critics claimed that the building's design was too eclectic, that the proportions more closely resembled those of pre-Mongol churches in Vladimir than the medieval structures characteristic of the Pskov region.[44] The chapel's helmet-like dome and vaulted roofs were criticized for being too Novgorodian in style while at the same time lacking the magnitude and grace of the neighboring region's medieval churches. On the whole, some felt, the chapel had failed to capture the essentially Pskovian elements that distinguished the region's architectural traditions from those of its historic neighbors; thus, an opportunity to assert Pskov's cultural uniqueness and significance in a national context had been missed.[45]

Critics contrasted the high-profile project to reconstruct the Chapel of St. Ol'ga with the fate of another local monument, the Anastasia Chapel. The latter had endured a difficult history. The original eighteenth-century chapel had been demolished in 1908 to make way for a bridge across the River Velikii, while, in 1969, the reconstructed chapel (1908–1911), which included internal wall paintings by the famous Russian artist Nikolai Roerich, was relocated to a spot fifty

FIGURE 13. The Anastasiia Chapel (1711, rebuilt 1911), Pskov, June 2009.

meters away to allow for construction work on the river's left bank.[46] Local restorers and preservationists nevertheless held that the chapel's cubic form, delicate cupola, and patterned walls rendered it an outstanding example of architecture in the "Pskov style," while Roerich's internal wall frescoes singled it out as an object of world heritage.[47] Nevertheless, the difficulty of marketing the building as part of a local brand (as the Chapel of St. Ol'ga had been in the 1990s) meant that its survival in the post-Soviet period was in jeopardy. At the end of the 2000s, the fate of the chapel was far from clear: the building was preserved in a severely dilapidated state, boarded up behind an iron fence and largely overlooked by passersby on the St. Ol'ga Bridge above it.

The 1100th-anniversary celebrations in Pskov in 2003 can be seen as a turning point in the development of the Ol'ga brand. While Ol'ga-promoting initiatives had, until this point, been driven by local actors and lobbies, the anniversary instigated a new phase in the myth's endorsement and promotion. In 2003, the town received two radically different visual representations of Ol'ga by prominent Muscovite artists: the first—a pious vision of the saint with her grandson Vladimir at her side, by the President of the Foundation for Slavic Literature and Culture, Viacheslav Klykov; the second—a more belligerent likeness of the local heroine, sword and shield in hand, by the notorious peddler of sculptural monstrosities Zurab Tsereteli.[48] This unusual coincidence had resulted from competing relationships of patronage within the local administration: Klykov's Ol'ga had been commissioned by Pskov's mayor, Mikhail Khoronen, while Tsereteli's Ol'ga had been authorized by the local governor, Evgenii Mikhailov.[49] In the lively public debate that dominated the local press in the weeks that followed, a consensus emerged favoring Klykov's devout figure over Tsereteli's bellicose vision.[50] Tsereteli's monument was consequently banished to the town's periphery on Riga Prospect, where, as the former director of the Pskov Restoration Workshop put it, "it could frighten away the foreign tourists," while Klykov's sculpture enjoyed pride of place on the central October Square.[51]

Ol'ga's elevation to the status of Pskov's patron saint reveals an interesting dynamic in region-center relations in the Putin era. An initiative to commemorate St. Ol'ga's memory in local culture, initiated by a pious local lobby, received national endorsement in the form of federal-level anniversary celebrations, monuments commissioned by nationally renowned sculptors, and, perhaps most influentially, formal acknowledgment in a presidential speech. The correspondence of local and national interests in this instance secured the success of the Pskov-based initiative, permitting it a degree of prestige and visibility

FIGURE 14. The sculpted head of St. Ol'ga on a pedestal outside the Church of Elijah the Prophet in Vybuty, Pskov region, July 2009.

that would be unimaginable in other more politically contested cases.[52] Yet without the promotion of the project at the grassroots level, it would not have achieved the impact it did among the local community. The integration of the

Ol'ga narrative in local cultural memory can thus be seen as a consequence of the close alignment of local and national rebranding agendas.

Rebranding Pskov II: Prokhanov's "Sacred Hill"

A second, more controversial initiative to enhance Pskov's cultural profile was the creation of the "Sacred Hill [*Sviashchennyi kholm*]" memorial in Izborsk, a project that originated with the Moscow-based ultranationalist critic and writer Aleksandr Prokhanov. Beginning as a relatively low-profile project and funded at Prokhanov's personal expense, the hill was constructed from "sacred soils" delivered to Izborsk from various sites that the writer considered to be of national political significance. The first stage of the monument's construction began in September 2007, during the Festival of the Exaltation of the Holy Cross, and involved the collection of soils from places of local renown, including Pushkin's Mikhailovskoe estate and the Pskov-Caves Monastery, as well as sites of national relevance, such as the train station in Dno (where Nikolai II signed his declaration of abdication) and the grounds of the Pskov Paramilitary Division, which had seen action during the Second Chechen War.

The second stage of the project's construction took place on the "Day of People's Unity," November 4, 2007. At this time soils were added from sites of national consequence—including the Moscow Kremlin complex and the territories of the State Hermitage and the Russian Museum—as well places of national mourning, such as the Poklonnaia Hill World War II Memorial Site in Moscow and the Piskarevskoe Memorial Graveyard (dedicated to the victims of the Leningrad Seige) in St. Petersburg. Soils were likewise conveyed from the lands of Slavic legend and mythology, namely Staraia Ladoga (the mythological first capital of the Varangian chieftain Rurik), the Solovetskii Islands (the location of a fifteenth-century Orthodox monastery and, in the twentieth century, the first Soviet Gulag), and Kulikovo Field (the historic site of Prince Dmitrii Donskoi's 1380 victory over the Golden Horde).[53]

The second phase in the Sacred Hill's construction was intended to establish a symbolic connection between the northwestern region and the political center, locating Pskov as a hub of Russian culture and spirituality through the ritualistic transplantation to the region of patriotic soils. This mystical subtext to the project received explication in Prokhanov's literary work *The Hill* (2008), written in parallel to the real-life Pskov-based project.[54] The fictional hill of Prokhanov's novel, which is likewise constructed in Pskov and formed of sacred soils collected from across Russia and former Russian territories, comprises a new spiritual center for the lost Russian Empire in the wake of Moscow's submission to the corrupting influence of international capital.[55] Given Prokhanov's tendency to blur boundaries between fictional worlds and political realities in his writing, one can assume that the project to create the Izborsk-based hill was governed by a similar neo-imperialist logic.[56]

Prokhanov's hill may well have remained the bizarre pet project of a marginal extremist had it not been for the patriotic turn in national politics that followed Putin's return to the Russian presidency in 2012. As official tastes for neo-imperialist ideas and the politics of spectacle grew, however, the project was co-opted by the political center and exploited as patriotic propaganda. In September 2012, Prokhanov and a number of his ultraconservative associates formed the anti-liberal think tank the "Izborsk Club," whose declared goal was "to formulate an ideology and strategy of breakthrough . . . essential to overcoming monstrous backwardness in all areas of Russian life."[57] Official support for this organization was indicated by the fact that both the Russian Minister of Culture Vladimir Medinskii and Pskov's pro-Putin governor, Andrei Turchak, were present at the club's inaugural meeting on September 7, 2012. At this meeting, the news agency Regnum reported, Turchak expressed his wish that the club become "a movement in constant interaction with government, which is in real need of this sort of support base."[58]

The Sacred Hill became an important prop in the performative rituals of the "Izborsk Club," whose membership nevertheless remained predominantly Muscovite throughout the 2010s.[59] These rituals intensified following the annexation of Crimea in 2014, when the club's members traveled to sites of Soviet military history in the peninsula, including Sapun-gora and the Malakoff Mound, to gather soils for the monument. Most controversially, in September 2014, following the military invasion of Eastern Ukraine, the club welcomed representatives of the so-called Novorossiia region to the Sacred Hill.[60] These military commanders, it was reported, delivered helmets full of soil from Savur-Mohyla, a strategic height on the Donetsk Ridge that had only days earlier been captured by pro-Russian rebels.[61]

The activities of the "Izborsk Club" were broadcast countrywide in a program on the state-owned news channel *Vesti.ru* in October 2014. As the primary contributor to this program, Prokhanov elaborated at self-indulgent length on the metaphysical basis for his project, explaining that, by unifying sacred soils, the monument had acquired a transformative spiritual energy that would shape the future of Russian government and culture. It is worth quoting Prokhanov's words at length here to get a sense of the mysticism and profound irrationality at the heart of the project:

> We had the idea of building a Hill, which would be a chalice [*chasha*], a sacred vessel, into which we could pour the Pskov lands, and, together with them, the Pskov times, and, together with them, the heroic feats of Pskov, and, together with them, the images and actions of Pskov's great military leaders, saints, and philosophers.
>
> This chalice would accept into itself all of these handfuls of soil and condense them so that all the Russian energy that had accumulated over the centuries would be compacted into a single ball of light, strength, and beauty, and it would fill our current age, and it would drench with its water of life the present-day Russian state. This energy will fill the hearts of our compatriots, themselves often weary, exhausted unbelievers, it will deliver unto them faith, strength, and triumphant, fiery beauty.[62]

Prokhanov's words revealed a heady mix of pagan esotericism, Russian chauvinism, and militant nostalgia for an imagined former Empire. More importantly, from the point of view of this discussion of territorial rebranding, they expressed a belief in the redemptive power of the Pskov region as a space of spiritual strength and military vigor that could help restore and renew the morally impoverished center. Pskov was presented in this speech as an alternative symbolic center to Moscow, a source of spiritual guidance and moral sustenance for the Russian nation. This gesture symbolically negated Russia's closed western border, which had rendered Pskov a literal dead end in territorial terms. The Sacred Hill thus reversed the act of division that had split the Soviet soils in 1991, reconstituting nation and empire through a rejection of politics and return to the language of the sacral.[63]

The initiative to create the Sacred Hill as a site of patriotic pilgrimage in Pskov was the work of a small group of metropolitan neo-traditionalists whose nationalistic ideas were co-opted by the political center in the wake of the Crimean annexation. The fact that the initiative attracted patronage from local elites—and from Pskov's regional governor, Andrei Turchak, in particular—is, however, worthy of note and deserves further comment. In September 2014, Pskov found itself at the center of a national controversy following the publication of several articles by Lev Shlosberg, the editor of the liberal local newspaper *Pskov Gubernia*, exposing the secret burial of two soldiers from the Pskov-based 76th Guards Air Assault

Division who had allegedly been killed in the conflict in Eastern Ukraine.[64] Shortly after the articles' appearance, Shlosberg was beaten unconscious near his home and hospitalized, seemingly as recompense for his challenge to the Kremlin's assertion that no serving Russian troops were fighting in the region.[65] In the context of this repressive violence, Turchak's involvement in the project and his statement at the ceremony welcoming the delivery of Crimean soils to Pskov—in which he called the hill "a place of unity for our people, a place of Russian historical strength and historical memory"— appeared particularly sinister.[66] The hill appeared part of a repressive symbolic vocabulary forced on the regions by the political center, a monumental statement of intolerance for particularistic narratives that challenged the officially endorsed understanding of national history and politics.

The incorporation of local heritage objects into performances of local and national identity can be placed within the broader context of the Putin administration's "politics of spectacle" in the twenty-first century. During the patriotic surge that accompanied the President's third term in office, historic architecture was used as a stage on which to perform nationalistic renditions of Russian history and culture. From the activities of the Kremlin-sponsored heavy metal bike gang the "Night Wolves," which included historical reenactments in Sevastopol, Stalingrad, and Petrozavodsk, to the pursuits of Russian Minister of Culture Vladimir Medinskii's "Russian Military History Society," which restaged battles in Borodino and Crimea—historical reenactments reinforced a narrative of Russian history that placed emphasis on military strength, Orthodox spirituality, and political unity.[67] The Crimean annexation and outbreak of war in Donbas in 2014 saw the campaign to promote national identity through performance intensify: Russian history began to be reimagined and restaged as a series of military victories and acts of heroic self-sacrifice in defense of the Russian people.

The local performances described in this chapter asserted a vision of the Northwest that corresponded with official narratives of Russian history in the Putin era. Novgorod was promoted at the 1150th anniversary celebrations as the birthplace of Russian nationhood rather than a recalcitrant region that historically resisted subordination to Moscow, while Pskov was marketed to the nation as a bastion of Russian defense and a center of Russian Orthodoxy. The local authorities' insistence on the national relevance of their regions can be explained by the exigencies of territorial marketing: in order to attract investment from the center and attention from domestic and foreign tourists, local elites prioritized national claims over the celebration of regional specificities. However, as the case of Turchak's involvement with the Sacred Hill project in Pskov demonstrates, there is also evidence of more coercive forms of territorial branding in the region. Efforts by local lobbies to promote local heritage initiatives were only likely to succeed if they corresponded with the political agenda and strategic ambitions of the center.

Such strategies of territorial marketing in the Russian Northwest were, in many ways, well established from the Soviet period. Local elites had abundant experience in managing regional heritage to respond to demands from the political center, and residents were used to participating in politicized displays of local culture for national audiences. Still, the question of how these practices were interpreted by those living in the historic region deserves further attention. While residents engaged enthusiastically in performances of local identity, they did not necessarily accept passively state-sponsored narratives about their regions' historical primacy or cultural uniqueness. Indeed, engagement with historic architecture happened in a variety of different spheres and contexts, engendering a diverse and multi-faceted understanding of the heritage landscape. The following chapter explores this relationship, drawing on oral testimony and participant observation work to examine the role of architectural heritage in forming local experience and identity.

6.

"EVERY CENTIMETER OF THIS GROUND IS HISTORY"

Heritage, Narrative, and Identity

In the Russian Northwest, architectural heritage constituted more than the museicized relics of a remote and remembered past. As a result of Soviet planning and the "organic integration" of old and new architecture into the urban landscape, it was an integral part of the lived environment. One of the things that immediately struck me on first visiting the historic region was the way that medieval churches jumped out unexpectedly from amid blocks of Soviet residential flats, or stood solemnly in the middle of a park or at the edge of an asphalted square. Far from exclusive sites of architectural appreciation or sacred reflection, these objects were an intimate part of the domestic landscape. The relationship of familiarity people had with heritage was reflected in the language they used to speak about historic buildings: many used the diminutive terms *tserkvushka* and *tserkovka*, for example, to refer to the region's medieval churches, a reference to the diminutive size of the buildings, but also a term of affection for the onion-domed "little churches" so typical of the local area.

While living in the Northwest, I visited many of the region's historic monuments, accompanying friends on guided tours of local monasteries and traveling independently to visit fortress ensembles or noble estates that I had been told held particular historic interest. This type of heritage tourism was popular among local residents, and particularly among older women, many of whom were Orthodox believers. My landlady in Vologda spent every Saturday traveling by coach to sites of historical interest, where she would take part in organized excursions around local churches and monasteries. An important part of this ritualistic consumption of local architecture was the taking and screening of digital photographs. I regularly joined members of the family on the folding bed that doubled up as a sofa in the flat's front room to view the slide shows of ornate churches and ascetic monasteries, which, after the first dozen or so images, blurred in my mind into one.

This chapter explores popular perceptions of heritage objects and the way that these perceptions have informed local identities, both in cultural and territorial terms. It begins with a discussion of the different kinds of knowledge about the heritage landscape that people have acquired, from the facts and figures learned in classrooms and museums to the more intimate forms of understanding rooted in social practice and personal experience. The social functions that historic architecture played in community identity and the different modes and registers residents employed to speak about heritage objects will receive particular attention. The chapter concludes with a look at the ways in which features of the architectural landscape were mapped onto the local character. Ultimately, popular perceptions of architectural heritage as an expression of the local community generated a range of emotions, from pride to frustration and even melancholy, in connection with the fate of historic buildings.

Oral History and the Narrative Construction of Identity

Oral history is an indefinite and contested realm of research activity that lies at the fruitful intersection of several established academic disciplines. For this reason, it has tended to be defined according to the disciplinary preferences of its practitioners: the folklorist and gender critic Elaine Lawless, for example, has described her work as "reciprocal ethnography," which places emphasis on the polyvocality inherent to her research and writing;[1] the oral historian of working-class politics Alessandro Portelli, by contrast, prefers the definition "history-telling," which reveals an understanding of oral testimony as one among a plurality of narrative forms that competes for dominance in the realm of public representations of the past.[2] The broad spectrum of disciplinary approaches to oral history has resulted in radically different forms of academic writing. In the field of Russian studies, these have ranged from the close semantic analyses of Marina Loskutova's *Memory of the Blockade* to the fluid essayistic prose of Svetlana Alexievich's *Second Hand Time*.[3]

This chapter follows Portelli in approaching oral testimony as a valuable source base that coexists alongside and complements traditional repositories of historical knowledge, such as the archive and the library. In terms of its approach to testimony, it takes inspiration from the work of the Russian anthropologists Nancy Ries and Dale Pesmen, both of whom have drawn on extensive interview work with local communities to identify patterns and tendencies in popular discourse and to locate these within a broader cultural framework. In her study of conversation during perestroika, for example, Ries determines a number of oral genres present in talk about Russian politics: she terms these genres "laments," "litanies of suffering," and "tales of total disintegration [*polnaia razrukha*]."[4] Pesmen likewise mines interview transcripts and media discourse for evidence of recurring motifs in connection with her theme.[5] Like these studies, this chapter has as its focus general tendencies in oral testimony that tell us something about a particular place or historical moment rather than the internal structure and content of any one individual interview.

The interview work from which this chapter draws was conducted over the course of a year and a half spent living and working in the Russian Northwest. During this time, I developed close friendships and professional relationships with a number of local residents who helped me to establish a broad network of contacts across the historic region. The people with whom I talked came from all walks of professional life and cultural backgrounds, and they ranged in age from twenty-six to seventy-seven. Our interviews took place during coffee breaks and over dinners that lasted into the early hours of the morning; they also took me to a variety of interesting and unusual locations: from an immaculately tended dacha garden, where I listened to a retired mining engineer complain bitterly about Pskov's decline into decadence and philistinism, to a makeshift literary salon in the back room of Vologda's "Museum of Forgotten Things," where I listened to the museum's director declaim poetry and recite literary tracts in an exhibition of patriotic love for her "little homeland."

While historic preservation cannot be considered a topic equal in political sensitivity to territorial displacement or military conflict, it occasionally led speakers into conversational domains that caused distress, anger, or melancholy. I quickly became aware of the questions that provoked such reactions: light-hearted reflections on local stereotypes could quickly turn into to acerbic comments about the capital's disparaging attitude toward the regions; fond memories of the towns' former landscapes could rapidly degenerate into bitter criticisms of today's corrupt local officials and their preservationist failures. A number of these commentaries could be categorized according to the oral genres identified by Ries in her study of Russian oral culture in the 1990s. The ritualistic lament—of preservationist failures, elite corruption, or governmental neglect, for example—was a common conversational trope. By the end of my residency in the towns, my feelings about the shortcomings in local preservationist policy matched those of many local residents, allowing me to add my own gripes to these "litanies of [local] suffering." While authentic in their emotional content, my contributions often established a more confessional mode to our conversations, which, over time, became increasingly candid and spontaneous.

Oral history practitioners have acknowledged the active role played by the researcher in determining the form and content of individual narrative. In her research on Donbas migrant narratives, Darya Tsymbalyuk notes the disparity of power between the interviewer and the interviewee in the context of oral history research. The interviewer, Tsymbalyuk points out, is the disproportionate beneficiary of oral history research: she is the one who determines the topic of the conversation and asks the questions, and she derives material benefit from the interaction in terms of a degree or publication that advances her academic career.[6] The feminist ethnographer Judith Stacey supports this view, noting the inevitability of "interpretation, evaluation, and judgement" on the part of the oral history researcher.[7] The postinterview process of deconstructing interview transcripts, selecting and extracting excerpts to support a particular academic argument has, moreover, been likened by the literary critic Julian Wolfreys to "dismemberment," a term that underlines the symbolic violence inherent to this kind of academic work.[8]

While the excerpts included in this chapter all pertain to questions of heritage politics and preservation, the themes treated in the interviews were much broader and richer than the discussion suggests. During the course of the many hours I spent talking with local residents, I heard stories of local experience that were astounding in their variety and emotional intensity. Leonid (1932), for example, spoke about his experiences fleeing the German invasion of Peterhof to the partisan-held countryside before being captured by German troops and resettled in Donbas; Valerii (1953) recounted an extraordinary life, which began in a prison camp in Irkutsk, before—following the rehabilitation of camp internees in 1956—taking a remarkable trajectory via Adygea to Pskov. I have not been able to represent all of these stories in this necessarily brief and thematically focused discussion. They nevertheless exist in the public domain, where the speaker has given permission, and constitute a uniquely valuable archive of personal biographies that shed new light on Soviet and post-Soviet identities and experiences beyond the capital.[9]

"A Little Russian Capital"

Residents of the historic Northwest demonstrated a remarkable knowledge of local architectural history. During walks around town with friends and colleagues, I was often struck by people's ability to remember the dates and events associated with historic buildings, their knowledge of the different phases in a monument's history, or the intricacies of its legal status. This understanding of the heritage landscape was undoubtedly rooted in the kraevedenie classes people had taken at school, the museum excursions they had attended, and the summers spent camping near Old Russian churches and monasteries, learning about local history and heritage. It also revealed an unusually high level of engagement with public debates about preservation, which simmered away in local newspapers and social media forums. This kind of heritage awareness was not limited to middle-class, middle-aged residents, as is often the case in European heritage cities.[10] Indeed, young people were just as likely as older residents to mobilize in defense of a historic building, thanks to online initiatives such as the "town groups" pages, featuring heritage-related matters, on the popular Russian-language blogging forum *LiveJournal* (*Zhivoi zhurnal*).[11]

Residents could switch into a romantic-patriotic mode when speaking about local heritage objects. Medieval churches, monasteries, and fortresses were often presented as evidence of the region's cultural "exceptionality" (*samobytnost'*), its Russian "authenticity" (*istinnost'*), and "antiquity" (*iskonnost'*). This tendency was particularly marked in the testimonies of non-native residents, some of whom had moved to the region from less culturally prestigious parts of Russia. My landlady in Pskov, Maggie (1955), who had relocated to the town with her family from Siberian Tomsk when she was eighteen, effervesced with enthusiasm for the town's architectural riches:

> Well, you see, when I first moved to Pskov, in, um, 1973, well I just immediately fell in love with the town! It just struck me as such an extra special [*osobyi-osobyi*] place. For one thing, those churches! In Siberia, I'd never seen anything like it: we didn't have any churches at all there. And here, well, it was an ancient Russian town [*starinnyi russkii gorod*], 900 or maybe more years old, and those churches! It just seemed to me like a little capital city! A little Russian capital city, and I thought: "This is my town!" and it really did become my town.

Tat'iana (1950), the director of Vologda's "World of Forgotten Things," spoke about her adopted town's wooden landscape in similarly nostalgic terms. She had relocated to the historic province from the industrial city Omsk and had been captivated by Vologda's folksy wooden architecture, which appeared to her something straight out of a Russian fairytale:

> I arrived in summer, in August, and in Vologda there were a lot more alleys and boulevards than there are now. They'd planted huge poplars all along our street. Well, I wandered around the town, going from one wooden house to the next, with no idea where I was going, sometimes I even managed to get lost and had to ask the locals how to get back to the center. Because, literally, those houses just cast a spell over you. They were incredible. Each house was lovely in its own way.

Outside of the Northwest, the region's associations with historic architecture and national traditions remained strong. The integration of materials about northwestern history and culture into the national curriculum, mass tourism to the region, and growing media interest in medieval Russian culture had succeeded in cementing a romantic ideal of the Northwest in the national imagination.[12] Responses to a 2018 survey conducted among university students in the southwestern provinces of Voronezh and Lipetsk confirmed this tendency: "For me, these three towns have strong links with the history of my country and the preservation of the monuments of medieval Rus'"; "these are ancient Russian towns, they're very beautiful. I've visited Novgorod and Pskov, so I know first-hand that there are ancient monuments everywhere you look." A number of individuals admitted never having visited the region but still had marked associations with the historic localities: "I can't say that I know much about these towns, since I haven't been to a single one. But I do know that they are indigenous Russian lands, for me they conjure up ideas of Old Russian government, ancient churches, monasteries and kremlin walls."[13]

Perceptions of the northwestern region as a "cradle of Russian civilization" were an obvious source of local pride. This did not mean, however, that residents were overly earnest or humorless in the ways that they engaged with local heritage. The "Alternative Kraevedenie Website of the Novgorod Region," a *Wikipedia*-style online initiative, was a striking example of the playful deconstruction of local patriotic discourse. The website parodied the superlative claims about cultural heritage found in tourist guidebooks to the region, asserting in their place a resolutely banal vision of local culture and traditions. Rather than onion-domed churches and kremlin walls, the website offered an excursion around Novgorod's least glamorous attractions: the local supermarket Lenta ("est. 2006"); the highly non-medieval

Turkish-style kebab, shashlik ("rumor has it that these shashliki are made from stale half-frozen meat, and the color and smell are chemically enhanced"); and universally hated local monuments, such as the World War II memorial "the Steed [*Kon'*]." The collaborative initiative of an Internet-savvy millennial generation, the website demonstrated awareness of traditional associations with the historic region, while at the same time exhibiting new tendencies to engage critically with established stereotypes and to assert local specificity and cultural value through innovative narrative techniques, such as self-parody and pastiche.

"The Feeling That Everything Here Is Mine"

Interactions with local monuments were not limited to museum excursions and kraevedenie lessons. A number of residents had a more intimate understanding of the towns' historic architecture via personal experience and social practice. During my time in the towns, I spoke with people who had lived in historic buildings that had been converted in the postwar period into temporary accommodation and continued to function in this capacity decades later. The experience of inhabiting a heritage object informed residents' attitudes toward the architectural landscape: the towns' historic monuments were not perceived as museicized relics of an irrelevant past, but rather as an intimate part of the lived environment.

"I grew up among ruins," stated Lena (b. 1956), a Novgorod artist who had lived for several decades at Novgorod's St. George's Monastery. The monastery had functioned as emergency accommodation for local residents after the war and had been converted into an artists' colony at the end of the 1970s.[14] Liudmila (b. 1954), a professional musician, had similar feelings about the St. Anthony's Monastery in Novgorod, where she and her family had lived until they had been forced to move in 1998. The monastery had been adapted for residential purposes in the postwar period and was recorded to have housed thirty-four families in 1964.[15] "I feel so melancholy walking around there now," she explained. "We lived on the grounds of the monastery itself, you see. . . . From my window you could see the Nativity of the Virgin Cathedral!" Everyday contact with heritage objects fostered a sentimental attachment to historic buildings. Viktoriia (b. 1954), an instructor at Novgorod's music college, housed within the historic kremlin, described the sensation as "that homely feeling [*domashnee oshchushchenie*], the feeling that everything here is mine."

Historic monuments had not only served as people's homes and workplaces but had also housed cinemas, museums, libraries, and other cultural facilities.[16] For residents who had frequented these places as children and young adults, their primary associations often remained their Soviet ones. For Galina (b. 1958), a schoolteacher from Vologda, the Intercession of the Virgin Church on Kozlenskaia Street (1704) was thus, first and foremost, a hunting ground for boyfriends; the church had functioned until 1991 as a preservice point for seventeen-year-old army recruits and was a renowned spot for parties in the 1970s. Igor' (b. 1940), a retired mining engineer from Pskov, had similar associations with the Alexander Nevsky Church (1908). As the former Soviet House of Officers, the church had been a popular venue for young recruits to watch films, attend dances, and listen to military bands. The reconsecration and high-profile refurbishment of the church in the 1990s had done little to diminish this association in Igor's mind.

More abstractly, heritage objects formed part of a landscape of childhood experience that was grounded neither in history nor in politics. As Marina Tsvetaeva suggests in her memoir-essay "My Pushkin," monuments are transformed in the childish imagination from symbols of cultural identity into mythical landmarks, as the goal of a race or the limit of a walk, for example.[17] Galina (b. 1971) spoke to me about this hidden meaning of the heritage landscape during a meeting at Pskov's Methodist Church. She remembered her experiences of exploring Pskov's old houses as a child; after demonstrations, she had been allowed to wander around the town with friends and would always return to the same buildings that held for the children an endless fascination. Irina (b. 1957), who talked with me at her historic wooden house on Zasodimskii Street in Vologda, remembered a similar thrill of childish transgression in connection with the neighborhood's old churches. The warders (*storozha*) of these churches would let the children beyond the barrier to play in the nearby field. The excitement of this experience continued to color Irina's feelings about the buildings, which retained, like Tsvetaeva's Pushkin Monument, a special place in her memory.

The sentimental attachment to heritage objects was even more pronounced in Vologda, where many older residents had personal experiences of inhabiting the town's historic wooden buildings. Indeed, the ubiquity of wooden housing, discussed in more detail in chapter 3, was a common feature of residents' memories of local life. Far from all of these memories were positive: Galina (b. 1966) listed the difficulties of life in an old wooden house, from the absence of basic sanitation to the extreme cold in winter ("it was so cold we had to walk around in felt boots [*valenki*]!"). Despite their material discomforts, however, wooden houses provided the everyday context for memories of childhood and adolescence, a focus of popular nostalgia.[18] The houses consequently featured in people's memories in fairytale-like terms, as the hub of family festivities, childhood games, and youthful rites of passage.

Some residents remembered the stoves that would heat their wooden houses, a crucial source of warmth in a region where temperatures could reach minus forty in winter.[19] Anel' (b. 1933) had grown up in a historic wooden mansion on Hertzen Street and recalled the handsome Russian stove that had stood in the center of their kitchen, in which her mother would bake fish, potato, and fresh berry pies in the summer ("Mama just loved cooking pies and we just loved eating them, as you can imagine!"). For Natalia (b. 1934), who guided me through her family photograph albums, memories of her childhood home on "Annunciation" Street were likewise bound up with moments of domestic intimacy and festivity. She recalled, for example, the huge New Year's tree that her father had brought home and that the family had decorated with real wax candles. On being discovered at play with these candles, she received a stern warning from her mother: "A thief may break in and take everything, but the walls will always remain. If a fire breaks out, everything will be destroyed!"

It was surely this intimate connection with the architectural landscape that prompted feelings of regret and melancholy in response to the disappearance of the town's historic wooden buildings in the 1960s and 1970s. The mass destruction of Vologda's wooden housing and its replacement by modern Soviet highrises improved many people's material well-being, but it also erased a landscape of memory.[20] The feeling that the experiences of childhood were disappearing along with the foundations of these buildings was expressed most succinctly by Anel' when remembering her family's move from their wooden house on Hertzen Street to a modern Soviet flat in the 1960s. In her narrative, Anel' shifted seamlessly from a description of the move to her memories of performing plays in the neighboring woodshed, demonstrating the connection between architectural and emotional landscapes:

> ANEL': It was around that time that they started to pull down our wooden houses. Mama, Papa, my brother and me, we were given a one-bedroom apartment in a forty-two apartment house, behind the theater, where the children's theater is now.
> VSD: And were you happy about the move?
> ANEL': It's hard to say if I was happy or not. They pulled down those wooden houses to put up new brick buildings, you see. And when we were still living in those

wooden houses, well, there was this huge woodshed next door, where we used to put on plays . . . we used to dress up and perform. I even used to sing. I also used to sing Russian folk songs in a choir in the Railwaymen's Palace of Culture. When I was in nursery school I even sang on the radio.

The intimate connection people had with historic buildings as homes, work-places, social spaces, and even playgrounds helps to explain the strength of their responses to the changes to the status of these objects after the collapse of social-ism. At her artist's studios in the Monastery of the Tithe in Novgorod, Galina (b. 1958) described the shifts in cultural politics that had led to her eviction from the St. George's Monastery complex in the early 1990s. She and her young family had moved to the site in the mid-1980s and had reveled in its bohemian atmosphere, which differed so considerably from that of the average Soviet town. In 1991, however, the monastery had been transferred from the Novgorod Museum to the local diocese, which immediately began to rebuild a monastic community on the site.[21] Galina's memories of this transitional moment in the monastery's history shed light on the human consequences of changes to preservationist politics in the early post-Soviet period:

> In the beginning they just returned the cathedral, but not . . . they didn't kick us out. They started to restore the churches, and services started being held, and then a priest arrived. That priest was replaced by Father Makarii, who's at the Khutyn Monastery now. He was a well-respected clergyman, a wonderful man. I know him well. I see him every now and again, and he always says to me: "I pray for you all the time." For the artists who lived there, he meant.

By 1995 the diocese had fully reoccupied the monastery and the last of the artists, some of whom had lived on the grounds for several decades, had been evicted. The shift in the monastery's status from architectural monument to sacred space resulted in a new hierarchy of exclusivity being imposed on the site; while art-ists and creative practitioners had been considered the rightful occupiers of the monastery during its time as a museum object, its reconceptualization in reli-gious terms meant that it was now off limits to anyone but the spiritually initiated. The appropriation of the monument's identity by the religious community was a source of obvious resentment for Galina, who described how her onetime home in St. George's southern corpus was now out-of-bounds for her and any other "tourist" who wanted to visit the complex:

GALINA: At some point they made a barrier, where the garden is by St. George's Church, and they don't let anyone go any further than that. There's a fence there and a sign that reads: "keep out." And behind it there's a garden and the southern corpus, where the workshops used to be. But now you're not allowed in there.

VSD: Do you still visit St. George's?

GALINA: Well, there's not really any point anymore. Sometimes we take visitors there. But only to the central part, to St. George's Church and the Exaltation of the Cross Church, where tourists are allowed to visit, and I suppose that's what we are too now [laughs]. There's no getting past that barrier.

Heritage as War Memory

The wartime devastation of Novgorod and Pskov was within living memory for some older residents. Yet, even for those born years after the towns' reconstruction, the experience of the war's aftermath was often reflected in their testimonials. The cultural memory of war was a fixture of local knowledge that was reinforced in school lessons, museum tours, tourist activities, and history books; it was also shaped by family experience and everyday conversation. On arriving in Novgorod for the first time in the summer of 2008, I was greeted by Viktor (b. 1981), a Novgorod native and an alumnus of the European University at St. Petersburg (EUSPb). Viktor had just graduated from a PhD program in history and had offered to give me a guided tour of his hometown. Like most graduating students at the EUSPb, Viktor spoke fluent English, and his comprehensive tour, which was delivered, it seemed, with little research or preparation, was packed with colorful detail and dates. Most striking, however, was the somber note on which he decided to end his excursion, as we rounded back to kremlin complex and approached the "Eternal Flame" memorial. "In Novgorod we never joke about the Second World War," he explained. "Everyone here has a family member who died or was affected by the war. It's not considered a laughing matter."

The cultural memory of World War II formed a central component of patriotic culture in Putin-era Russia.[22] And in Novgorod and Pskov, where the towns' reconstructed heritage landscapes functioned as a memorial complex of sorts, residents were particularly conscious of this history. Alla (b. 1950), a technical translator at a local factory, described her early memories of life in Novgorod. She was just old enough to remember Novgorod's postwar appearance and recalled her first impressions of the town on arriving in 1955:

I was five when we first came to Novgorod. We came via the bridge across the Volkhov, not the route that you walk along, the route for cars. . . . And when we arrived in
the town, on the right, I remember, by the old factory, Planeta, there was this carcass
of a house without a roof. Well, it was probably covered by something, but there was
definitely no roof on it. And there were these little trees growing out of the roof of
that house! That image really struck me as a five-year old. Trees growing out of the
roofs of houses! Well, I just stared and stared! And that's remained with me as a
memory of how badly damaged Novgorod was.

These personal recollections of postwar Novgorod quickly gave way to established
cultural narratives.[23] Alla added detail to her picture of wartime devastation in the
form of institutional memory and folk knowledge. Her description of the war-ravaged landscape included several fixtures of the local historical narrative that had
been reinforced in school textbooks and referenced in popular literature and art.
It also demonstrated the place of heritage preservation in the construction of the
Soviet myth of Novgorod, which emerged in her telling as a symbolic center of
national identity and tradition:

Well, what you have to understand is that Novgorod was completely ruined. All that
was left here were the carcasses of forty houses. Just carcasses of houses, all the rest
was destroyed . . . all the churches, like Sasha just said. And Novgorod, just after it
was liberated, the monument, you know about that, right? That it was completely
destroyed, the Millennium of Russia Monument? And all those figures of famous
people were lying around . . . do you know that painting by Kukryniksy, *Flight of
the Fascists from Novgorod*?[24] And all the figures are lying around the monument in
the snow, right? And then later, the government passed an order about the reconstruction of fifteen Russian towns.[25] And Novgorod was included on that list of
fifteen towns. Vladimir, Novgorod, and so on . . . Yaroslavl, maybe. The very, very
most . . . the ones that were considered the roots [*korni*] of Russia. And they were
reconstructed first so that people could see that Russia was alive and well and that
everything was going swimmingly [laughs].

The association of heritage objects with a patriotic myth of war was even stronger
in Pskov. The town's contemporary significance as a center of Russian military
life—as the location of the 76th Guards Air Assault Division, which had seen
action in Chechnya and other conflict zones—meant that many of its heritage
objects were infused with military-patriotic meaning. The connection between

the historic landscape and acts of local military heroism had been emphasized over the decades in Soviet-era kraevedenie materials, museum displays, and theatrical performances. The Soviet kraeved Savelii Iamshchikov, for example, had presented Pskov's monuments as symbols of military heroism in a publication dedicated to the town's architecture in 1979. As he wrote in the conclusion to this guide, "Every fortress wall, chapel, and graceful belfry speaks of the heroic courage and mighty deeds of their defenders."[26]

What locals saw when they looked at heritage objects was consequently colored by the military patriotism that dominated local education and culture.[27] Sitting on the banks of the River Velikii in the summer, Ol'ga (b. 1973) told me about a historic reconstruction of the "Liberation of Pskov" that she had witnessed as a child. The recreation of Pskov's recapture from German occupation had taken place each year, on July 23, and had involved local actors scrambling across a reconstructed pontoon bridge to the other bank of the river, where they had penetrated the Pskov Kremlin in a dramatic reimagining of the historic event. Ol'ga recalled that she had encountered a local veteran at one of these performances who had embroidered the scene unfolding before her with vivid eyewitness detail:

> I remember this one time, I was six years old, we were watching the forced crossing and standing next to us was this old man who'd clearly fought at the time, you know, in the Liberation of Pskov. And he says to us: "It might all look very beautiful now, but back then it was just a river of blood with pilots' bodies floating down it." Because so many people died, you see . . . we used to celebrate that festival, the "Liberation of Pskov," every year.

Ol'ga's words provide a vivid illustration of the condition that Marianne Hirsch has called, with reference primarily to remembrance of the Holocaust, "postmemory." Hirsch describes this condition as "the relationship of the second generation to powerful, often traumatic, experiences that preceded their births but that were nevertheless transmitted to them so deeply as to seem to constitute memories in their own right."[28] While one can claim that all of Russian society was, in some sense, a community of "postmemory" of the war, the close proximity of trauma in Pskov arguably left a deeper mark on local culture. This condition of inherited mourning, combined with the hyper-militarized nature of everyday life in the town, helps explain the local reverence for heritage objects and war memory, more generally.

FIGURE 15. A mother photographing her daughter beside a machine gun during Pskov's "Days of the Town" celebrations, July 2009.

Heritage Discourses in the Narrative Construction of Identity

In the historic Northwest, speaking about heritage could serve different social functions. Knowledge of the Soviet-era preservationist idiom could help demonstrate one's intelligentsia credentials or dissent from contemporary politics, while more pragmatic statements about heritage could serve to distinguish "real love" for one's town from mere academic interest in the historic landscape. Heritage objects also formed a foundation for social knowledge that delimited the boundaries of local identity. Understanding the folkloric meaning of a historical building or site helped to situate one within a privileged circle of "insiders" (*svoi*), as opposed to "tourists" (*turisty*), "out-of-towners" (*priezzhie*) or other kinds of cultural "outsiders" (*chuzhie*).

As the public commentaries discussed in earlier chapters demonstrate, local residents were well versed in the preservationist idiom. Exposure to preservationist ideas in schools, museums, clubs, and the media created a shared vocabulary for talking about heritage that people deployed in strategic ways. The most fluent in the preservationist discourse were, unsurprisingly, individuals who had worked in the towns' cultural sectors as museum curators, archivists, or excursion guides. These speakers would sometimes slip into a performative mode when asked about local heritage politics, substituting personal anecdote and recollection for more polemical statements about the value of local monuments and the urgency of preservationist matters. This is not to suggest, however, that these statements were in any way disingenuous or emotionally inauthentic. On the contrary, such performances revealed the importance of heritage debates to the speaker's social identity.

Tat'iana (b. 1950) provided perhaps the most striking example of this sort of performative patriotism in an answer to a question about the changes to Vologda's architectural landscape in the post-Soviet period. In her description of the shortcomings of contemporary politics, she made effortless use of the lexicon of architectural preservation, shifting seamlessly from her own reflections on Vologda's fate to the preservationist lyrics of the early twentieth-century émigré poet Marina Tsvetaeva. This sort of intertextual commentary, in which preservationist sentiments were interwoven across time and space, was a frequent feature of Tat'iana's speech. The technique had clearly been honed as an excursion guide, though it also revealed the speaker's erudition and breadth of literary and cultural reference:

> I have no taste at all for Vologda's contemporary architecture. The town is losing its character [*litso*], its individuality [*individual'nost'*]. If in the nineteenth century, an architect would look at a map as a whole and build something new, he would never destroy the old. He would blend his work in [*vpisival'sia*] with the landscape. There are a couple of high-rises here, but no one can see them because it's all united [*tsel'noe*]. It's all unified [*edinoe*]. And Vologda was always a wooden town, and wood, unfortunately, does not stand the test of time well. It has to be changed. . . . If these policies continue then in ten years Vologda will be no different [*ni chem ne otlichat'sia*] from any other town. There will be no wood left at all. It'll all be high-rise, paneled houses. As Marina Tsvetaeva wrote in her time, back at the start

of the twentieth century, about the old houses in Moscow: "Little houses marked by pedigree / With the look of pedigree's keepers / You've been changed for hulking monsters / Six-stories from the ground. / The householders—it is their right! / And so you perish too / Glory of languishing grandmothers / Little houses of old Moscow."[29] And the same can be said about Vologda. In Moscow, it's all disappeared already, and in Vologda it's disappearing before our very eyes.

While few residents were as fluent in the preservationist idiom as Tat'iana, a number echoed her sentiments in displays of enlightened local patriotism. "Sensible people feel pride in their town's cultural heritage," Liudmila (b. 1954) remarked, "Educated [razvitye] people love it all, of course." Leonid (b. 1946), whose struggle to save his own wooden house I have discussed in more detail in chapter 3, likewise saw preservation as a patriotic duty. Concluding a long monologue on the virtues of local heritage, he expressed sentiments that could have belonged to Soviet preservationists over half a decade earlier: "What is patriotism but love for your little homeland [malaia rodina], for the place you grew up in as a child? It's something that you can't live without. If people live in these brick houses how will anyone feel any sort of patriotism?"

Other residents took a more pragmatic approach to heritage questions. Their views were more closely aligned with those of the Soviet modernizers of the 1960s who had criticized preservationist lobbies for wanting to stop historic towns from becoming "modern" and "lively" and saw them only as places "to gather material for their dissertations."[30] For example, Tat'iana (b. 1959), a housewife from Vologda, associated the region's wooden houses with the "wretched suburbs" (zakholustnye regiony), overrun by "dirt and squalor" while new developments in areas such as Leningrad Street were, in her opinion, a real cause for local pride. The disappearance of the traditional architecture in this neighborhood was, for Tat'iana, secondary to the town's more general "improvement," its transition from sleepy province into a modern regional capital:

> They've started to build LOTS of new buildings, beautiful ones, unusual ones . . . not like the ones they used to build, block after block, all the same. Like prison cells, they were, all the same! These days, it's a pleasure to see these buildings going up, all in different styles. . . . Take Leningrad Street, for example, it's a completely new street, spacious, and filled with chic buildings with little towers and columns on them. It's just a new, modern style of building. It's a completely new region. It's a real feast for the eyes [glaz raduet!]!

Some residents went further, accusing preservationists of being elitist and out of touch with the everyday reality of town life. A revealing exchange on this theme took place on the social networking site *LiveJournal*, following a post about the appropriateness of the new streetlights erected around the Novgorod Kremlin as part of the 1150th Jubilee renovations in 2009. The author of the post was subjected to an onslaught of derision following a photograph of the offending lights and a statement that read: "Convince me that the color and structural 'delicacy' of these streetlights is in keeping with the architecture of an ancient town."[31] Such slavish adherence to preservationist protocol, as some perceived it, prompted a flurry of snide remarks: "What kind [of streetlights] did you want? Ones made of birch bark?" one commentator wrote; "What do you mean 'old-fashioned'? Chandeliers with candles, or what? Old-fashioned electricity in a bast shoe?"[32] The vitriol of these attacks revealed contempt for preservationist posturing; the comments asserted an alternative kind of patriotism, one rooted in the lived experience rather than historical memory.

If statements about heritage allowed residents to exhibit their patriotic credentials, they also formed a means of asserting local belonging. Knowledge of the cultural associations or folkloric meanings of a historic site situated one within a community of insiders, establishing the parameters of local identity. This kind of knowledge was often intuitive rather than factual. After working together for several months at the Novgorod Museum archives, situated within the Novgorod Kremlin complex, Valentina (b. 1948) confided in me that she, like many other local residents, disliked the atmosphere inside the fortress, which had historically witnessed so much violence: "Lots of people envy us for working here, but we have this bad feeling about the place," she explained. "There's something not quite right about it." Conversely, Tat'iana (b. 1950) revealed the hidden identity of Leningrad Street in Vologda, on which her museum was located, and which local experts had confirmed was the spiritual center of the town. "This area is the very best place with the most positive energy," she insisted. "It's because there are two churches nearby, the kremlin's just over there and there are churches right next door as well."

The destruction of the Saviour of All the Town Cathedral in Vologda, which I have discussed in chapter 4, had likewise engendered its own folk mythology. While few had witnessed the scene of the church's demolition first hand, the well-known photographs, displayed at local museums and published in local history books, had etched the event into people's imaginations. Valentina (b. 1958) thus remarked that everyone had known about the church's legend and had "looked

FIGURE 16. The Varlaam Khutynskii Church (1780) near Leningrad Street, Vologda, February 2009.

upon [its demolition] with horror." Galina (b. 1966) added folkloric detail to the narrative: "[My friend] told me that all the people who had pulled it down had died, that within ten years they'd all died. That just goes to show that you shouldn't touch a sacred space."

Folk knowledge of the landscape extended to the meaning of individual sculptures that adorned historical buildings. Stroking the paw of the lion sentry to the right of the entrance to the Novgorod Museum was said to bring luck in love, while caressing the leg of the lion sculpture to the left of the entrance could hasten a windfall.[33] In Vologda, rubbing the boot of the Konstanin Batiushkov Monument outside the kremlin walls ensured creative success, while stroking the finger of the nearby figurine granted the participant a wish.[34] Monuments also had unofficial social functions established by local communities over time. The Pushkin Monument in Pskov, for example, had acquired a reputation as a meeting place for literary-minded youngsters in the Soviet period and, after 1991, for Europhile subcultures, such as goths and "emo" fans.[35] By contrast, Soviet monuments in newer parts of the towns, such as the Monument to the Heroes of the October Revolution in Vologda, were renowned as the hangouts of hard-drinking and anti-social gangs, a place to avoid on one's walk home at night.[36]

Heritage as an Expression of Local Identity

It is not uncommon for local stereotypes to be rooted in the natural landscape. The romantic myth of Scotland, for example, as a land of mist, heather, hills and glens, has been successfully linked with the imagined character traits of bravery, purity, and integrity—a link that has been solidified in Hollywood blockbusters such as *Highlander* (1986) and *Braveheart* (1995), which combine rugged scenery with epic tales of heroism and self-sacrifice. Less common, perhaps, is the tendency to root local stereotypes in the architectural landscape, to perceive buildings as a reflection of the local mentality. In the Russian Northwest, however, where heritage was celebrated and marketed to the nation as an ideal of Russian culture, architecture was purposefully associated with the local character. The legacy of this work has continued to inform residents' understanding of local identity into the twenty-first century.

Writing in 1976, the kraevedy of the Russian Northwest V. Gippenreiter, E. Gordienko, and S. Iamshchikov had the following to say of the links between Novgorod's historic landscape and the character of the local people:

> Just one look at the strong, sturdy monuments of Novgorod the Great is enough to understand the ideal Novgorodian—a good warrior, not too well-mannered, rustic, but with his head screwed on (that's how he managed to get his freedom long

before the other peoples, not by following the example of his neighbors; and how he colonized the whole gigantic North); his buildings are just like him: strong walls devoid of any annoying decoration, which, from his point of view is "good for nothing," mighty silhouettes, masses that exude energy. The ideal of the Novgorodian is strength and its beauty—the beauty of strength. Not always smooth around the edges, but always magnificent, strong, noble, and triumphant.[37]

Residents of the historic town were aware of this cultural stereotype. As Natalia (b. 1966), the director of a local children's charity, explained, "you meet people from other parts of Russia and they say: 'Oh Novgorod! That's a town of great culture, antiquity and all that. And as for Novgorodians, they're independent people, brave, strong, courageous, decisive.'" The more robust association, however, and one that was likewise rooted in the heritage landscape, was of Novgorodians as "cultured" people. This notion was linked to the town's Soviet past and, specifically, its role as a center of architectural restoration in the postwar period, which had made it a magnet for world-class architects, archaeologists, and historians. A number of residents with whom I spoke rehearsed this idea, while regretting the shifts to the region's cultural profile, and the concomitant out-migration of local intellectual capital, that had followed the collapse of socialism.

Strength, purity and simplicity were likewise traits that were emphasized in the literature dealing with Pskov's architectural heritage. In kraevedenie materials, repeated mention was made of the "severe" or "austere" character of Pskov's monasteries, while the "authentic" credentials of the region's "Old Russian" architecture were often singled out for praise.[38] These architectural features were mapped onto the local stereotype of Pskovichi (Pskovians) as "ironmongers" (skobari), hardened characters, war-beaten like the local landscape, performing their patriotic duty. In 2014, this stereotype was lent official endorsement by the unveiling of the "Ironmonger" Monument in Pskov's Children's Park. This archetypal Pskovian, cast in the sculpture as a muscular and mustachioed Slav extending a newly forged horseshoe in an act of friendship, was presented as a respected folkloric hero.

The insistence on the "laconicism" of Pskov's architecture was echoed in residents' (more negative) comments about the characteristic reservedness or taciturnity of the local people. "Pskovichi are unfriendly [neprivetlivye] and taciturn [nerazgovorchivye], you never know what's going on in their heads," explained my landlady in Pskov, Margarita (b. 1955). Liudmila (b. 1948), who had moved to Pskov from northern Murmansk, agreed that, by contrast with people from other parts of Russia, Pskovichi "were a bit on the closed side [nemnozhko zamknuty]."

Igor' (b. 1940) drew the most explicit link between the hostility of local people and Pskov's landscape. The specificities of the local mentality, he explained, were a result of the town's historic status as a "borderland [*porubezhnaia zemlia*]":

> Some nations are happy, but here people are . . . people are hard [*tiazhelyi*]. But you have to ask yourself why. Why are they hard? It's because historically there was always fighting on their territory. With the Fascists and before that with all those others, with the Germans, with Lithuania, and Poland, and then with the Germans again and the Baltic Countries, there was always a war going on here, because it's a borderland. That's the reason that people are the way they are.

Vologda's traditional wooden architecture produced a separate set of local stereotypes. The popular, "democratic" character of the town's folk landscape was linked to the "authentic Russianness" of local people in a way that recalled the works of the Russian Village Prose writers. Speaking about the noble "reserve" (*nemnogoslovnost'*) of local residents, Tat'iana (b. 1950) illustrated this point with reference to the local architectural style, demonstrating the perceived link between the town's architectural and social "fabrics":

> Character-wise Vologzhane [Vologdians] are very constrained. I remember, just after I started working at the museum, some foreigners came in, Italians. They were always asking why people here don't smile. I told them, this is the North, it's very cold here and that's the reason why people here don't smile. In Italy where it's nice and warm and clear, everyone goes around grinning. But that doesn't mean that Vologzhane are mean people. They're just made that way. Even their houses—their wooden houses, especially the two-story ones, on the first floor they have small windows—that's to keep the warmth in.

The association of the local character with the traditional architectural landscape made the destruction of the latter a source of particular regret. This was especially true of Vologda's ornately decorated wooden mansions, which were linked in the minds of locals with the region's vibrant folk culture, crafts, and the melodic local dialect. The disappearance of Vologda's vernacular architecture and the standardization of the region's folk traditions were consequently presented as associated cultural phenomena. Both were indications of a worrying loss of cultural identity, the replacement of an authentic Russian way of life with rootless cultural imports.

Efforts to market the Northwest as a center of Russian culture and heritage continued to inform perceptions of local identity into the twenty-first century. Despite being located in the geographic heart of European Russia, many residents rejected the notion of their localities as "European towns" and instead connected their cities with "authentic" or "ancient" Russianness, recalling the preservationist discourses of the postwar period. Responding to a request to sum up her home-town in several words, Ol'ga (b. 1973) thus explained that Pskov was "more like . . . an ancient Russian town [*starinnyi russkii gorod*] because, it seems to me that it has more of those kinds of traits than European ones." Irina (b. 1972), whose son Vitalii sat beside her as she spoke, reiterated this idea, making explicit the role she perceived architectural heritage to play in shaping the town's "authentically Russian" identity:

> IRINA: Pskov is more modern now, with its festivals, and, you know, modern life. There are lots of signs in foreign languages, there never used to be anything like that, but nevertheless it's still . . .
> VITALII: European?
> IRINA: European, maybe yes! Though I don't think that it will ever become fully European. And maybe it doesn't need to since it's a nice authentically Russian town [*khoroshii samobytnyi russkii gorod*]. Even historically, before the Soviet period even, there were so many streets in the town, so many chapels and churches. And if you looked at the town from above, right, you'd see that there were those cupolas of Orthodox churches on every street corner.

This statement perhaps most succinctly revealed the impact of decades of pro-moting the Northwest as a symbolic center of Russian identity. Pskov emerged in Irina's telling as an inherently Russian cultural space; a town whose architectural, spiritual and cultural values asserted difference from "Europe," a cultural con-struct that continued to form in the twenty-first century a significant constituent "Other" against which Russia defined itself.

While this chapter does not pretend to represent in its entirety the broad spec-trum of opinions on preservationist matters present in the Northwest, the local voices that it showcases nevertheless exhibit some revealing tendencies. A the-matic strand connecting almost all of the testimonies, for example, was the feeling of pride in local cultural heritage. This pride manifested itself in a range of ways:

from the eulogistic celebration of the architectural landscape to the castigations of contemporary politicians who failed to defend the integrity of historic buildings. Feelings of pride were in some cases linked to perceptions of northwestern heritage as something intrinsically Russian, a construct that I have argued in this book has its roots in the patriotic politics of the postwar period. The conflation of local and national heritage, I would suggest, had been strengthened by performances of patriotic identity, both in formal contexts, such as school presentations and museum excursions, and in informal ones, such as walks around town with visitors and conversations with family and friends.

Residents of the historic Northwest had different registers for talking about preservationist matters. A number were versed in the preservationist idiom and able to exploit this mode to demonstrate their general erudition and intelligentsia credentials. Talking about heritage, however, had other less obvious social functions. Childhood memories of exploring historic buildings, personal associations with local monuments, and knowledge of the rumors and superstitions connected with particular historic places served to reinforce the boundaries of community identity. I had my own personal experience of the social inclusivity that came with learning about heritage objects. As I discovered more from residents about the hidden meanings of monuments, I was able to gain credibility as an interlocutor. Sharing my feelings and experiences of a local place—the Novgorod Kremlin where I worked in the museum archives for several months, for example—could create a space of shared intimacy that allowed for a more confessional mode of conversation.

Most striking, however, were the negative emotions expressed in connection with the preservationist failures of the present-day political authorities. It would appear that local knowledge of the value of the heritage landscape, reinforced in Soviet classrooms and museums, made the systematic neglect of heritage objects in the twenty-first century (particularly in Pskov and Vologda) a source of particular resentment. Moreover, the association of heritage objects with the local population, the conflation of aesthetic traditions and local character traits, resulted, I would argue, in heritage being perceived as an embodiment of the local community. The abuse and destruction of local architecture was consequently understood in very personal terms. At a time when local economies were stagnating and politics were perceived to be particularly undemocratic, neglected historical monuments formed evocative metaphors for the Russian provincial condition more generally.

CONCLUSION

In an article that appeared in 2008 on the website of the Russian current affairs magazine *Skepsis*, Ivan Leshchinskii described a new human life form that had emerged in the Russian regions.[1] Half "One Dimensional Man" (the creature of uniform dress, thoughts, and false desires imagined by Herbert Marcuse), half illiterate peasant, the caricature was intended as a critique of cultural degeneration outside of the nation's capitals. Leshchinskii's text could be situated within a long tradition of denigrating the regions, which had its origins in the satirical portrayals of Russian provincial elites in the prerevolutionary era. From the scathing sketches of Gogol and Saltykov-Shchedrin in the nineteenth century to the ultrableak cinema (*chernukha*) of the perestroika era, cultural representations of the provinces had succeeded in establishing Russia beyond its capital cities as a site of ignorance, corruption, and, perhaps most importantly, monotony in the national imagination.

Given the tendency to denigrate cultural life in the regions, it is striking that the Russian Northwest has so often been seen as a "center" or "capital" of cultural production. Since the end of the war, the region has been imagined variously as a heartland of authentic Russian traditions, a preserve of "Old Russian" architecture, a hub of Russian folk culture, and even a chalice containing the sacred soils of Russian history. The exceptional status of the Northwest in the national imaginary is due in part to its celebration by Russian patriots and nationalists, who seized upon the region's associations with ideas of Russian cultural authenticity to promote their own cultural agendas. Yet, as I have argued in this book, it is also a consequence of the Soviet nation-building politics of the postwar era. The strategic endorsement of northwestern heritage at moments of political crisis in the second half of the twentieth century resulted in the region becoming not only a showcase of Russian traditions, but also a focus of Soviet identity politics.

While interested in the political rationale behind the Soviet state's decision to endorse northwestern heritage after the war, this book has focused primarily on the local consequences of preservationist policies in the Russian Northwest. The main actors in this story are thus not national politicians, writers, or dissidents, but rather the local practitioners and grassroots activists who mobilized in response to the state-sponsored drive to preserve and promote the region's historic architecture. These restorers, kraevedy, folklorists, and preservationists were the human face of the politics of cultural memory that shaped the region's cultural identity after 1945. They were not merely administrators of policy decisions devised in Moscow, however. Local elites, comprising world experts in the fields of architectural restoration, history, and folklore studies, formed formidable lobbies for the cultural interests of the region in the postwar period that were able to exploit the discourse of state patriotism to challenge and make far-reaching demands of the political center.

The first four chapters of this book have traced the formation and development of local lobbies for cultural preservation in the Russian Northwest. While these chapters are divided according to spheres of cultural work—restoration, tourism, museum work, and preservation—the activities and actors that populate each discussion must be seen as interwoven parts of the fabric of local cultural life. With each strategic affirmation of the preservationist cause, local lobbies gained authority and assertiveness, articulating their criticisms of Soviet policy with greater impact over time. By the Gorbachev era of political restructuring, preservationist lobbies had evolved into veritable movements for social change, absorbing, in some cases, more extremist nationalist groups. After the collapse of socialism, conservationist movements were consequently able to draw support not only from a heritage-savvy minority, but also from a much broader constituency in their campaign to defend local culture from the destructive consequences of Yeltsin-era liberal market reforms.

How representative were these developments of changes to cultural life in other Russian regions? How far does this story map part of a broader localist turn in postwar Soviet politics? The conditions that gave rise to the preservationist culture in the Russian Northwest are, in many ways, specific to this region. In the case

of Novgorod and Pskov, the wartime devastation of the towns' rich heritage landscapes prompted the formation of expert restoration workshops, whose members
were outspoken patrons of local culture and traditions. Likewise in Vologda, the
town's prerevolutionary history as a hub of intellectual activity, combined with an
uncommonly well-preserved folk landscape, encouraged preservationist interest
in the region. The status of these indigenous preservationist communities was
reinforced in the Brezhnev era, when efforts were made to contain the growth
of Russian nationalism through the strategic endorsement of Russian themes. At
this time, the Russian Northwest was once more privileged in national politics,
witnessing the elevation of its local traditions to the status of symbols of national
culture and identity.

This is not to suggest that the rise of cultural preservationism had no impact
in other regions of Soviet Russia. The visibility of preservationist debates in the
national media, combined with the enforcement of national legislation supporting the conservation of architectural heritage and the promotion of kraevedenie
work, stimulated popular engagement with local history and heritage across the
USSR. An indication of the national reach of preservationist ideas was provided in
1982 following an interview, published in *Spark*, with Dmitry Likhachev, in which
the historian condemned VOOPIiK for its inactivity at the Soviet periphery.[2] The
interview generated a lively response from residents of historic towns across
the Soviet territory, including the regions of Omsk, Simferopol', Yaroslavl', and
Irkutsk, who wrote to the editors to add their own local gripes to the criticisms
of the medieval historian.[3] Such popular engagement with preservationist themes
increased following the collapse of state socialism, when the failure of inept and
corrupt regional authorities to ensure the integrity of heritage objects prompted
resentment and outrage from local communities all over Russia.[4]

While it is useful to locate local developments within a national context, it is also
important to place this national picture within a broader global frame. The rise in
preservationist thinking in Russia did not occur in isolation. On the contrary, the
postwar period saw a growth in cultural retrospection across Europe. As Michael
Hunter has noted, in Britain, World War II catalyzed prewar concerns about heritage preservation, resulting in the pioneering regulations for listing buildings in
the Town and Country Planning Acts of 1944 and 1947.[5] Other European states
took similar steps to transform the amorphous notion of historic preservation
into concrete legislation at this time. The French "Malraux Law" of 1962 gave rise
to a flurry of restoration work in cities such as Chartres, Lyon, and Colmar in the
1960s, while the postwar period in Italy saw the adoption of a number of laws for

the protection of historic buildings and towns, such Venice in 1953, Assisi in 1957, and Urbino in 1968.[6] All over the continent, it would appear, the material traces of the past were in the process of being catalogued, categorized, and rehabilitated.

The roots of the retrospective turn in European culture are most certainly located in the events of World War II and the policies of reconstruction and urban regeneration that followed. As in Russia, the mass transfer from the country to the town that marked the 1950s and 1960s in France, Italy, and Germany had socially transformative consequences, not least in the domain of urban planning.[7] The crash construction of new residential areas and the creation of an infrastructure of public services and leisure facilities transformed European landscapes "beyond recognition," giving rise to preservationist concerns about the survival of national traditions and the maintenance of heritage objects. The events of the mid-twentieth century might therefore be compared to other civilizational ruptures in the eighteenth and nineteenth centuries—the French Revolution or the Industrial Revolution, for example—which prompted similar bouts of nostalgic retrospectivism, both in terms of public ritual and private practice.[8]

What, then, was different about the movement for cultural preservation in Soviet Russia, and what does this tell us about the localist and nationalist tendencies that emerged in the country in the late Soviet and post-Soviet periods? Firstly, it is important to acknowledge the genuinely mass nature of the movement for cultural preservation in the postwar Soviet Union. This fact is reflected in the VOOPIiK membership figures for this period. While the National Trust in the United Kingdom achieved a membership of around one million (or 1.7 percent of the national population) by 1981,[9] individual VOOPIiK membership in Vologda (in 1983) and Novgorod (in 1978) alone was 125,000 (or 49.2 percent of the local population) and 85,000 (47.2 percent of the local population), respectively.[10] Being a Soviet preservationist, moreover, involved much more than simply sporting a bumper sticker and occasionally visiting a stately home. Residents of the Northwest attended conferences and exhibitions, participated in trips to sites of historical interest, and even acted as patrons of individual heritage objects. These activities were reinforced by kraevedenie work involving local museums, schools, and tourist activities. Soviet citizens were thus significantly more "heritage aware" than their neighbors in Western Europe, not to mention fluent in a preservationist discourse that they deployed to praise or condemn local developments in public forums, from museum response books to local newspapers.

Secondly, as I have argued throughout this book, Soviet preservation was characterized by a fundamental contradiction between the affirmation of local identity, on the one hand, and the centripetal tendencies of the authoritarian Soviet state, on the other. This book has pinpointed occasions on which this tension culminated in open conflict between regional and national authorities: the clashes between local restorers and urban modernizers in the immediate postwar period; the debates over the value of folk architecture and its preservation during the Brezhnev years; and local preservationists' defense of heritage objects against the pressures of liberal market reforms after socialism. While the authority to determine heritage politics remained at the political center, local lobbies were increasingly prepared to challenge this authority throughout the late Soviet period. Appealing to alternative sources of cultural influence, from prominent cultural critics, such as Likhachev, to the Soviet people themselves, regional elites petitioned the national authorities, successfully in some instances, in the interests of local communities and culture.

This last point leads to a broader observation regarding the late Soviet "Russian revival." It has generally been held that Russian heritage and traditions were privileged in late Soviet cultural politics as part of a two-pronged strategy to distract from more pressing social and economic concerns, and to contain Russian nationalist potential.[11] If this is true, this book nevertheless demonstrates that the primacy placed on Russian national culture did not necessarily equate to the endorsement of Russian regional identity; indeed, these two tendencies were often located in a relationship of tension and conflict. This was even true of the historic Northwest, a region whose traditions and heritage were celebrated, and even fetishized, by the Russian patriotic elite. In the postwar period, cultural memory in the Northwest was subjected to homogenizing forces that erased references to local recalcitrance and emphasized politically resonant themes such as collectivism, militarism, and national patriotism. This process might be compared to the "Russocentric etatism" described by David Brandenberger in his account of Stalinist state-building.[12] In this instance, however, the tools of censorship were directed not only against non-Russian historical traditions but also against local memory within Russia itself, substituting a multivoiced national narrative for a hegemonic discourse of unity and integration.[13]

At the center of this study of cultural preservation are people: those who restored the Northwest's historic monuments, composed museum displays, and focused the tourist gaze on the landscape, and those whose lives and understanding of themselves and their communities were shaped by this activity. The last two chapters of this book present a closer look at the social legacy and impact of the Soviet-era work marketing the Northwest as a symbolic center of national identity. According to these chapters' findings, the local administrations' efforts to boost regional economies by rebranding the region in the twenty-first century were heavily influenced by Soviet-era cultural politics: rebranding agendas demonstrated a preoccupation with asserting the national significance of the regions—as birthplaces, bastions, and spiritual centers of Russian identity—while, at the same time, fixating on heritage objects as a means to signify cultural specificity. Whether issuing from local lobbies, regional governors, or Muscovite neo-nationalists, the politics of local cultural memory in the twenty-first century continued to be played out on a heritage stage.

A more complicated question is how the systematic exploitation of northwestern heritage for political ends influenced and informed the attitudes of communities living in the region. The interview excerpts presented in the final chapter of this book shed valuable light on the everyday consequences of this sort of political maneuvering. Sustained engagement with heritage objects, both at an institutional level and in more intimate contexts, created a heightened awareness of heritage questions that shaped people's appreciation for the historic landscape. Perhaps only in St. Petersburg, where preservation was likewise high on the cultural agenda, were historic buildings so closely identified with the local experience. The consequences of this situation were various. On the one hand, it resulted in a pronounced sense of the region's cultural specificity and historical significance, giving rise to feelings of local pride and patriotism; on the other, it created a gap between popular expectations and reality in connection with preservationist policy. The inability of local administrators to protect regional heritage was seen as part of a broader malaise afflicting Russian politics, as an institutional failure to represent the authentic interests of the Russian people.

Traveling to the Russian Northwest today, one has the feeling that heritage objects have fallen victim to the vicissitudes of transitional politics. The condition of "Old Russian" churches, monasteries, kremlin complexes, and folk architecture varies remarkably depending on the patrons who have assumed responsibility for the buildings' maintenance. An Orthodox church, restored to glimmering grandeur by the local diocese, can stand next to a crumbling wooden house whose owners have lobbied the local authorities in vain for the building's restoration. And yet, when the political circumstances demand it, both buildings are hastily restored and presented as evidence of the region's status as a sanctuary of national traditions, spiritual and cultural life. These inconsistencies in preservationist politics cannot fail to rankle communities nourished on the preservationist arguments of the late Soviet era. For many residents, the most recent pages of the Northwest's "stone chronicles" thus tell stories of opportunism, uncertainty, and thwarted hopes with little prospect of a happy ending.

APPENDIX

This book draws on interviews and participant observation work carried out in Novgorod, Pskov, and Vologda between October 2007 and August 2012. I have also quoted from interviews conducted as part of a collaborative project, "From the Plough to the Factory Furnace: Retracing the Paths of Soviet Urban Migration in Northwest Russia," sponsored by *Geschichtswerkstatt Europa Programme* and carried out in 2010: http://www.geschichtswerkstatt-europa.org/expired-project-details/items/plough-furnace.html. A number of interviews were conducted by colleagues as part of the AHRC project "National Identity in Russia after 1961: Traditions and Deterritorialization." A number of the interview transcripts are held at the *Oxford Russian Life History Archive*: http://www.ehrc.ox.ac.uk/lifehistory/.

Novgorod Interviews

(Interviewers: Victoria Donovan and Svetlana Podrezova)

1. ALEKSANDR (1948–2009), born in Novgorod; worked as a physics teacher at School No. 21; Russian.
2. ALESHA (1975), born in Germany; moved to Novgorod in 1979; formerly worked for local authorities; ethnically Russian but self-identifies as Jewish.
3. ALLA (1950), born in the Moscow region; moved to Novgorod in 1955; works as a technical translator at a local factory; Russian.
4. EKATERINA (1953), born in the Tver region; moved to Novgorod in 1962; studied at Leningrad Order of Lenin State Conservatory named after N. A. Rimskii-Korsakov; teaches at the Novgorod Regional College of Art, named after S. V. Rakhmaninov; Russian.
5. GALINA (1958), born in Arkhangelsk; moved to Novgorod with husband after graduating from Leningrad Academy of Art and Industry in 1988; lived and worked for several years at the St. George's Monastery complex; professional artist; Russian.
6. IRINA (1973), born in Novgorod; studied economics at Novgorod State Agricultural University, now the Institute for Agricultural and Natural Resources within the Novgorod State University named after Yaroslav the Wise; works as an accountant at the tourist firm "Ark-Tur"; volunteers at the "Alexandria Club" in Novgorod; Russian.
7. LIUDMILA (1954), born in the Moscow area; moved to Novgorod in 1979 to study at the Novgorod Musical College; violin teacher at the Musical School named after A. Arenskii; Russian.
8. NATALIIA (1977), born in Novgorod; studied economics at Novgorod State University; works as a manager in the tourist firm "Ark-Tur"; volunteer administrator at Novgorod's "Alexandria Club"; Russian.
9. VALENTINA (1948), born in the village of Ruska in the Novgorod region; studied French and German at the Novgorod Pedagogical Institute; worked at the "Birch Tree" tourist store and, later, at the Novgorod State Regional Museum archive; Russian.

10. VIACHESLAV (1953), born in Novgorod; studied for PhD in Leningrad; worked in the Faculty of Foreign Languages at the Novgorod Pedagogical Institute for fifteen years; works as a translator at a local factory; Russian.

11. VIKTORIIA (1954), born in Leningrad; studied at Leningrad Order of Lenin State Conservatory named after N. A. Rimskii-Korsakov; moved to Novgorod in 1989 to work at the Musical College; now teaches at the Novgorod Regional College of Arts named after S. V. Rakhmaninov; Russian.

Pskov Interviews

(Interviewer: Victoria Donovan)

1. DMITRII (1979), born in Pskov; moved to St. Petersburg for postgraduate study at the European University at St. Petersburg in 2005; works as a teacher and independent scholar; Russian.

2. GALINA (1971), born in Ukraine; moved to Pskov in 1977; studied languages at Pskov Pedagogical Institute (English, German, Latin); works as an English language teacher; Ukrainian with Carpathian Cossack roots.

3. IGOR' (1940), born in Ulaanbaatar, Mongolia; moved to Pskov in 1946; studied at the Leningrad Mining Institute; worked in Murmansk before returning to Pskov in the 1960s to help secure accommodation for his mother; retired; Russian.

4. IRINA (1962), born in a village 30 km from Pskov; moved to Pskov in 1979; studied languages at the Pskov Pedagogical Institute; works as an English language teacher; Russian.

5. IRINA (1972), born in Pskov; moved to St. Petersburg in 1990 to study journalism; works as a journalist at the *St. Petersburg Times*; Russian.

6. LEONID (1932), born in Peterhof; parents moved to a nearby village when war broke out in 1941; was transported to Germany by occupying German army; returned to Russia in 1945 and lived temporarily in Donbas; moved to Pskov to live with relatives in 1946; worked at the radio engineering factory as a technical engineer and as an engineer for 76th Guards Division; retired; Russian.

7. LIUDMILA (1948), born in Murmansk, where she worked for 12 years in a factory as a lab technician; mother worked in the Murmansk gorispolkom and secured them shares in a cooperatively owned house in Pskov; moved to Pskov in 1977; worked as a senior shop assistant; retired; Russian.

8. MARGARITA (1955), born in the Komsomolsk settlement in the Tomsk region; moved to the Pskov region (first to Velikii Luki and then to Pskov) in 1973; studied at the Pedagogical Institute at the Faculty of Foreign Languages; worked as an English-language teacher at the "Liberal Institute" in Pskov until its closure in 2010; published several volumes of poetry; Russian.

9. MIKHAIL (1963), born in Ostrov to a Russified Roma family; studied at a practical college with a specialization in tractor driving; works as a driver and loader; Russified Rom.

10. NATAL'IA (1968), born in Pskov; works as a hairdresser; Russian.

11. OL'GA (1973), born in Pskov; studied at the Pskov Pedagogical Institute; works as a teacher in a primary school; Russian.

12. TAT'IANA (1961), born in Pskov; worked at the radio engineering factory as a quality control manager; Russian.

13. VALERII (1953), born in a camp in Irkutsk where his mother (Polish) and father (Armenian) were prisoners; on his father's release in 1956 the family returned to the Maikopsk region in Adygea and worked on the local kolkhoz; specialized in military engineering but had problems finding work after graduating because of his father's record; eventually found work at the radio engineering factory in Pskov, where he relocated in 1974; was a deputy of the Pskov gorsovet for four years after 1991; retired; Armenian.

14. VIACHESLAV (1974), born in Pskov; studied to become a gas welder; worked as a professional soldier; now works as a professional driver; Russian.

Vologda Interviews

(Interviewer: Victoria Donovan)

1. ALEKSANDR (1958), born in Vologda; works as university lecturer at the pedagogical institute; father was a locally renowned "Village Prose" writer; Russian.
2. ALENA (1983), born in Vologda; works as a college lecturer; Russian.
3. ANEL' (1933), born in Vologda; worked as an engineer-planner; retired; Russian.
4. EVGENII (1958), born in the Molochnoe settlement; moved to Vologda in 1983; worked as a structural engineer; Russian.
5. GERMAN (1934), born in Vologda; worked as a senior specialist in sanitary engineering in the planning institute; Russian.
6. IRINA (1957), born in Vologda; works as seamstress and toy maker; Russian.
7. LEONID (1946), born in Vologda; works as a photographer and kraeved; published several books on Vologda history and culture; Russian.
8. MARIIA (1968), born in Vologda; deputy head of the Vologda library; Russian.
9. NATAL'IA (1962), born in Novgorod; moved to Vologda in 1975; works as a librarian at the Vologda State Library; Russian.
10. NATALIIA (1934), born in Vologda; studied at Vologda Pedagogical Institute; worked as a math teacher; retired; Russian.
11. RIMMA (1934), born in the village of Vokhma in the Kostroma region; moved to Velikii Ustiug and then to Vologda; formerly an accountant; retired; Russian.
12. SVETLANA (1965), born in Vologda; works as a computer programmer in the department of social welfare; Russian.
13. TAT'IANA (1950), born in Omsk; studied at Vologda Pedagogical Institute; works as director at the "World of Forgotten Things"; Russian.
14. TAT'IANA (1959), born in the Molochnoe region of the Vologda oblast; moved to Vologda in 1983; worked as Deputy Head of Studies for the Legal Academy; Russian.
15. VALENTINA (1958), born in Vologda; worked as manager of the pedagogical sector at Vologda Pedagogical Institute; Russian.
16. IURII (1961), born in the village of Novgorodovo in the Vologda region; grew up in Kharachevo (a large settlement near Vologda); studied at Vologda Pedagogical Institute; now works as a master of ceremonies (*tamada*) and event planner; Russian.

Other Interviews

1. Oxf/AHRC-SPb-08 AP PF. Aleksandr Davidovich Margolis. Interview conducted by Aleksandra Piir, 29.01.2008.
2. Oxf/AHRC-SPb-08 AP PF2. Oleg Mikhailovich Ioannisian. Interview conducted by Aleksandra Piir, 25.03.2008.

SELECT BIBLIOGRAPHY

I. Archives

NOVGOROD

Novgorod State Museum-Zapovednik (NGOM)

> Op. 1 (1944–1966)
> Op. 2 (1967–1979)
> Op. 3 (1980–1992)
> Op. 4 (1993–1994)

Novgorod Regional State Archive (GANO)

> F. R-3994. Cultural authorities of the Novgorod oblispolkom
> F. R-4063. Professional councils of the Novgorod region. Council for tourism and excursions. Department for travel and excursions
> F. R-4137. Special scientific restoration production workshop. Cultural authorities of the ispolkom of the Novgorod regional council of workers' deputies
> F. R-4563. VOOPIiK council of the Novgorod regional department

PSKOV

State Archive of the Contemporary History of Pskov (GANIP)

> F. 1060. Senior party organization of the Pskov historical-artistic museum

Pskov Regional State Archive (GAPO)

> F. R-1855. Cultural authorities of the executive committee of the Pskov regional council of workers deputies. Planning and finance departments

VOLOGDA

Vologda Regional State Archive (GAVO)

> F. 134. Cultural authorities of the Vologda gorispolkom
> F. 843. Regional department of the All-Russian Society for the Preservation of Historical and Cultural Monuments
> F. 4795. Cultural authorities of the Vologda oblispolkom

VOLOGDA REGIONAL KRAEVEDENIE MUSEUM (VOKM)

> Op. 1 (1923–1979)
> F. 52 (separate file)

II. Newspapers

I have drawn on a range of national and regional newspapers in this study, some of which will be familiar to Russian scholars, and some of which may not be. As an aid to future research on the region, I provide below a list of the most popular regional newspapers together with a short description of each publication's character and political outlook.

NOVGOROD

> *Novgorodskaia pravda* (Soviet-era publication and regional branch of the official KPSS newspaper *Pravda*); disseminated weekly; continues to exist in the region today, albeit with a radically reduced readership.
>
> *Novgorod* (popular weekly with a circulation of around 104,000); founded by the Novgorod Duma; source of government-friendly news and local information.

PSKOV

> *Pskovskaia pravda* (Pskov branch of KPSS publication *Pravda*); disseminated weekly; rebranded in the 2000s as government-friendly e-journal with an emphasis on family values and campaigns for social justice.
>
> *Pskovskaia lenta novosti* (popular e-newspaper founded in 2000); source of news and local information; draws a lively community of commentators on local affairs.
>
> *Pskovskaia guberniia* (regional newspaper whose declared intention is to provide "comprehensive and full information to citizens about events taking place in Pskov and in Russia more generally"); directed and edited by head of the Pskov regional branch of "Yabloko," Lev Shlosberg; the newspaper has drawn attention for its outspoken criticism of the Russian government.

VOLOGDA

> *Khronometr* (scandal-loving tabloid founded in 1999 under the auspices of the publishing house "Provintsiia"); the newspaper claims to pride itself on its "universality" and "non-aligned" nature: in reality it trades in local scandal, poverty porn, and gratuitous misogyny.
>
> *Prem'er* (broadly liberal weekly tabloid founded in 1997, with a circulation of 15,000); specializes in coverage of politics and society; excellent source of polls and survey work with the local population.
>
> *Krasnyi sever* (Soviet-era publication founded in 1917); remains in circulation today, funded by the Vologda regional government; newspaper holds exclusive rights to publication of official government documents; circulation of around 28,000.
>
> *Nash region* (Vologda weekly focusing on news and current events); ceased activity in 2006, seemingly as a consequence of the scandal resulting from its republication of the cartoons of Muhammad first featured in the Danish newspaper *Jyllands-Posten* in 2005.
>
> *Vologodskaia nedelia* (free local weekly, founded in 2009); the most widely read newspaper in the region, with a circulation of around 107,000; the publication has a pronounced regional focus with an emphasis on local politics and society.

III. Published Sources in English and Russian

Abashev, V. V. *Perm' kak tekst: Perm' v russkoi kul'ture i literature XX veka*. Perm: Izd-vo Permskogo universiteta, 2000.

Abashin, Sergei. *Natsionalizmy v Srednei Azii: V poiskakh identichnosti*. St. Petersburg: Ateleiia, 2007.

Alexievich, Svetlana. *Vremia sekond khend*. Moscow: Vremia, 2014.

———. Nobel Lecture by Svetlana Alexiévich (in Russian). NobelPrize.org. Nobel Media AB 2018. October 1, 2018. https://www.nobelprize.org/prizes/literature/2015/alexievich/25414-nobel-lecture-by-svetlana-aleksievitch-in-russian/.

"Analiz praktiki sub"ektivizatsii v rannestalinskom obshchestve." Interviews with Igal Halfin and Jochen Hellbeck; essays by Aleksandr Kustarev, David L. Hoffmann, Jeremy Smith, Svetlana Boym, Il'ia Gerasimov, Alla Sal'nikova, Dietrich Beyrau, and Yashiro Matsui; "Concluding Thoughts" by Halfin and Hellbeck. *Ab Imperio* 3 (2002): 209–418.

Andreev, V. F. *Novgorod*. Leningrad: Lenizdat, 1985.

Arkashuni, O. K. *Predchuvstvie: Vospominaniia o Iurii Pavloviche Spegal'skom*. Leningrad: Lenizdat, 1987.

Assmann, Jan, and John Czaplicka. "Collective Memory and Cultural Identity." *New German Critique* 65 (1995): 125–133.

Balina, Marina, and Evgeny Dobrenko. *Petrified Utopia: Happiness Soviet-style*. London: Anthem Press, 2009.

Baranov, N. V., and A. I. Naumov. "General'nyi plan vosstanovleniia i razvitii Pskova." Leningradskii gorodskoi sovet deputatov trudiashchikhsia ispolnitel'nii komitet. Upravleniia po delam arkhitektury. Pskov, 1945.

Bassin, Mark, and Catriona Kelly, eds. *Soviet and Post-Soviet Identities*. Cambridge: Cambridge University Press, 2012.

Bedina, N. N. "Obraz sviatoi kniagini Ol'gi v drevnerusskoi knizhnoi traditsii (XII–XVI v.)." *Drevniaia Rus', Voprosy medievistiki* 4, no. 30 (2007): 8–12.

Belov, Vasilii. *Plotnitskie rasskazy*. Arkhangel'sk: Severo-Zapadnoe Knizhnoe Izdatel'stvo, 1968.

———. "Privychnoe delo." *Sever* 1 (1966): 7–92.

Berdiaev, Nikolai. "Literaturnoe napravlenie i 'sotsial'nyi zakaz.'" *Put'* 29 (1931): 80–92.

Beumers, Birgit, Stephen Hutchings, and Natalia Rulyova, eds. *The Post-Soviet Russian Media: Conflicting Signals*. London: Routledge, 2009.

Bhabha, Homi K. *The Location of Culture*. London: Routledge, 2012.

Bittner, Stephen. *The Many Lives of Khrushchev's Thaw: Experience and Memory in Moscow's Arbat*. Ithaca: Cornell University Press, 2008.

Bocharov, G. and V. Vygolov. *Vologda, Kirillov, Ferapontovo, Belozersk*. Moscow: Iskusstvo, 1969.

Bulkin, B. A., and O. V. Ovsiannikov, *Uchenyi, zodchii, kamenshchik*. Leningrad: Lenizdat, 1983.

Brandenberger, David. *National Bolshevism: Stalinist Mass Culture and the Formation of Modern Russian National Identity, 1931–1956*. Cambridge, MA: Harvard University Press, 2002.

———. "Proletarian Internationalism, 'Soviet Patriotism' and the Rise of Russocentric Etatism During the Stalinist 1930s." *Left History* 6, no. 2 (2000): 80–100.

———. *Propaganda State in Crisis: Soviet Ideology, Indoctrination and Terror under Stalin, 1927–1941*. New Haven: Yale University Press, 2011.

Brandenberger, David, and Kevin M. F. Platt. *Epic Revisionism: Russian History and Literature as Stalinist Propaganda*. Madison, WI: University of Wisconsin Press, 2006.

Brooks, Jeffrey. *Thank You, Comrade Stalin!: Soviet Public Culture from Revolution to Cold War*. Princeton, NJ: Princeton University Press, 2000.

Brudny, Yitzhak. *Reinventing Russia: Russian Nationalism and the Soviet State*. Cambridge, MA: Harvard University Press, 1998.

Brunov, N. I. "O poslednikh issledovaniiakh arkhitektury sobora Sofii v Novgorode." *Materialy k VII sessii Akademii arkhitektury SSSR*, 3–23. Moscow, 1946.

Bush, Anne. "Reviewing Rome: The Guidebook as Liminal Space." *Visual Communication* 1 (2002): 370–377.

Cantacuzino, Sherban, ed. *Architectural Conservation in Europe*. Bedford: The Architectural Press Ltd., 1975.

Clark, Katerina. "Eisenstein's Two Projects for a Film about Moscow." *Modern Language Review* 101 (2006): 184–200.

Clark, Martin. *Modern Italy 1871–1995*. London: Longman, 1996.

Clowes, Edith. *Russia on the Edge: Imagined Geographies and Post-Soviet Identities.* Ithaca, NY: Cornell University Press, 2011.

Clowes, Edith, Gisela Erbslöh, and Ani Kokobobo, eds. *Russia's Regional Identities: The Power of the Provinces.* New York, NY: Routledge, 2018.

Confino, Alon. *The Nation as a Local Metaphor: Württemberg, Imperial Germany, and National Memory, 1871–1918.* Chapel Hill: University of North Carolina Press, 1997.

Corney, Frederick C. *Telling October: Memory and the Making of the Bolshevik Revolution.* Ithaca; London: Cornell University Press, 2004.

Cothren, Larry. *Outcast Visionary: Yurii Pavlovich Spegal'skii and the Reconstruction of Pskov.* Interweave Australia, 2017.

Danilina, Natalia. "The Zapovedniks of Russia." *The George Wright Forum* 18, no. 1 (2001): 48–55.

Davies, Robert William. *Soviet History in the Yeltsin era.* Basingstoke: Macmillan, 1997.

Diefendorf, Jeffry M. *In the Wake of War: The Reconstruction of German Cities after World War II.* Oxford: Oxford University Press, 1993.

Dobson, Miriam, and Benjamin Ziemann, eds. *Reading Primary Sources of Texts from Nineteenth and Twentieth Century History.* London: Routledge, 2008.

Donovan, Victoria. "'How Well Do You Know Your Krai?': The Kraevedenie Revival and Patriotic Politics in Late-Khrushchev Era Russia." *Slavic Review* 74, no. 3 (Fall 2015): 464–483.

——. "The 'Old New Russian Town': Modernization and Architectural Preservation in Russia's Historic North West, 1961–1982." *Slavonica* 19, no. 1 (April 1, 2013): 18–35.

Dovlatov, Sergei. *Zapovednik.* Ann Arbor, MI: Ermitazh, 1983.

Due Enstad, Johannes. "Prayers and Patriotism in Nazi-Occupied Russia: The Pskov Orthodox Mission and Religious Revival, 1941–1944." *Slavonic and East European Review* 94, no. 3 (July 2016): 468–496.

Dunlop, John B. *The Faces of Contemporary Russian Nationalism.* Princeton, NJ: Princeton University Press, 1983.

——. *The New Russian Nationalism.* New York: Praeger, 1985.

Dunnage, Jonathan. *Twentieth Century Italy: A Social History.* London: Pearson Education Limited, 2002.

Elfimov, Alexei. *Russian Intellectual Culture in Transition: The Future in the Past.* New Brunswick: Transaction Publishers, 2003.

Etkind, Alexander. *Internal Colonization: Russia's Imperial Experience.* Cambridge, MA: Polity, 2011.

Evtuhov, Catherine. *Portrait of a Russian Province: Economy, Society, and Civilization in Nineteenth-Century Nizhnii Novgorod.* Pittsburgh: University of Pittsburgh Press, 2011.

Faraldo, José M. "Medieval Socialist Artifacts: Architecture and Discourses of National Identity in Provincial Poland, 1945–1960." *Nationalities Papers* 29, no. 4 (2001): 606–632.

Fekhner, M. V. *Arkhitektura gorodov SSSR: Vologda.* Moscow: Gosudarstvennoe izdatel'stvo literatury po stroitel'stvu, arkhitekture i stroitel'nym materialam, 1958.

Filimonov, A. V. *Podniatyi iz ruin: Poslevoennoe vosstanovlenie i razvitie Pskova (1944– nachalo 1950 gg.).* Pskov: Pskovskaia oblastnaia tipografiia, 2008.

Finkelstein, Sidney Walter. *Composer and Nation: The Folk Heritage in Music.* London: Lawrence & Wishart, 1960.

Fitzpatrick, Sheila. "Revisionism in Soviet History." *History and Theory: Studies in Philosophy of History* 46, no. 4 (December 2007): 77–91.

Forty, Adrian, and Susanne Küchler, eds. *The Art of Forgetting.* Oxford: Berg, 1999.

Fritzsche, Peter. *Stranded in the Present: Modern Time and the Melancholy of History.* London: Harvard University Press, 2004.

Fürst, Juliane. *Stalin's Last Generation: Soviet Post-War Youth and The Emergence of Mature Socialism.* Oxford: Oxford University Press, 2010.

Gillespie, David. *Valentin Rasputin and Soviet Russian Village Prose.* London: Modern Humanities Research Association, 1986.

Gippenreiter, V., E. Gordienko, and S. Iamshchikov. *Novgorod (Fotoal'bom).* Moscow: Planeta, 1976.

Gleason, Abbot, Peter Kenez, and Richard Stites. *Bolshevik Culture: Experiment and Order in the Russian Revolution*. Bloomington, IN: Indiana University Press, 1989.

Gololobov, I., H. Pilkington, and Y. B. Steinholt. *Punk in Russia: Cultural Mutation from the "Useless" to the "Moronic."* London: Routledge, 2014.

Golubev, Alexey. "'A Wonderful Song of Wood': Heritage Architecture of North Russia and the Soviet Quest for Historical Authenticity." *Rethinking Marxism* 29, no. 1 (2017): 142–172.

Golubeva, I. B., V. D. Sarab'ianov. *Sobor Rozhdestva bogoroditsy Snetogorskogo monastyria*. Moscow: "Severnyi palomnik," 2002.

Gor'kii, Maksim [Maxim Gorky]. "Vozzvanie o sokhranenii proizvedenii iskusstva." *Rech'*, March 8, 1917.

Gorsuch, Anne E. "'There's No Place like Home': Soviet Tourism in Late Stalinism." *Slavic Review* 62, no. 4 (2003): 760–785.

Grabar, Igor. "The Restoration of Russian Architectural Monuments." *American Slavic and East European Review* 4, nos. 1–2 (1945): 182–184.

Grant, Bruce. "New Moscow Monuments, or, States of Innocence." *American Ethnologist* 28, no. 2 (2001): 332–362.

Griffiths, Edmund, *Aleksandr Prokhanov and Post-Soviet Esotericism*. Stuttgart: ibidem Press, 2017.

Halfin, Igal. *From Darkness to Light: Class, Consciousness, and Salvation in Revolutionary Russia*. Pittsburgh: University of Pittsburgh Press, 2000.

———, ed. *Language and Revolution: Making Modern Political Identities*. London: Frank Cass, 2002.

Hirsch, Marianne. "The Generation of Postmemory." *Poetics Today* 29, no. 1 (2008): 103–128.

Hosking, Geoffrey. *Beyond Socialist Realism: Soviet Fiction Since Ivan Denisovich*. London: Elek, 1980.

———. *The Awakening of the Soviet Union*. Cambridge, MA: Harvard University Press, 1991.

Hosking, Geoffrey, and Vasilii Belov. "Vasilii Belov—Chronicler of the Soviet Village." *Russian Review* 34, no. 2 (April 1975): 165–185.

Hunter, Michael, ed. *Preserving the Past: The Rise of Heritage in Modern Britain*. Stroud, Gloucestershire: Alan Sutton Publishing Limited, 1996.

Hutchings, Stephen. "V-Day: The (De-)construction of Nationhood on Russian TV." *Art Margins* [online]. August 14, 2009. http://www.artmargins.com/index.php/8-archive/489-v-day-the-de-construction-of-nationhood-on-russian-tv-.

Ianin, V. L. *Novgorodskie posadniki*. Moscow: Izd-vo Moskovskogo universiteta, 1962.

Iashin, Aleksandr. "Vologodskaia svad'ba." *Novyi mir* 12 (1962): 3–26.

Iun'ev, I. S. *Kraevedenie i turizm*. Moscow, 1974.

Ivanov, E. P., ed. *Pskovskii krai v istorii Rossii*. Pskov: Izd-vo Pskov. obl. in-ta povysheniia kvalifikatsii rabotnikov obrazovaniia, 2000.

Johnson, Emily D. *How St Petersburg Learned to Study Itself: The Russian Idea of Kraevedenie*. University Park, PA: Pennsylvania State University Press, 2006.

Johnson, Richard, et al., eds. *Making Histories: Studies in Historical Writing and Politics*. Minneapolis, MN: University of Minnesota Press, 1982.

Jones, Polly. *Myth, Memory, Trauma: Rethinking the Stalinist Past in the Soviet Union, 1953–1970*. New Haven: Yale University Press, 2013.

Karamzin, N. M. *Istoriia gosudarstva rossiiskogo v dvenadtsati tomakh*. Vol. 9, ch. 5. Moscow: OLMA-Press, 2003.

Karger, M. K. *Novgorod Velikii*. Leningrad: Iskusstvo, 1961.

Kaulen, Maria. *Muzeefikatsiia istoriko-kul'turnogo naslediia Rossii*. Moscow: Eterna, 2012.

Kelly, Catriona. "'Ispravliat'' li istoriiu? Spory ob okhrane pamiatnikov v Leningrade 1960–1970-kh godov." *Neprikosnovennyi zapas* 2, no. 64 (2009). http://www.intelros.ru/readroom/nz/nz_64/3858-ispravljat-li-istoriju-spory-ob-okhrane.html.

———. *Remembering St Petersburg*. Triton Press, 2014.

———. *Socialist Churches: Radical Secularization and the Preservation of the Past in Petrograd and Leningrad, 1918–1988*. DeKalb, IL: Northern Illinois University Press, 2016.

————. *St Petersburg: Shadows of the Past*. New Haven: Yale University Press, 2014.

————. "The Shock of the Old: Architectural Preservation in Soviet Russia." In *Nations and Nationalism* 24, no. 1 (2018): 88–109.

Kirschenbaum, Lisa A. *The Legacy of the Siege of Leningrad, 1941–1995: Myth, Memories, and Monuments*. Cambridge: Cambridge University Press, 2006.

Knabe, G. S., ed. *Moskva i "moskovskii tekst" russkoi kul'tury: Sbornik statei*. Moscow: Rossiiskii gosudarstvennyi gumanitarnyi universitet, 1998.

Knox, Zoe. *Russian Society and the Orthodox Church: Religion in Russia after Communism*. Oxford: Routledge, 2005.

Kolotilova, S. I. and I. P. Shaskol'skii. *Pskov: Ocherki istorii. Sbornik*. Leningrad: Lenizdat, 1971.

Kovalev, B. N. *Povsednevnaia zhizn' naseleniia Rossii v period natsistskoi okkupatsii*. Moscow: Molodaia gvardiia, 2011.

Kozlov, Denis. "The Historical Turn in Late Soviet Culture: Retrospectivism, Factography, Doubt, 1953–91." *Kritika: Explorations in Russian and Eurasian History* 2, no. 3 (2001): 577–600.

Krasnorech'ev, L. E. *Narodnoe dereviannoe zodchestvo Novgorodchiny*. Novgorod: Novgorod muzei-zapovednik, 2012.

Kushnir, M. I. *Arkhitektura Novgoroda*. Leningrad: Lenizdat, 1982.

————. *Novgorod*. Leningrad: Stroiizdat, 1967.

Kuz'menko, M. A. et al., eds. *Muzeia divnoe prostranstvo: Khram pamiati, nauk i muz*. Pskov: Pskovskii gosudarstvennyi ob"edinennyi istoriko-arkhitekturnyi i khudozhestvennyi muzei-zapovednik, 2002.

Lagunin, I. I. *Pskov. Izborsk*. Leningrad: Lenizdat, 1984.

Lambourne, Nicola. *War Damage in Western Europe: The Destruction of Historic Monuments During the Second World War*. Edinburgh: Edinburgh University Press, 2001.

Laskovskii, V. P. *Putevoditel' po Novgorodu: Sofiiskaia storona*. St. Petersburg: Alabord, 2007.

————. *Putevoditel' po Novgorodu: Torgovaia storona*. St. Petersburg: Alabord, 2007.

Laruelle, Marlène. *In the Name of the Nation: Nationalism and Politics in Contemporary Russia*. New York: Palgrave Macmillan, 2009.

————, ed. *Russian Nationalism and the National Reassertion of Russia*. London: Routledge, 2009.

Lawless, Elaine J. *Holy Women, Wholly Women: Sharing Ministries of Wholeness through Life Stories and Reciprocal Ethnography*. Philadelphia: University of Pennsylvania Press, 1993.

Lebedev, Evgenii. *Iubilei—dovmontovskii i pushkinskii*. Pskov: tip. Gub. zemstva, 1899.

Lenger, Friedrich, ed. *Towards an Urban Nation: Germany since 1780*. Oxford: Berg, 2002.

Leshchinskii, Ivan. "Novye Liudi." *Nauchno -prosvetitel'skii zhurnal Skepsis*, August 2008. http://scepsis. ru/library/id—2149.html.

le Torrivellec, Xavier. "Entre steppes et stèles. Territoires et identités au Bachkortostan." *Cahiers du monde russe* 41, no. 2/3 (April–September 2000): 369–400.

Likhachev, D. S. "Chetvertoe izmerenie." *Literaturnaia gazeta*, June 10, 1965.

————. "Iz letnikh puteshestvii." *Literaturnaia gazeta*, September 14, 1965.

————. *Novgorodskie letopisnye svody XII v*. Avtoref. Diss. kand. Filol. Nauk. Isvestiia AN SSSR. Otd. literatury i iazyka. 1944.

————. *Novgorod Velikii: Ocherk istorii kul'tury Novgoroda XI–XII vv*. Moscow: Izdatel'stvo Sovetskaia Rossiia, 1959.

————. "Novgorod Velikii, rovesnik russkoi istorii." *Sovetskii soiuz*, 5 (1966): 37–41.

————. "Pamiat' istorii sviashchenna." *Ogonek* 29 (July 1982): 18–20.

————. *Russkaia kul'tura*. Moscow: Iskusstvo, 2000.

————. *Zemlia rodnaia: Kniga dlia uchashchikhsia*. Moscow: "Prosveshchenie," 1983.

Lipovetsky, Mark. "Anything Goes: How the Russian News Became a Postmodern Game Without Rules." *The Calvert Journal*, March 10, 2015. http://calvertjournal.com/comment/show/3736/political-steampunk-postmodern-game-mark-lipovetsky.

Livers, Keith. "The Tower or the Labyrinth: Conspiracy, Occult, and Empire-Nostalgia in the Work of Viktor Pelevin and Aleksandr Prokhanov." *The Russian Review* 69, no. 3 (2010): 477–503.

Loskutova, M. V., ed. *Pamiat' o blokade: Svidetel'stva ochevidtsev i istoricheskoe sozdanie obshchestva. Materialy i issledovaniia.* Moscow: Novoe izdatel'stvo, 2006.

Lounsbery, Anne. "'No, this is not the provinces!' Provincialism, Authenticity, and Russianness in Gogol's Day." *The Russian Review* 64, no. 2 (2005): 259–280.

———. "'To Moscow, I Beg You!': Chekhov's Vision of the Russian Provinces." *Toronto Slavic Quarterly* 9 (2004). http://sites.utoronto.ca/tsq/09/lounsbery09.shtml.

Lovell, Stephen, *Destination in Doubt: Russia Since 1989.* New York: Zed Books, 2006.

———. *The Shadow of War: Russia and the USSR, 1941 to the Present.* Oxford: Wiley-Blackwell, 2010.

Lunacharsky, Anatoly. "Krasota proshlogo." *Krasnaia gazeta,* August 5–6, 1926.

Maddox, Steven, *Saving Stalin's Imperial City: Historic Preservation in Leningrad, 1930–1950.* Bloomington, IN: Indiana University Press, 2015.

Maksakova, L. V. *Spasenie kul'turnykh tsennostei v gody Velikoi Otechestvennoi voiny.* Moscow: Nauka, 1990.

Malkov, V. M. *Vologda.* Vologda: Vologodskoe knizhnoe izdatel'stvo, 1964.

Merridale, Catherine. *Red Fortress: The Secret Heart of Russia's History.* London: Allen Lane, 2013.

Mil'chik, M. I., ed. *Arkhitekturnoe nasledie Velikogo Novgoroda i Novgorodskoi oblasti.* St. Petersburg: Spas. Fond sodeistviia restavratsii pamiatnikov istorii i kul'tury "Liki Rossii," 2008.

Mitrokhin, Nikolai. *Russkaia partiia: Dvizhenie russkikh natsionalistov v SSSR 1953–1985 gody.* Moscow: Novoe literaturnoe obozrenie, 2003.

Nekrasov, Iu. K., ed. *Vologda v minuvshem tysiacheletii: Ocherki istorii goroda,* 2nd ed. Vologda: Drevnosti Severa, 2006.

Nora, Pierre. "Between Memory and History: Les Lieux de Memoire." *Representations* 26 (1989), 7–24.

Oboznyi, K. P. *Istoriia Pskovskoi Pravoslavnoi Missii 1941–1944 gg.* Moscow: Izd. Krutitskogo podvoria, 2008.

Okhrana pamiatnikov istorii i kul'tury: Sbornik dokumentov. Moscow: Sovetskaia Rossiia, 1973.

Opolovnikov, Alexander. *Kizhi.* 2nd ed. Moscow: Stroiizdat, 1976.

———. *The Wooden Architecture of Russia: Houses, Fortifications, Churches.* London: Thames and Hudson, 1989.

Oushakine, Serguei A. *The Patriotism of Despair: Nation, War, and Loss in Russia.* Ithaca: Cornell University Press, 2009.

———. "Remembering in Public: On the Affective Management of History." *Ab Imperio* 1 (2013): 269–302.

Ovechkin, Evgenii. "Iurii Spegal'skii – arkhitektor, restavrator, verkholaz." *Russkoe geograficheskoe obshchestvo 'Klub Al'pinistov 'Sankt-Peterburg.'* October 1, 2018. http://www.alpklubspb.ru/ass/a476.htm.

Pallot, Judith. "Rural Depopulation and the Restoration of the Russian Village under Gorbachev." *Soviet Studies* 42, no. 4 (1990): 655–674.

Parmenov, V. D. *Portret na fone Vologdy. Vospominaniia, razmyshleniia, dokumenty.* Vologodskaia gorodskaia duma i administratsiia goroda Vologdy: Vologda, 2007.

Parthé, Kathleen. *Russian Village Prose: The Radiant Past.* Princeton, NJ: Princeton University Press, 1992.

Pesmen, Dale. *Russia and Soul: An Exploration.* Ithaca: Cornell University Press, 2000.

Petro, Nicolai N. *Crafting Democracy: How Novgorod Has Coped with Rapid Social Change.* New York: Cornell University Press, 2004.

Pomerantsev, Peter. *Nothing is True and Everything is Possible: Adventures in Modern Russia.* London: Faber and Faber, 2015.

Popov, V., L. Tyntareva, and S. Troianovskii. "Nachalo: Iz khaosa ruin." *Novgorod* 6 (1995): 1–10.

Portelli, Alessandro. *The Battle of Valle Giulia: Oral History and the Art of Dialogue.* Madison: The University of Wisconsin Press, 1997.

Poslevoennoe vosstanovlenie pamiatnikov: Teoriia i praktika XX veka. St. Petersburg: IPK "Beresta," 2014.

Prokhanov, Aleksandr. *Kholm: Roman.* Moscow: Vagrius, 2008.

——. "Ne kniaz' Vladimir vybral, eto pravoslavie izbralo ego i Rus.'" *Izborskii klub,* http://www.dynacon.ru/content/articles/7282/.

——. "Sviashchennyi kholm: Replika Aleksandra Prokhanova." *Vesti.ru.* October 3, 2014. http://www.vesti.ru/doc.html?id=2018082.

Pskovskaia guberniia. Izbrannye stranitsy, 2000–2005. Pskov: ANO "Svobodnoe slovo," 2005.

Qualls, Karl D. *From Ruins to Reconstruction: Urban Identity in Soviet Sevastopol after World War II.* Ithaca: Cornell University Press, 2009.

Ries, Nancy. *Russian Talk: Culture and Conversation During Perestroika.* Cornell University Press: Ithaca, 1997.

Russkie pisateli, XX vek. Biobibliograficheskii slovar', vol 2. Moscow: Prosveshchenie, 1998.

Sakwa, Richard. *Gorbachev and His Reforms, 1985–1990.* New York: Philip Allan, 1990.

Samuel, Raphael. *Theatres of Memory: Past and Present in Contemporary Culture.* Rev. ed. London: Verso, 2012.

Sazonov, A. I. *Takoi gorod v Rossii odin.* Vologda: PF "Poligrafist," 1993.

Sazonov, A. I., and E. A. Starikov. *Moia Vologda: Gorod nashei pamiati.* Vologda: Drevnosti Severa, 2007.

Schönle, Andreas. *Architecture of Oblivion: Ruins and Historical Consciousness in Modern Russia.* DeKalb, IL: Northern Illinois University Press, 2011.

Semanov, S. N. *Pamiatnik "Tysiacheletie Rossii:" Fotoal'bom.* Moscow: Sovetskaia Rossiia, 1974.

Semenov, A. I. *Istoricheskie pamiatniki Novgorodskogo kremlia.* Novgorod: Novgorodskaia pravda, 1959.

——. *Novgorodskii kreml'.* Novgorod: Novgorodskaia pravda, 1964.

Shalamov, Varlam. "Chetvertaia Vologda." In *Sobranie sochenenii v chetyrekh tomakh.* Moscow: Khudozhestvennaia literatura "Vagrius," 1998.

Shchenkov, A. S., ed. *Pamiatniki arkhitektury v Sovetskom soiuze. Ocherki istorii arkhitekturnoi restavratsii.* Moscow: Pamiatniki istoricheskoi mysli, 2004.

Shchusev, A. V. "Pamiatniki zodchestva v sotsialisticheskoi rekonstruktsii goroda." *Arkhitektura i stroitel'stvo* 12 (1948), 3–7.

——. "Proekt vosstanovleniia Novgoroda." Presented at the consortium "Proekty planirovaniia vosstanavlivaemykh gorodov" on July 14, 1944. Published in *Voprosy vostanovitel'nogo stroitel'stva,* 30–31. Moscow, 1945.

Shkarovskii, M. *Tserkov' zovet k zashchite Rodiny: Religioznaia zhizn' Leningrada i Severo-Zapada v gody Velikoi Otechestvennoi voiny.* St. Petersburg: Izd. "Satis" Derzhava, 2005.

Shulakov, T. V. *Khramy Pskova. Arkhitekturnyi putevoditel'.* Pskov, Pskovskii Volnyi institut, 2005.

Smith, Kathleen E. "An Old Cathedral for a New Russia: The Symbolic Politics of the Reconstituted Church of Christ the Saviour." *Religion, State and Society: The Keston Journal* 25, no. 2 (1997): 163–175.

Smith, Steve. "Contentious Heritage: the Preservation of Churches and Temples in Communist and Post-Communist Russia and China." In *Heritage in the Modern World,* edited by Paul Betts and Corey Ross, 178–213. *Past and Present Supplement* 10 (2015).

Smith-Peter, Susan. "How to Write a Region: Local and Regional Historiography." *Kritika: Explorations in Russian and Eurasian History* 5, no. 3 (2004): 527–542.

Soloukhin, Vladimir. "Chernye doski." *Moskva* 1 (1969): 129–187.

——. *Vladimirskie proselki.* Moscow: Gosudarstvennoe izdatel'stvo khudozhestvennoi literatury, 1958.

Spegal'skii, Iu. P. *Po Pskovu XVII veka: Al'bom risunkov.* Leningrad: Lenizdat, 1974.

——. *Pskov.* Khudozhestvennye pamiatniki. Leningrad: Iskusstvo, 1963.

——. *Pskov.* 2nd ed. Arkhitekturno-khudozhestvennye pamiatniki XII-XVII vv. Leningrad: Iskusstvo, 1978.

——. "Rekonstruktsiia tserkvi Nikoly so Usokhy v Pskove." *Pamiatniki kul'tury. Issledovanie i restavratsiia* 3 (1961).

Stacey, Judith. "Can There Be a Feminist Ethnography?" In *Women's Words: The Feminist Practice of Oral History,* edited by Sherna Gluck Berger and Daphne Patai, 111–121. London: Routledge, 1991.

Stroev, V. M. *Zhivopisnyi Karamzin, ili Russkaia istoriia v kartinakh.* St. Petersburg: Andrei Prevo, 1836–1844.

Suny, Ronald Grigor. *The Revenge of the Past: Nationalism, Revolution and the Collapse of the Soviet Union.* Stanford: Stanford University Press, 1993.

Suslov, Mikhail, and Per-Arne Bodin, eds. *The Post-Soviet Politics of Utopia: Language, Fiction and Fantasy in Russia.* London: I.B. Tauris, 2018.

Suzdalev, V. E. *Kolomenskoe: Gosudarstvennyi muzei-zapovednik XVI-XIX vekov. Putevoditel'.* Moscow: Moskovskii rabochii, 1986.

Sviatoi Dovmont-Timofei, kniaz' Pskovskii: (K 600-letiiu blazhennoi konchiny ego). Pskov: tip. Gub. zemstva, 1899.

Sviatyi blagovernyi kniaz' Dovmont Pskovskii: V pamiat' shestistoletiia so dnia ego konchiny, 1299–1899. St. Petersburg: tipo-lit. R. Golike, 1899.

Takahashi, Sanami. "Church or Museum? The Role of State Museums in Conserving Church Buildings, 1965–85." *Journal of Church and State* 3 (2009): 502–517.

Taylor, Brandon. *Art and Literature under the Bolsheviks.* Concord, MA: Pluto Press, 1991–1992.

Thum, Gregor. *Uprooted: How Breslau Became Wrocław during the Century of Expulsions,* trans. Tom Lampert, Allison Brown, W. Martin, and Jasper Tilbury. Princeton, NJ: Princeton University Press, 2011.

Tikhomirov, M. N., ed. *Novgorod k 1100-letiiu goroda: Sbornik statei.* Moscow: Nauka, 1964.

Titarenko, Larissa, and Anna Shirokanova. "The Phenomenon of Minsk: The City Space and the Cultural Narrative." *Limes: Borderland Studies* 4, no. 1 (2011): 21–35.

Tolstoy, Vladimir, et al. *Street Art of the Revolution: Festivals and Celebrations in Russia, 1918–1933.* London: Thames and Hudson, 1990.

Toporov, Vladimir. *Mif. Ritual. Simvol. Obraz: Issledovaniia v oblasti mifopoeticheskogo.* Moscow: Progress, 1995.

Tsvetaeva, Marina. *A Captive Spirit: Selected Prose,* trans. by J. Marin King. London: Virago, 1983.

Tumarkin, Nina. *The Living and the Dead: The Rise and Fall of the Cult of World War II in Russia.* New York: Basic Books, 1994.

Urry, John. *The Tourist Gaze.* London: Sage, 2002.

Verkhovskii, A., and F. Kozhevnikova, eds. *Radikal'nyi russkii natsionalizm.* Moscow, Tsentr "Sova," 2009.

Von Geldern, James. *Bolshevik Festivals, 1917–1920.* Berkeley: University of California Press, 1993.

Wolfreys, Julian. *Readings: Acts of Close Reading in Literary Theory.* Edinburgh: Edinburgh University Press, 2000.

Yamshchikov, Savely et al., eds. *Pskov, Art Treasures and Architectural Monuments.* Leningrad: Aurora Art Publishers, 1978.

Young, Michael, and Peter Willmott. *Family and Kinship in East London.* London: Routledge and Kegan Paul, 1986.

Zabello, S., V. Ivanov, and P. Maksimov. *Russkoe dereviannoe zodchestvo.* Moscow: Izd-vo Akademiia arkhitektury SSSR, 1941.

Zaionts, L. O., ed. *Geopanorama russkoi kul'tury: Provintsiia i ee lokal'nye teksty.* Moscow: Iazyki slavianskoi kul'tury, 2004.

Zasodimskii, P., *Lesnoe tsarstvo.* Moscow: Izd-vo I.D. Sytinam 1908.

III. Websites

Andrei Turchak. Gubernator Pskovskoi oblasti: Voprosy i problemy, http://turchak.ru
Velikii Novgorod—rodina Rossii, http://1150.novgorod.ru
Izborskii klub, http://www.izborsk-club.ru
Rossiiskii fond kul'tury, http://fond.culture.ru
Vabla.ru, http://wobla.ru/forum/Default.aspx?postid=214558

IV. Unpublished sources in English and Russian

i) MA AND PhD DISSERTATIONS

Fein, Julia. "Cultural Curators and Provincial Publics: Local Museums and Social Change in Siberia, 1887–1941." PhD diss., University of Chicago, August 2012.

Kosenkova, Iu. L. "Sovetskii gorod 1940-kh—pervoi poloviny 1950-kh godov. Ot tvorcheskikh poiskov k praktike stroitel'stva." PhD diss., Rossiiskaia akademiia arkhitektury i stroitel'nykh nauk nauchno-issledovatel'skii institut teorii arkhitektury i gradostroitel'stva, Moscow, 2000.

Tsymbalyuk, Darya. "Agency, Meaning-Making and Displacement in Two Stories from Donbas, Ukraine." MA thesis, University of St Andrews, 2017.

ii) CONFERENCE PAPERS

Brouwer, Sander. "Centre and Borders in Dugin and Prokhanov." Paper presented at the interdisciplinary workshop "Russia on Edge: Reclaiming the Periphery in Contemporary Russian Culture." December 11–12, 2009. CRASSH, University of Cambridge.

MacFadyen, David. "Russian Popular Music and Song Today. Sounds beyond the Mainstream." Unpublished conference paper presented at the Dashkova Centre seminar series, Edinburgh, September 2015.

Melnikova, Ekaterina. "Celebrating Locality in an Era of Territorial Branding: Rituals and Symbols of Local Solidarity after 1992." Unpublished conference paper presented at ASEEES Annual Convention in San Antonio, November 2014.

Parts, Lyudimila. "How is Voronezh not Paris? Branding in the Russian Provinces." Unpublished conference paper presented at the conference "Centrifugal Forces: Reading Russia's Regional Identities." March 26–8, 2015.

"Sozdanie Komiteta po delam arkhitektury pri SNK SSSR i ego rol' v organizatsii rabot po poslevoennomu vosstanovleniiu pamiatnikov arkhitektury." Paper presented at the conference "Poslevoennoe vosstanovlenie pamiatnikov: Teoriia i praktika XX veka." St. Petersburg, December 4–5, 2014.

NOTES

Notes to Introduction

1. Iu. P. Spegal'skii, *Pskov* (Leningrad: Iskusstvo, 1978), 11.

2. D. S. Likhachev, "Kraevedenie kak nauka i kak deiatel'nost'" (Vsesoiuznaia konferentsiia po istoricheskomu kraevedeniiu, Poltava, 1987), *Russkaia kul'tura* (Moscow: Iskusstvo, 2000), 162.

3. Alon Confino, *The Nation as a Local Metaphor: Württemberg, Imperial Germany, and National Memory, 1871–1918* (London: UNC Press Books, 1997), 4.

4. Ibid., 8.

5. Ibid.

6. For the most authoritative evaluation of this period, see Valentin Ianin, *Novgorodskie posadniki* (Moscow: Izd-vo Moskovskogo universiteta, 1962).

7. See, for example, the publications released in 1899 to commemorate the 600th anniversary of King Daumantas's death: *Sviatoi Dovmont-Timofei, kniaz' Pskovskii: (K 600-letiiu blazhennoi konchiny ego)* (Pskov: tip. Gub. zemstva, 1899); Evgenii Lebedev, *Iubilei – dovmontovskii i pushkinskii* (Pskov: tip. Gub. zemstva, 1899); *Sviatyi blagovernyi kniaz' Dovmont Pskovskii: V pamiat' shestistoletiia so dnia ego konchiny, 1299–1899* (St. Petersburg: tipo-lit. R. Golike, 1899).

8. Illustrations by B. A. Chorikov in V. M. Stroev, *Zhivopisnyi Karamzin, ili Russkaia istoriia v kartinakh* (St. Petersburg: Andrei Prevo, 1836–1844).

9. N. M. Karamzin, *Istoriia gosudarstva rossiiskogo v dvenadtsati tomakh*, vol. 9, ch. 5 (Moscow: OLMA-PRESS, 2003), 509 (translation my own).

10. Geoffrey A. Hosking and Vasilii Belov, "Vasilii Belov—Chronicler of the Soviet Village," *Russian Review* 34, no. 2 (April 1975): 165–185 (166).

11. I discuss the "Vologda School" of Village Prose writing in more detail in chapter 3.

12. See, in particular, Sergei Abashin's work on the reinvention of the past in Central Asia: *Natsionalizmy v Srednei Azii: V poiskakh identichnosti* (St. Petersburg: Ateleiia, 2007); and Xavier le Torrivellec's work on the Volga region: "Entre steppes et stèles. Territoires et identités au Bachkortostan," *Cahiers du monde russe* 41, no. 2/3 (April–September 2000): 369–400.

13. There is a substantial secondary literature on Soviet preservation and preservationist legislation, including: Steve Smith, "Contentious Heritage: The Preservation of Churches and Temples in Communist and Post-Communist Russia and China," in *Heritage in the Modern World*, ed. Paul Betts and Corey Ross, *Past and Present Supplement* 10 (2015), 178–213; and Catriona Kelly, "The Shock of the Old: Architectural Preservation in Soviet Russia," *Nations and Nationalism* 24, no. 1 (2018): 88–109. The most comprehensive Russian-language guide to developments in architectural preservation in the Soviet period is *Pamiatniki arkhitektury v Sovetskom soiuze. Ocherki istorii arkhitekturnoi restavratsii*, ed. A. S. Shchenkov (Moscow: Pamiatniki istoricheskoi mysli, 2004).

14. See, for example, Maksim Gor'kii, "Vozzvanie o sokhranenii proizvedenii iskusstva," *Rech'*, March 8, 1917; and Anatoly Lunacharsky's preservationist treatises, "Krasota proshlogo," *Krasnaia gazeta*, August 5–6, 1926.

15. Richard Stites has discussed the tension between iconoclastic and preservationist impulses during and immediately after the 1917 revolution in his chapter "Iconoclastic Currents in the Russian Revolution: Destroying and Preserving the Past," in *Bolshevik Culture: Experiment and Order in the*

Russian Revolution, ed. Abbot Gleason, Peter Kenez and Richard Stites (Bloomington, IN: Indiana University Press, 1989), 55–56.

16. See "Churches in the Socialist City: Crash Industrialization, Rational Atheism, and City Planning, 1929–1940," in Catriona Kelly, *Socialist Churches: Radical Secularization and the Preservation of the Past in Petrograd and Leningrad, 1918–1988* (DeKalb: Northern Illinois University Press, 2016), 95–139.

17. For complete lists of the historic churches destroyed in Novgorod, Pskov, and Vologda in the Soviet period, see https://ru.wikipedia.org/wiki/Список_храмов_Новгород; https://ru.wikipedia.org/wiki/Список_храмов_Псков; https://ru.wikipedia.org/wiki/Список_храмов_Вологды.

18. For the post-war legislation on the preservation of cultural monuments, see *Okhrana pamiatnikov istorii i kul'tury: Sbornik dokumentov* (Moscow: Sovetskaia Rossiia, 1973), 104–110.

19. See, for example, Stephen Bittner's account of architectural preservation in Moscow during these years: *The Many Lives of Khrushchev's Thaw: Experience and Memory in Moscow's Arbat* (Ithaca: Cornell University Press, 2008).

20. M. P. Pavlova, "Sostoianie okhrana pamiatnikov arkhitektury i organizatsii restavratsionnykh rabot v 1940-e–1960-e gg.," in *Pamiatniki arkhitektury v Sovetskom soiuze. Ocherki istorii arkhitekturnoi restavratsii*, ed. A. S. Shchenkov (Moscow: Pamiatniki istoricheskoi mysli, 2004), 228–297 (287).

21. GANO, f. R-3994, op. 5–66, d. 317 (Correspondence between the Novgorod oblispolkom and the restoration workshop on the subject of fulfilling the plan for the restoration of architectural monuments in 1962), 31.

22. Catriona Kelly, "'Ispravliat' li istoriiu? Sbory ob okhrane pamiatnikov v Leningrade 1962–1990," *Neprikosnovennyi zapas* 2, no. 64 (2009), http://magazines.russ.ru/nz/2009/2/kk7.html.

23. See, for example, D. S. Likhachev, "Pamiat' istorii sviashchenna," *Ogonek* 29 (July 17, 1982): 18–20.

24. See, for example, Yitzhak Brudny, *Reinventing Russia: Russian Nationalism and the Soviet State, 1953–1991* (Cambridge MA: Harvard University Press, 1998); John B. Dunlop, *The Faces of Contemporary Russian Nationalism* (Princeton, NJ: Princeton University Press, 1983); and Nikolai Mitrokhin, *Russkaia partiia: Dvizhenie russkikh natsionalistov v SSSR 1953–1985 gody* (Moscow: Novoe literaturnoe obozrenie, 2003).

25. For related remarks about the exaggeration of links between architectural preservation and Russian chauvinism in scholarly commentary, see Kelly, "The Shock of the Old."

26. For an account of kraevedenie and its evolution in the early Soviet period, see Emily Johnson, *How St Petersburg Learned to Study Itself: The Russia Idea of Kraevedenie* (University Park, PA: Pennsylvania State University Press, 2006).

27. Stephen Lovell, *The Shadow of War: Russia and the USSR, 1941 to the Present* (Oxford: Wiley-Blackwell, 2010), 178.

28. Edith Clowes, *Russia on the Edge: Imagined Geographies and Post-Soviet Identities* (Ithaca, NY: Cornell University Press, 2011), 6.

29. Clowes, *Russia on the Edge*, chapters 2 and 5.

30. Catherine Evtuhov, *Portrait of a Russian Province: Economy, Society, and Civilization in Nineteenth-Century Nizhnii Novgorod* (Pittsburg: University of Pittsburg Press, 2011), 6; on the provincialisms of the cultural capitals, see also Catriona Kelly, *St Petersburg: Shadows of the Past* (New Haven: Yale University Press), 94.

31. Evtuhov, *Portrait of a Russian Province*, 9.

32. Of relevance here are the many excellent Russian-language studies of regional and urban culture, beginning with Vladimir Toporov's seminal "Peterburg i 'Peterburgskii tekst russkoi literatury' (Vvedenie v temu)," in *Mif. Ritual. Simvol. Obraz: Issledovaniia v oblasti mifopoeticheskogo* (Moscow: Progress, 1995); other semiotic studies of urban culture published in recent years include *Moskva i "moskovskii tekst" russkoi kul'tury: Sbornik statei*, ed. G. S. Knabe (Moscow: Rossiiskii gosudarstvennyi gumanitarnyi universitet, 1998), and V. V. Abashev, *Perm' kak tekst: Perm' v russkoi kul'ture i literature XX veka* (Perm: Izd-vo Permskogo universiteta, 2000).

33. Homi K. Bhabha, *The Location of Culture* (London: Routledge, 2012).

34. Svetlana Alexievich, Nobel Lecture, December 7, 2015. Transcript available on the Nobel Prize website: https://www.nobelprize.org/nobel_prizes/literature/laureates/2015/alexievich-lecture_ en.html.

35. For an account of this movement by one of its most influential proponents, see Sheila Fitzpatrick, "Revisionism in Soviet History," *History and Theory: Studies in Philosophy of History* 46, no. 4 (December 2007): 77–91.

36. Evtuhov, *Portrait of a Russian Province*, 7.

37. Denis Kozlov, "The Historical Turn in Late Soviet Culture: Retrospectivism, Factography, Doubt, 1953–91," *Kritika: Explorations in Russian and Eurasian History* 2, no. 3 (2001): 577–600.

38. Susan Smith-Peter, "How to Write a Region: Local and Regional Historiography," *Kritika: Explorations in Russian and Eurasian History* 5, no. 3 (2004): 527–542.

39. Serguei Oushakine, *The Patriotism of Despair: Nation, War, and Loss in Russia* (Ithaca: Cornell University Press, 2009); *Soviet and Post-Soviet Identities*, ed. Mark Bassin and Catriona Kelly (Cambridge: Cambridge University Press, 2012); I. Gololobov, H. Pilkington, and Y. B. Steinholt, *Punk in Russia: Cultural Mutation from the "Useless" to the "Moronic"* (London: Routledge, 2014).

40. Italics are added. Evtuhov, *Portrait of a Russian Province*, 15.

41. Mark Lipovetsky, "The Strange Case of a Regional Cultural Revolution: Sverdlovsk in the Perestroika Years," in *Russia's Regional Identities: The Power of the Provinces*, ed. Edith W. Clowes, Gisela Erbslöh, Ani Kokobobo (London: Routledge, 2018).

42. David MacFadyen, "Russian Popular Music and Song Today. Sounds beyond the Mainstream," unpublished conference paper presented at the Dashkova Centre seminar series, Edinburgh, September 2015. The Far From Moscow project can be accessed here: http://www.farfrommoscow.com/.

43. A compelling analysis of this relationship is provided by Ronald G. Suny in his chapter "The Contradictions of Identity: Being Soviet and National in the USSR and After," in *Soviet and Post-Soviet Identities*, 17–36.

44. David Brandenberger, *National Bolshevism: Stalinist Mass Culture and the Formation of Modern Russian National Identity, 1931–1956* (Cambridge MA: Harvard University Press, 2002).

45. Brudny, *Reinventing Russia*.

46. Confino, *The Nation as a Local Metaphor*, 4.

47. "The Difference Between Patriotism and Nationalism," *Merriam-Webster*, https://www.merriam-webster.com/words-at-play/patriotism-vs-nationalism.

48. *Entsiklopediia gosudarstva i prava*, vol. 3 (Moscow, 1937), s.v. "Patriotizm," by P. Stuchka, 252–254, cited in David Brandenberger, "Proletarian Internationalism, 'Soviet Patriotism' and the Rise of Russocentric Etatism During the Stalinist 1930s," *Left History* 6, no. 5 (1999): 80–100 (84).

49. Karl Radek's article on "Soviet patriotism," published in *Pravda* in 1936, was influential in this regard. K. B. Radek, "Sovetskii patriotizm," *Pravda*, May 1, 1936, 6, cited in David Brandenberger, *Propaganda State in Crisis: Soviet Ideology, Indoctrination and Terror under Stalin, 1927–1941* (New Haven: Yale University Press, 2011), 106.

50. David Brandenberger, *National Bolshevism*, 4.

51. "Sovetskii patriotizm," *Pravda*, March 19, 1935, cited in Brandenberger, *National Bolshevism*, 9.

52. Ronald Grigor Suny, "The Contradictions of Identity," in Bassin and Kelly, *Soviet and Post-Soviet Identities*, 17–36 (26).

53. Brandenberger, *National Bolshevism*, chapter 9.

54. The phrase "supranational but Russified patriotism" is taken from Suny, "The Contradictions of Identity," in Bassin and Kelly, *Soviet and Post-Soviet Identities*, 27.

55. Victoria Donovan, "'How Well Do You Know Your Krai?': The Kraevedenie Revival and Patriotic Politics in Late-Khrushchev Era Russia," *Slavic Review* 74, no. 3 (Fall 2015): 464–483.

56. Ibid., 466.

57. For an overview of Khrushchev-era kraevedenie revival, see Emily Johnson, 178–182.

58. Donovan, "'How Well Do You Know Your Krai?'"

59. There is a vast literature dedicated to the state-sponsored revival of Russian national consciousness in the Brezhnev and late Soviet eras. See, for example, John B. Dunlop, *The Faces of Contemporary*

Russian Nationalism, and John B. Dunlop, *The New Russian Nationalism* (New York: Praeger, 1985); Mitrokhin, *Russkaia partiia.* Perhaps the most influential study of this topic and the source of the idea of Brezhnev-era "inclusionary politics," discussed in more detail below, is Yitzhak Brudny's *Reinventing Russia.*

60. See, in particular, Brudny, *Reinventing Russia,* chapters 3 and 4.

61. Mitrokhin, *Russkaia partiia.*

62. Marlène Laruelle, "Rethinking Russian Nationalism: Historical continuity, political diversity, and doctrinal fragmentation," in *Russian Nationalism and the National Reassertion of Russia,* ed. Marlène Laruelle (London: Routledge, 2009), 13–49 (18).

63. Suny, "The Contradictions of Identity," in Bassin and Kelly, *Soviet and Post-Soviet Identities,* 30.

64. See my discussion of these organizations and their limited appeal for preservationists in the Northwest in chapter 3.

65. Catriona Kelly and Mark Bassin, "Introduction: National Subjects," in *Soviet and Post-Soviet Identities,* 3–16, (4).

66. On the various manifestations of the Russian far right, see, for example, *Radikal'nyi russkii natsionalizm,* ed. A. Verkhovskii and F. Kozhevnikova (Moscow, Tsentr "Sova," 2009); Edmund Griffiths, *Aleksandr Prokhanov and Post-Soviet Esotericism* (Stuttgart: ibidem Press, 2017); and Edith Clowes, "Postmodernist Empire Meets Holy Rus': How Aleksandr Dugin Tried to Change the Eurasian Periphery into the Sacred Center of the World," in *Russia on the Edge,* 43–67.

67. Marlène Laruelle, "Rethinking Russian Nationalism," 24.

68. Ibid., 25.

69. Valerie Sperling, "Making the Public Patriotic: Militarism and Anti-Militarism in Russia," in Laruelle, *Russian Nationalism and the National Reassertion of Russia,* 218–245.

70. On the cultural memory of World War II in Putin's Russia, see, for example, Stephen Hutchings and Natalia Rulyova, "Commemorating the Past/Performing the Present: Television Coverage of the Second World War Victory Celebrations and the (De)construction of Russian Nationhood," in *The Post-Soviet Russian Media: Conflicting Signals,* ed. Birgit Beumers, Stephen Hutchings, and Natalia Rulyova (London: Routledge, 2009), 137–155; and Serguei A. Oushakine "Remembering in Public: On the Affective Management of History," *Ab Imperio* 1 (2013): 269–302.

71. Brudny, *Reinventing Russia*; Dunlop, *The Faces of Contemporary Russian Nationalism*; Mitrokhin, *Russkaia partiia*; Alexei Elfimov, *Russian Intellectual Culture in Transition: The Future in the Past* (New Brunswick: Transaction Publishers, 1983).

72. Raphael Samuel, *Theatres of Memory: Past and Present in Contemporary Culture,* rev. ed. (London: Verso, 2012), 7.

73. Popular Memory Group, "Popular Memory: Theory, Politics, and Method," in *Making Histories: Studies in Historical Writing and Politics,* ed. Richard Johnson, et al. (Minneapolis, MN: University of Minnesota Press, 1982), 207–210.

74. Karl D. Qualls, *From Ruins to Reconstruction: Urban Identity in Soviet Sevastopol after World War II* (Ithaca: Cornell University Press, 2009).

75. Steven M. Maddox, *Saving Stalin's Imperial City: Historic Preservation in Leningrad, 1930–1950* (Bloomington, IN: Indiana University Press, 2015).

76. Lisa A. Kirschenbaum, *The Legacy of the Siege of Leningrad, 1941–1995: Myth, Memories, and Monuments* (Cambridge: Cambridge University Press, 2006); Catriona Kelly, *St Petersburg: Shadows of the Past,* as well as *Socialist Churches.* Also see Kelly's *Remembering St Petersburg* (Triton Press, 2014).

77. Kirschenbaum, 15.

78. For a full list and short biographies of the interviewees, see the appendix to this book.

79. This literature has tended to focus on the practices of subjectivation in the early Soviet and Stalin eras. See, for example, Igal Halfin, *From Darkness to Light: Class, Consciousness, and Salvation in Revolutionary Russia* (Pittsburgh: University of Pittsburgh Press, 2000); Igal Halfin, ed., *Language and Revolution: Making Modern Political Identities* (London: Frank Cass, 2002); "*Analiz praktiki sub"ektivizatsii v rannestalinskom obshchestve*" (Interviews with Igal Halfin and Jochen Hellbeck;

essays by Aleksandr Kustarev, David L. Hoffmann, Jeremy Smith, Svetlana Boym, Il'ia Gerasimov, Alla Sal'nikova, Dietrich Beyrau, and Yashiro Matsui; "Concluding Thoughts" by Halfin and Hellbeck), *Ab Imperio* 3 (2002): 209–418.

80. Spegal'skii, 11.

Notes to Chapter 1

1. On the "de-Germanization" of Poznań's city silhouette, see José M. Faraldo, "Medieval Socialist Artifacts: Architecture and Discourses of National Identity in Provincial Poland, 1945–1960," *Nationalities Papers* 29, no. 4 (2001): 606–632; on the re-Polonization of Breslau/Wrocław, see Gregor Thum, *Uprooted: How Breslau Became Wrocław during the Century of Expulsions,* trans. Tom Lampert, Allison Brown, W. Martin, and Jasper Tilbury (Princeton, NJ: Princeton University Press, 2011).

2. Jeffry M. Diefendorf, *In the Wake of War: The Reconstruction of German Cities after World War II* (Oxford: Oxford University Press, 1993), 83–90.

3. On the symbolic work of transforming Minsk into a Soviet capital in the postwar period, see Larissa Titarenko and Anna Shirokanova, "The Phenomenon of Minsk: The City Space and the Cultural Narrative," *Limes: Borderland Studies* 4, no. 1 (2011): 21–35.

4. Karl D. Qualls, *From Ruins to Reconstruction: Urban Identity in Soviet Sevastopol after World War II* (Ithaca: Cornell University Press, 2009).

5. David Brandenberger, *National Bolshevism: Stalinist Mass Culture and the Formation of Modern Russian National Identity, 1931–1956* (Cambridge, MA: Harvard University Press, 2002).

6. B. N. Kovalev, *Povsednevnaia zhizn' naseleniia Rossii v period natsistskoi okkupatsii* (Moscow: Molodaia gvardiia, 2011), 7.

7. For a description of the fate of Novgorod's architectural monuments during wartime, see I. Orlov, "Razrushenie pamiatnikov arkhitektury Novgoroda v gody Velikoi Otechestvennoi voiny," in *Arkhitekturnoe nasledie Velikogo Novgoroda i Novgorodskoi oblasti,* ed. M. I. Mil'chik (St. Petersburg: Spas. Fond sodeistviia restavratsii pamiatnikov istorii i kul'tury "Liki Rossii," 2008), 489–493.

8. Marina Safronova, "Pskov pod nemtsami," *Pskovskaia guberniia* (July 13–19, 2011), 4.

9. "Osobaia provintsiia Velikoi Germanii," from the "Stranitsy istorii" on the website of the Pskov Library, http://bibliopskov.ru/pskov-history.htm.

10. Ibid.

11. "Ot 'turistov' do okkupatsii, ot evakuatsii do osvobozhdeniia," *Novgorod*, January 20, 2011, http://gazetanovgorod.ru/arhiv/item/21313-ot-turistov-do-okkupatsii-ot-evakuatsii-do-osvobozhdeniia.

12. Ibid.

13. On the history of the "Pskov Orthodox Mission," see K. P. Oboznyi, *Istoriia Pskovskoi Pravoslavnoi Missii 1941–1944 gg.* (Moscow: Izd. Krutitskogo podvoria, 2008); and M. Shkarovskii, *Tserkov' zovet k zashchite Rodiny: Religioznaia zhizn' Leningrada i Severo-Zapada v gody Velikoi Otechestvennoi voiny* (St. Petersburg: Izd. "Satis" Derzhava, 2005).

14. Johannes Due Enstad, "Prayers and Patriotism in Nazi-Occupied Russia: The Pskov Orthodox Mission and Religious Revival, 1941–1944," *Slavonic and East European Review* 94, no. 3 (2016): 468–496 (473).

15. Ibid.

16. See, for example, the presentation of the wartime destruction of the architectural landscape in the architectural guides to the city produced in the 1950s and 1960s: A. I. Semenov, *Istoricheskie pamiatniki Novgorodskogo kremlia* (Novgorod: Novgorodskaia pravda, 1959), 7–8; and M. N. Tikhomirov, *Novgorod k 1100-letiiu goroda: Sbornik statei* (Moscow: Nauka, 1964), 22.

17. Nicola Lambourne, *War Damage in Western Europe: The Destruction of Historic Monuments During the Second World War* (Edinburgh: Edinburgh University Press, 2001), 52. On the destruction of Lübeck and Rostock, see Lambourne, 52–53, and 93–95.

18. Orlov, "Razrushenie pamiatnikov arkhitektury," 489–493.

19. Il'ia Kushnir, *Novgorod* (Leningrad: Stroiizdat, 1967), 87.

20. Excerpts from this report are quoted by Ekaterina Mikhailovna in "Iz materialov deiatel'nosti komissii po ustanovleniiu i rassledovaniiu zlodeianii nemetsko-fashistskikh zakhvatchikov," *Novaia Novgorodskaia gazeta* (January 21, 2009), http://novarchiv.org/2009-02-25-12-48-57/65.

21. Orlov, "Razrushenie pamiatnikov arkhitektury," 493.

22. Ibid.

23. Likhachev dedicated numerous works to Novgorod's literary and architectural heritage, including his doctoral dissertation *Novgorodskie letopisnye svody XII v* (Avtoref. Diss. Kand. Filol. Nauk. Isvestiia AN SSR. Otd. Literatury I iazika, 1944); see also Dmitrii Likhachev, *Novgorod Velikii: Ocherk istorii kul'tury Novgoroda XI–XII vv.* (Moscow: Izd-vo Sovetskaia Rossiia, 1959).

24. D. S. Likhachev, "Novgorod Velikii, rovesnik russkoi istorii," *Sovetskii soiuz* 5 (1966): 37–41 (41).

25. "Osobaia provintsiia Velikoi Germanii."

26. E. P. Ivanov, "Iz istorii kul'turnoi zhizni Pskovshchiny, 1945–1994," in *Pskovskii krai v istorii Rossii*, ed. E. P. Ivanov (Pskov: Izd-vo Pskov. obl. in-ta povysheniia kvalifikatsii rabotnikov obrazovaniia, 2000), http://edapskov.narod.ru/pskov/pskovrus.htm#19. For a more detailed account of Pskov's wartime destruction, see A.V. Filimonov, *Podniatyi iz ruin: Poslevoennoe vosstanovlenie i razvitie Pskova (1944 – nachalo 1950 gg.)* (Pskov: Pskovskaia oblastnaia tipografiia, 2008).

27. Ibid.

28. For a detailed overview of the damage inflicted on Pskov's architectural landscape during the years of wartime occupation and recapture, see Iu. A. Seliverstov and M. P. Pavlova, "Restavratsiia pamiatnikov Pskova," in *Pamiatniki arkhitektury v Sovetskom soiuze, ocherki istorii arkhitekturnoi restavratsii*, ed. A. S. Shchenkov (Moscow: Pamiatniki istoricheskoi mysli, 2004), 372–386.

29. "Vekhi istorii: Pskov v gody Velikoi Otechestvennoi voiny," *Gorod Pskov*, May 8, 2009, http://www.pskovgorod.ru/news.html?id=2644.

30. M. P. Pavlova, "Organizatsiia dela okhrany i restavratsii pamiatnikov arkhitektury s 1941 po 1946 g.," in Shchenkov, 228–259 (230).

31. On exhibitions of architectural ruins in wartime Leningrad, see Steven M. Maddox, *Saving Stalin's Imperial City: Historic Preservation in Leningrad, 1930–1950* (Bloomington, IN: Indiana University Press, 2015), 14; on the exhibitions of architectural ruins at Tolstoy's estate in Yasnaya Polyana, see L. V. Maksakova, *Spasenie kul'turnykh tsennostei v gody Velikoi Otechestvennoi voiny* (Moscow: Nauka, 1990), 119.

32. Andreas Schönle, *Architecture of Oblivion: Ruins and Historical Consciousness in Modern Russia* (DeKalb: Northern Illinois University Press, 2011), 155.

33. Schönle, 169.

34. As Lisa Kirschenbaum argues, the reconstruction of the city's ruins was an attempt "not merely to manage memory but to obliterate it," involving the closure of the Museum of the Heroic Defense of Leningrad and the almost total exclusion the Blockade from Soviet histories of the war after the Leningrad Affair of 1949. Lisa A. Kirschenbaum, *The Legacy of the Siege of Leningrad, 1941–1995: Myth, Memories, and Monuments* (Cambridge: Cambridge University Press, 2006), 124.

35. Iu. A. Nekhoroshev, "Ekonomicheskie i organizatsionnye aspekty poslevoennogo vosstanovleniia pamiatnikov arkhitektury," in *Poslevoennoe vosstanovlenie pamiatnikov: Teoriia i praktika XX veka* (St. Petersburg: IPK "Beresta," 2014), 154–163 (156–157).

36. M. P Pavlova, "Organizatsiia dela okhrany i restavratsii pamiatnikov arkhitektury v 1946–1966," in Shchenkov, 260–297 (264).

37. M. P. Pavlova, "Sostoianie okhrana pamiatnikov arkhitektury i organizatsii restavratsionnykh rabot v 1940-e – 1960-e gg.," in *Pamiatniki arkhitektury v Sovetskom soiuze. Ocherki istorii arkhitekturnoi restavratsii*, ed. A. S. Shchenkov (Moscow: Pamiatniki istoricheskoi mysli, 2004), 228–259 (229).

38. Catriona Kelly, "'Ispravliat' li istoriiu?' Spory ob okhrane pamiatnikov v Leningrade 1960–1970-kh godov," *Neprikosnovennyi zapas* 2, no. 64 (2009).

39. Stephen Bittner, *The Many Lives of Khrushchev's Thaw: Experience and Memory in Moscow's Arbat* (Ithaca: Cornell University Press, 2008), 145.

40. Pavlova, "Sostoianie okhrana pamiatnikov arkhitektury," 229.

41. I. E. Grabar', "Vosstanovlenie pamiatnikov stariny," *Sovetskoe iskusstvo* 928 (November 28, 1944). Cited from Igor Grabar, "The Restoration of Russian Architectural Monuments," *American Slavic and East European Review* 4, nos. 1–2 (1945): 182–184 (182).

42. The legislation is published online on a website dedicated to the 70th Anniversary of Pskov's Liberation from Nazi Occupation in 2014. "70 let osvobozhdeniiu goroda Pskova ot nemetsko-fashistskikh zakhvatchikov," http://www.archive.pskov.ru/pskov70/pages/occupation/index.html.

43. *Okhrana pamiatnikov istorii i kul'tury: Sbornik dokumentov* (Moscow: Sovetskaia Rossiia, 1973), 104–110.

44. V. A. Iadryshnikov, "'Velikii razbeg': Sergei Nikolaevich Davydov i novgorodskaia restavratsiia," in *Poslevoennoe vosstanovlenie pamiatnikov,* 266–279 (266).

45. Pavlova, "Sostoianie okhrana pamiatnikov arkhitektury," 246.

46. Ibid.

47. M. I. Mil'chik, ed., *Arkhitekturnoe nasledie Velikogo Novgoroda* (St. Petersburg: Spas. Fond sodeistviia restavratsii pamiatnikov istorii i kul'tury "Liki Rossii," 2008), 43.

48. Iadryshnikov, "'Velikii razbeg,'" 268.

49. Ibid., 269.

50. V. A. Iadryshnikov, "L.M. Shuliak," Prilozhenie 3, in Mil'chik, *Arkhitekturnoe nasledie,* 502–503.

51. Iadryshnikov, "'Velikii razbeg,'" 270.

52. N. I. Brunov, "O poslednikh issledovaniiakh arkhitektury sobora Sofii v Novgorode," *Materialy k VII sessii Akademii arkhitektury SSSR* (Moscow, 1946), 3–23 (5).

53. Orlov, "Razrushenie pamiatnikov arkhitektury," 493.

54. Mil'chik, *Arkhitekturnoe nasledie,* 102.

55. M. P. Pavlova and A. S. Shchenkov, "Restavratsionnaia praktika Novgoroda," in Shchenkov, *Pamiatniki arkhitektury v Sovetskom soiuze,* 358–372 (361).

56. Pavlova and Shchenkov, "Restavratsionnaia praktika Novgoroda," 358–372.

57. Iadryshnikov, "'Velikii razbeg,'" 271.

58. Pavlova, "Sostoianie okhrana pamiatnikov arkhitektury," 245.

59. M. Kniazeva, "Spustia 44 godov," *Novgorodskaia pravda,* January 26, 1961, 4.

60. Karl D. Qualls, *From Ruins to Reconstruction: Urban Identity in Soviet Sevastopol after World War II* (Ithaca: Cornell University Press, 2009).

61. The zoning principle had its roots in the early Soviet concept of the "museum city" (*muzei-gorod*) advocated by conservators, including the Novgorod kraeved Nikolai Porfiridov, in the 1920s. See Maria Kaulen, *Muzeefikatsiia istoriko-kul'turnogo naslediia Rossii* (Moscow: Eterna, 2012), 228.

62. Iu. L. Kosenkova, "Sovetskii gorod 1940-kh–pervoi poloviny 1950-kh godov. Ot tvorcheskikh poiskov k praktike stroitel'stva" (PhD diss., Rossiiskaia akademiia arkhitektury i stroitel'nykh nauk nauchno-issledovatel'skii institut teorii arkhitektury i gradostroitel'stva, Moscow, 2000).

63. On the General Plans of 1944 and 1945, see G. N. Iakovleva, "Istoricheskoe samosoznanie i problemy naslediia v sovetskoi kul'ture vo vremia Velikoi Otechestvennoi voiny," in Shchenkov, 201–208, (207).

64. Victoria Donovan, "The 'Old New Russian Town': Modernization and Architectural Preservation in Russia's Historic North West, 1961–1982," *Slavonica* 19, no. 1 (April 2013): 18–35.

65. Larry Cothren, *Outcast Visionary: Yurii Pavlovich Spegal'skii and the Reconstruction of Pskov* (Interweave Australia, 2017), 182.

66. Comments to the "Lengiprogor" project, quoted in Kosenkova, 71.

67. L. V. Rudnev, quoted in Kosenkova, 71.

68. "Proekt vosstanovleniia Novgoroda," report by A. V. Shchusev presented at the consortium "Proekty planirovaniia vosstanavlivaemykh gorodov," on July 14, 1944. Published in *Voprosy vosstanovitel'nogo stroitel'stva* (Moscow, 1945), 30–31.

69. Ibid.

70. On the fate of the Committee for Architectural Affairs, see "Sozdanie Komiteta po delam arkhitektury pri SNK SSSR i ego rol' v organizatsii rabot po poslevoennomu vosstanovleniiu

pamiatnikov arkhitektury," paper presented at the conference "Poslevoennoe vosstanovlenie pamiatnikov: Teoriia i praktika XX veka," St. Petersburg, December 4–5, 2014.

71. The Leningrad Affair was a series of criminal cases fabricated in the late Stalin era in order to accuse a number of prominent politicians and members of the Communist Party of treason and conspiring to create an anti-Soviet power base in Leningrad. Iadryshnikov, "'Velikii razbeg,'" 278.

72. Ibid.

73. V. Popov, L. Tyntareva, S. Troianovskii, "Nachalo: Iz khaosa ruin," *Novgorod* 6 (1995): 1–10.

74. I. I. Kushnir, *Arkhitektura Novgoroda* (Leningrad: Lenizdat, 1982), 159.

75. Ibid., 162.

76. I. I. Kushnir, *Novgorod* (Leningrad: Stroiizdat, 1967), 89, 108, and 118.

77. D. S. Likhachev, "Iz letnikh puteshestvii," *Literaturnaia gazeta*, September 14, 1965, 2; for further criticisms of socialist planning in Novgorod and Pskov, see Dmitrii Likhachev, "Chetvertoe izmerenie," *Literaturnaia gazeta*, June 10, 1965.

78. A. V. Shchusev, quoted in A. V. Filimonov, *Podniatyi iz ruin: Poslevoennoe vosstanovlenie i razvitie Pskova (1944 – nachalo 1950 gg.)* (Pskov: Pskovskaia oblastnaia tipografiia, 2008), 122.

79. Postanovlenie SNK RSFSR ot 20.11.1945 N 670 "O neotlozhnykh meropriiatiiakh po sokhraneniiu pamiatnikov arkhitektury g. Pskova i Pskovskoi oblasti." http://lawru.info/dok/1945/11/20/n1194009.htm.

80. Evgenii Ovechkin, "Iurii Spegal'skii – arkhitektor, restavrator, verkholaz." *Russkoe geograficheskoe obshchestvo 'Klub Al'pinistov 'Sankt-Peterburg'.*" October 1, 2018. http://www.alpklubspb.ru/ass/a476.htm.

81. Ibid.

82. Lev Shlosberg, "Krest Spegal'skogo." *Pskovskaia guberniia* 2, January 21–27, 2009. http://gubernia.pskovregion.org/number_423/04.php.

83. On Spegal'skii's disregard for Soviet bureaucracy, see Cothren, *Outcast Visionary*, chapters 5 and 6.

84. GAPO, f. 1767, op. 1, d. 4, l. 5–6.

85. Filimonov, *Podniatyi iz ruin*, 123.

86. PGIKhMZ, f. 16547/1007(3). l. 1, quoted in Filimonov, *Podniatyi iz ruin*, 126.

87. Iu. A. Seliverstov, A. S. Shchenkov, "Restavratsiia pamiatnikov Pskova," in Shchenkov, 372–386.

88. Iurii Spegal'skii, "Rekonstruktsiia tserkvi Nikoly so Usokhy v Pskove," *Pamiatniki kul'tury. Issledovanie i restavratsiia* 3 (1961).

89. Ibid.

90. Lev Shlosberg, "Krest Spegal'skogo."

91. Baranovskii, cited in Cothren, *Outcast Visionary*, 160.

92. N. V. Baranov, A. I. Naumov, "General'nyi plan vosstanovleniia i razvitii Pskova," Leningradskii gorodskoi sovet deputatov trudiashchikhsia ispolnitel'nii komitet. Upravleniia po delam arkhitektury (Pskov, 1945), 6.

93. For a dramatized account of Spegal'skii's efforts to lobby central and regional authorities for the implementation of his plan, see O. K. Arkashuni, *Predchuvstvie: Vospominaniia o Iurii Pavloviche Spegal'skom* (Leningrad: Lenizdat, 1987), 74–75.

94. B. A. Bulkin, O. V. Ovsiannikov, *Uchenyi, zodchii, kamenshchik* (Leningrad: Lenizdat, 1983), 16.

95. Baranov and Naumov, "General'nyi plan," 16.

96. Ibid.

97. Filimonov, *Podniatyi iz ruin*, 52.

98. Ibid., 55.

99. Ibid., 56.

100. The subject was the focus of fierce debate at the conference "Iu.P. Spegal'skii i istoriko-kul'turnoe nasledie Pskovskoi zemli," held in Pskov on June 2–3, 2009.

101. This archive was closed for restoration in 2007–2009, when I conducted my research in Pskov, and was closed again in 2017–2018 for major refurbishment work in preparation for the Hanseatic Days celebrations in 2018.

102. Cothren, *Outcast Visionary*, chapter 7.

103. Spegal'skii, quoted in Cothren, *Outcast Visionary*, 193.

104. Ibid., 192.

105. Cothren, *Outcast Visionary*, 217.

106. Ibid., 200.

107. Lev Shlosberg, "Krest Spegal'skogo."

108. *Pskov: Khudozhestvennye pamiatniki*, 5.

109. *Pskov: Khudozhestvennye pamiatniki*, 5.

110. Iu. P. Spegal'skii, *Po Pskovu XVII veka: Al'bom risunkov* (Leningrad: Lenizdat, 1974).

111. Filimonov, *Podniatyi iz ruin*, 130.

112. Seliverstov and Pavlova, "Restavratsiia pamiatnikov Pskova," 374–378.

113. Filimonov, *Podniatyi iz ruin*, 130.

114. Declaration of the Council of Ministers of the RSFSR of 22 August 1952 "On the Means to Reconstruct the Pskov Kremlin," LibUSSR.ru, Biblioteka normativno-pravovykh aktov Soiuza Sovetskikh Sotsialisticheskikh Respublik, http://www.libussr.ru/doc_ussr/ussr_4864.htm.

115. Seliverstov and Pavlova, "Restavratsiia pamiatnikov Pskova," 382–383.

116. Filimonov, *Podniatyi iz ruin*, 135.

117. Ibid.

Notes to Chapter 2

1. For a detailed account of Khrushchev's "Secret Speech" and its political implications, see Polly Jones, *Myth, Memory, Trauma: Rethinking the Stalinist Past in the Soviet Union, 1953–1970* (New Haven: Yale University Press, 2013).

2. Anne E. Gorsuch, "'There's No Place Like Home': Soviet Tourism in Late Stalinism," *Slavic Review* 62, no. 4 (2003): 760–785 (772).

3. Ibid.; see, also, Katerina Clark's appraisal of Soviet Moscow as "the acme in the symbolic system of the country, the end point in a spatial hierarchy that is simultaneously temporal and anthropological." Katerina Clark, "Eisenstein's Two Projects for a Film about Moscow," *Modern Language Review* 101 (2006): 184–200 (186).

4. This phrase is taken from Gorsuch, 771.

5. NGOM, op. 1, d. 30 (materials about the organization of discussion-seminars of workers at architectural museum-reserves of the RSFSR in Novgorod [plans, protocols]), 2.

6. Natalia Danilina, "The Zapovedniks of Russia," *The George Wright Forum* 18, no. 1 (2001): 48–55 (48).

7. NGOM, op. 1 (Historical note), 1–2.

8. Museum exhibits included fourteen buildings from within the Novgorod Kremlin complex; ten historic churches from the Yaroslav's Yard complex on the "Trade Side"; and eleven other buildings from various suburbs, including the Transfiguration Church on Il'in Street, the Savior on Nereditsa church, and the St. George's Monastery Cathedral. NGOM, op. 1, d. 407 (Report on the work of the Novgorod historical-architectural museum-zapovednik in 1961), 15.

9. Ibid., 2.

10. NGOM, op. 1, d. 30, 9.

11. Ibid.

12. Ibid.

13. *Arkhitekturnoe nasledie Velikogo Novgoroda i Novgorodskoi oblasti*, ed. M. I. Mil'chik (St. Petersburg: Spas. Fond sodeistviia restavratsii pamiatnikov istorii i kul'tury "Liki Rossii," 2008), 176, 193, and 267.

14. NGOM, op. 1, d. 407, 15.

15. NGOM, op. 1, d. 376, 22–24.

16. S. Ruzhentsev, I. Kushnir, and V. Ershov, "Sokrovishcha – v dobrykh rukakh," *Novgorodskaia pravda*, September 13, 1966, 3.

17. *Muzeia divnoe prostranstvo: Khram pamiati, nauk i muz*, ed. M. A. Kuz'menko, et al. (Pskov: Pskovskii gosudarstvennyi ob''edinennyi istoriko-arkhitekturnyi i khudozhestvennyi muzei-zapovednik, 2002), 11.

18. I discuss the growth in visitor numbers to the historic towns throughout the 1960s and 1970s in more detail below.

19. GAPO, f. P-1855, d. 226 (Correspondence with the Ministry of Culture [reports, information about preservation of architectural and historical-artistic monuments in the Pskov region]), 95.

20. Kuz'menko, 11.

21. "Muzei v XX-XXI vv.," *Pskovskii gosudarstvennyi ob''edinennyi istoriko-arkhitekturnyi i khudozhestvennyi muzei-zapovednik*, http://museums.pskov.ru/istoriya_muzeya/istoriya.

22. GAPO, op. 1, d. 226, l. 109

23. Ibid.

24. Ibid., 118.

25. GAPO, f. P-1855, d. 226, 118.

26. GAVO, f. 4795, op. 1, d. 232 (Correspondence on museum work and the preservation of monuments), 72.

27. GAVO, f. 4795, op. 6, d. 76 (Surveys, information, reports, and other correspondence about the condition of local cultural monuments), 128–130.

28. GAVO, f. 4795, op. 6, d. 138 (Surveys, information, reports and other correspondence on the condition of local cultural monuments in 1966), 27.

29. GAVO, f. 4795, op. 4, d. 20 (Surveys, information, and reference material about the condition of local cultural monuments), 99.

30. GAVO, f. 4795, op. 6, d. 138, 129.

31. NGOM, op. 1, d. 407, 19; NGOM, op. 1, 407, 18; NGOM, op. 1, 504 (Report on the work of the Novgorod historical-architectural museum-zapovednik in 1966), 9.

32. GAPO, f R-1855, op. 1, d. 164 (Annual reports of museums for 1962), 57; GAPO, f. R-1855, op. 1, d. 517 (Reports of museums [Pskov district, Velikoluki district, Pechery district, Porkhov district, and Sebezh district]), 1.

33. VOKM, op. 1, d. 403 (Reports on museum work in 1961), 14; VOKM, op. 1, d. 678 (Reports and information about the work of the museum and its branches in 1970), 29.

34. The following figures are based on research carried out in conjunction with librarians at the Russian National Library in St. Petersburg.

35. These statistics are based on work carried out in conjunction with local librarians in Novgorod, Pskov, and Vologda, in 2008–2009.

36. Programma KPSS, section 1, part 1, August 2, 1961.

37. NGOM, op. 1, d. 398 (Materials about the preservation and restoration of architectural monuments (plans, work, information, correspondence), 127.

38. On the transformation of the Moscow Kremlin complex during these years, see Catherine Merridale, *Red Fortress: The Secret Heart of Russia's History* (London: Allen Lane, 2013), particularly chapter 10.

39. NGOM, op. 1, d. 398, 127.

40. Ibid., 128.

41. NGOM, op. 1, d. 429 (Report on the work of the Novgorod historical architectural museum-zapovednik in 1962), 5.

42. Ibid.

43. Mil'chik, *Arkhitekturnoe nasledie*, 102.

44. Ibid., 195–196.

45. NGOM, op. 1, d. 479 (Declarations of OK KPSS, decisions, orders and instructions from oblispolkom and the department of culture), 1.

46. Ibid., 2.

47. Ibid.

48. Dmitrii Likhachev, "Chetvertoe izmerenie," *Literaturnaia gazeta*, June 10, 1965; and Dmitrii Likhachev, "Iz letnikh puteshestvii," *Literaturnaia gazeta*, September 14, 1965.

49. This quotation refers back to the document on the museum exploitation of the St. Sophia Cathedral, cited above: NGOM, op. 1, d. 429, 5.

50. For an overview of the history of this church in the prerevolutionary and Soviet periods, see Mil'chik, *Arkhitekturnoe nasledie*, 267–269.

51. NGOM, op. 2, d. 634 (Report on the work of the Novgorod historical-architectural museum-zapovednik), 15–16.

52. NGOM, op. 2, d. 653 (Program plan for the restoration and museicization of Church of the Transfiguration on Il'in Street), 6–8.

53. For details of both these projects, see NGOM, op. 2, d. 805 (Reports for 1974), 9–10.

54. GANIP, f. 1060, op. 1, sv. 2, d. 19 (Minutes of party meetings), 11.

55. Ibid.

56. The "tourist gaze," according to the originator of the phrase, John Urry, refers to the way that touristic activities and texts regulate and order the relationship with the tourist environment. See John Urry, *The Tourist Gaze* (London: Sage, 2002).

57. NGOM, op. 1, d. 407, 6

58. Trainee guides at the Novgorod State Museum received kraevedenie lectures on physical geography, local history, (prerevolutionary and Soviet themes), and Novgorodian art. GANO, d. 270a (Materials on the training of excursion guides [declarations], plans, information, etc.), 21ob.

59. The courses attended by local excursion guides were described by A. Protsenko, the head of the Novgorod Tourist Excursion Authorities, in an interview with *Novgorod Pravda* in 1960. A. Protsenko, "V turisticheskie pokhody," *Novgorodskaia pravda*, April 14, 1960, 4.

60. GANO, f. R-4063, op. 2–4, d. 42 (Reports by tourists on excursions around Novgorod), 19.

61. Ibid.

62. GANO, f. R-4063, op. 2–10, d. 140a (Response and suggestion book for the Novgorod Council for Tourism and Excursions for 1968–1972), 2.

63. Ibid., 3.

64. Ibid., 9.

65. Anne Bush, "Reviewing Rome: The Guidebook as Liminal Space," *Visual Communication* 1 (2002): 370–377.

66. V. P. Laskovskii, *Putevoditel' po Novgorodu: Sofiiskaia storona* (St. Petersburg: Alabord, 2007); and V. P. Laskovskii, *Putevoditel' po Novgorodu: Torgovaia storona* (St. Petersburg: Alabord, 2007). These publications are rereleases of Laskovskii's 1910 guides to the town.

67. A. I. Sazanov and E. A. Starikov, *Moia Vologda: Gorod nashei pamiati* (Vologda: Drevnosti Severa, 2007).

68. M. K. Karger, *Novgorod Velikii* (Leningrad: Iskusstvo, 1961), 147, 172.

69. A. I. Semenov, *Novgorodskii kreml'* (Novgorod: Novgorodskaia pravda, 1964), 3.

70. S. N. Semanov, *Pamiatnik "Tysiacheletie Rossii:" Fotoal'bom* (Moscow: Sovetskaia Rossiia, 1974), 35.

71. V. F. Andreev, *Novgorod* (Leningrad: Lenizdat, 1985), 63.

72. S. I. Kolotilova and I. P. Shaskol'skii, *Pskov: Ocherki istorii. Sbornik* (Leningrad: Lenizdat, 1971), 35.

73. I. I. Lagunin, *Pskov. Izborsk* (Leningrad: Lenizdat, 1984), 4.

74. M. V. Fekhner, *Arkhitektura gorodov SSSR: Vologda* (Moscow: Gosudarstvennoe izdatel'stvo literatury po stroitel'stvu, arkhitekture i stroitel'nym materialam, 1958), 42.

75. G. Bocharov and V. Vygolov, *Vologda, Kirillov, Ferapontovo, Belozersk* (Moscow: Iskusstvo, 1969), 6.

76. See the Decree of the Central Committee of the KPSS and the Council of Ministers of the USSR of 4 November 1955 No. 1871 "On the Elimination of Decorative Extravagances in Design and Construction Work," *Sovarkh: Proekt Sovetskaya arkhitektura*: http://www.sovarch.ru/postanovlenie55/.

77. Bocharov and Vygolov, *Vologda, Kirillov, Ferapontovo, Belozersk*, 6.

78. See, for example, I. I. Kushnir, *Novgorod* (Leningrad: Stroiizdat, 1967), 35 and 53; and Fekhner, *Arkhitektura gorodov SSSR*, 53.

79. Fekhner, *Arkhitektura gorodov SSSR*, 59.

80. Iu. P. Spegal'skii, *Pskov: Khudozhestvennye pamiatniki* (Leningrad: Iskusstvo, 1963), 117–118.

81. NGOM, op. 1, d. 407, 19.

82. Tourists visiting Novgorod as part of these excursions left entries in response books in 1970 and 1976. See NGOM, op. 2, d. 611 (Response book of the exhibition of decorative and applied arts at the Faceted Palace [April 3, 1969–October 18, 1970]) and NGOM, op. 2, d. 812 (Response book of the St. Sophia Cathedral [March 7, 1974–January 8, 1976]).

83. On the usefulness of Soviet public commentary as a historical resource, see Miriam Dobson, "Letters," in *Reading Primary Sources of Texts from Nineteenth and Twentieth Century History*, ed. Miriam Dobson and Benjamin Ziemann (London: Routledge, 2008), 57–73.

84. VOKM, op. 1, d. 406 (Vologda regional kraedevenie museum response and suggestion book, 1961–1962), 4.

85. VOKM, op. 1, d. 661 (Vologda regional kraedevenie museum response and suggestion book, 1969–1971), 41ob.

86. NGOM, op. 2, d. 611 (Response book for the Novgorod state integrated museum-zapovednik, 1969), 29ob.

87. NGOM, op. 2, d. 812 (Response book: St Sophia Cathedral), 25.

88. On the Khrushchev-era kraevedenie revival, see Victoria Donovan, "'How Well Do You Know Your Krai?': The Kraevedenie Revival and Patriotic Politics in Late-Khrushchev Era Russia," *Slavic Review* 74, no. 3 (Fall 2015): 464–483; Emily Johnson also deals briefly with the kraevedenie revival in the late Khrushchev era, in *How St Petersburg Learned to Study Itself: The Russian Idea of Kraevedenie* (University Park, PA: Pennsylvania State University Press, 2006), 178–182; on the expansion of tourist excursions with local populations and local history propaganda in Leningrad, see Catriona Kelly, *Remembering St Petersburg* (Triton Press, 2014), 90.

89. I. S. Iun'ev, *Kraevedenie i turizm* (Moscow, 1974), 11.

90. V. Shevchenko, "A pochemu ne Novgorod?," *Novgorodskaia pravda*, October 19, 1966, 3.

91. NGOM, op. 1, d. 407, 19.

92. GANO, f. R-4063, op. 2–57, d. 908 (Description of tourist routes), 11.

93. NGOM, op. 1, d. 410 (Materials on the work of the museum [plans, reports, information, correspondence]), 24.

94. Ibid.

95. VOKM, op. 1, d. 403 (Reports on museum work for 1961), 8.

96. VOKM, op. 1, d. 784 (Report from 1974 on the conditions of community and industrial museums in the Vologda region), 59–60.

97. See the report on the expeditions of the Novgorod museum collective to villages in the Novgorod region for the collection of museum exhibits. NGOM, op. 1, d. 429, 17.

98. G. Melomedov, "O gorode moem rodnom," *Novgorodskaia pravda,* January 6, 1967, 4.

99. GAVO, f. 843, op. 1, d. 229 (Documents on questions of restoration and exploitation of historical and cultural monuments, letters and complaints from residents), 10.

100. GAVO, f. 843, op. 1, d. 213 (Documents on questions of restoration and exploitation of historical and cultural monuments, letters, complaints, and correspondence of workers with party and soviet organs), 37.

101. Ibid., 38.

102. NGOM, op. 1, d. 407, 18.

103. GAVO, f. 4795, op. 6, d. 76, 11.

104. GAPO, op. 1, d. 1652 (Reports and information about the work of cultural institutions, presented to the Ministry of Culture, the party obkom and the oblispolkom), 79.

105. Iu. A. Seliverstov, M. P. Pavlova, "Restavratsiia pamiatnikov Pskova," in *Pamiatniki arkhitektury v Sovetskom soiuze. Ocherki istorii arkhitekturnoi restavratsii,* ed. A. S. Shchenkov (Moscow: Pamiatniki istoricheskoi mysli, 2004), 374–378.

106. For a sardonic literary portrayal of the work of the Mikhailovskoe museum-zapovednik, see Sergei Dovlatov, *Zapovednik* (Ann Arbor, MI: Ermitazh, 1983).

107. A. Akhmatova, et al., "Pis'mo k redaktsii: Zapovednik ili turbaza?," *Literaturnaia gazeta*, May 13, 1965, 3.

108. Ibid.

109. GAPO, f. R-1855, op. 1, d. 1185 (Reference materials and information about the work of cultural institutions, presented to the Ministry of Culture, party obkom and oblispolkom for 1980), 223.

110. GAPO, f. R-1855, op. 1, d. 513 (Materials on the preservation and equipment of historical and cultural monuments), 2.

111. GAVO, f. 843, op. 1, d. 57 (Documents on the work of town and regional departments of the Society for 1971), 162.

112. V. Molotkov, "O nashikh gostiakh," *Novgorodskaia pravda*, August 4, 1961, 3.

Notes to Chapter 3

1. Cf. the literature on the Brezhnev-era "Russian revival": John B. Dunlop, *The Faces of Contemporary Russian Nationalism* (Princeton, NJ: Princeton University Press, 1983) and John B. Dunlop, *The New Russian Nationalism* (New York: Praeger, 1985); perhaps the most influential study of this topic and the source of the idea of Brezhnev-era "inclusionary politics," discussed in more detail below, is Yitzhak Brudny's *Reinventing Russia: Russian Nationalism and the Soviet State, 1953–1991* (Cambridge, MA: Harvard University Press, 1998).

2. I. N. Shurgin, "Restavratsiia pamiatnikov dereviannoi arkhitektury v Rossii," in *Pamiatniki arkhitektury v Sovetskom soiuze. Ocherki istorii arkhitekturnoi restavratsii*, ed. A. S. Shchenkov (Moscow: Pamiatniki istoricheskoi mysli, 2004), 440–452.

3. Shurgin, in Shchenkov, 441.

4. For an account of the early history of this museum, see V. E. Suzdalev, *Kolomenskoe: Gosudarstvennyi muzei-zapovednik XVI–XIX vekov. Putevoditel'* (Moscow: Moskovskii rabochii, 1986).

5. On the strategic sponsorship of Russian patriotism during wartime, see David Brandenberger, *National Bolshevism: Stalinist Mass Culture and the Formation of Modern Russian National Identity, 1931–1956* (Cambridge, MA: Harvard University Press, 2002), and *Epic Revisionism: Russian History and Literature as Stalinist Propaganda*, ed. David Brandenberger and Kevin Platt (Madison, WI: University of Wisconsin Press, 2006), in particular chapters 10 and 15.

6. S. Zabello, V. Ivanov, P. Maksimov, *Russkoe dereviannoe zodchestvo* (Moscow: Izd-vo Akademiia arkhitektury SSSR, 1941).

7. Opolovnikov established an influential methodology for the restoration of historic wooden architecture after the war. It became well known in the West following the publication of his *The Wooden Architecture of Russia: Houses, Fortifications, Churches* (London: Thames and Hudson, 1989).

8. Shurgin, in Shchenkov, 442.

9. Alexey Golubev, "'A Wonderful Song of Wood': Heritage Architecture of North Russia and the Soviet Quest for Historical Authenticity," *Rethinking Marxism* 29, no. 1 (2017): 142–172.

10. Aleksandr Opolovnikov, *Kizhi*, 2nd edition, (Moscow: Stroiizdat, 1976), 100, quoted in Golubev, 157; see also the discussion of wooden folk architecture in Sanami Takahashi, "Church or Museum? The Role of State Museums in Conserving Church Buildings, 1965–85," *Journal of Church and State* 3 (2009): 502–517.

11. Golubev, 162.

12. Ibid.

13. Vladimir Soloukhin, *Vladimirskie proselki* (Moscow: Gosudarstvennoe izdatel'stvo khudozhest-vennoi literatury, 1958); Vladimir Soloukhin, "Chernye doski," *Moskva* 1 (1969): 129–187.

14. Vladimir Soloukhin, "Chernye doski," LiveLib version: https://www.livelib.ru/book/1000514238-vladimirskie-proselki-vladimir-solouhin.

15. Kathleen F. Parthé, *Russian Village Prose: The Radiant Past* (Princeton, NJ: Princeton University Press, 1992), ix–x; on the cultural relevance of the Soviet Village Prose movement, see also David

Gillespie, *Valentin Rasputin and Soviet Russian Village Prose* (London: Modern Humanities Research Association, 1986).

16. Geoffrey A. Hosking and Vasilii Belov, "Vasilii Belov – Chronicler of the Soviet Village," *Russian Review* 34, no. 2 (April 1975): 165–185 (166).

17. On the legacy of exile and Vologda's cultural identity, see Varlam Shalamov, "Chetvertaia Vologda," in *Sobranie sochenenii v chetyrekh tomakh* (Moskva: Khudozhestvennaia literatura "Vagrius," 1998); more generally, on the role of exile in Russian provincial culture, see Julia Fein, "Cultural Curators and Provincial Publics: Local Museums and Social Change in Siberia, 1887–1941" (PhD diss., Chicago, IL, August 2012).

18. The following biographical information is taken from *Russkie pisateli, XX vek. Biobibliograficheskii slovar'*, vol. 2 (Moscow: Prosveshchenie, 1998), 652–655.

19. Aleksandr Iashin, "Vologodskaia svad'ba," *Novyi mir* 12 (1962): 3–26. See, also, Lib.Ru version: http://www.lib.ru/PROZA/YASHIN/ryabina.txt.

20. Vasilii Belov, *Plotnitskie rasskazy* (Arkhangel'sk: Severo-Zapadnoe Knizhnoe Izdatel'stvo, 1968).

21. The influence of oral tradition on Belov's writing was acknowledged by the author in his co-authored article with Geoffrey Hosking, "Vasilii Belov – Chronicler of the Soviet Village."

22. Belov, "Privychnoe delo," *Sever* 1 (1966): 7–92.

23. Belov, "Privychnoe delo," 7.

24. Geoffrey Hosking, *Beyond Socialist Realism: Soviet Fiction Since Ivan Denisovich* (London: Elek, 1980), 58.

25. For a discussion of Khrushchev's agricultural policies and their consequences, see Judith Pallot, "Rural Depopulation and the Restoration of the Russian Village under Gorbachev," *Soviet Studies* 42, no. 4 (1990): 655–674.

26. Parthé discusses the relationship between urban migration and nostalgia for rural traditions in chapter 1 of *Russian Village Prose*; see also David Gillespie, *Valentin Rasputin and Soviet Russian Village Prose* (London: Modern Humanities Research Association, 1986).

27. On the use of the term "derevenshchik" to refer to Village Prose writers, and certain writers' resistance to the term, see Parthé, 12; for an example of the contemporary use of the term "derevianshchik," to refer to a scholar of wooden folk architecture, see V. A. Popov, "Vstupitel'naia stat'ia," in L. E. Krasnorech'ev, *Narodnoe dereviannoe zodchestvo Novgorodchiny* (Novgorod: Novgorod muzei-zapovednik, 2012), 5.

28. The biographical details that follow are taken from Popov, "Vstupitel'naia stat'ia."

29. Order of the Ministry of Culture of the RSFSR "On the Means to Improve the Preservation of Wooden Architecture," January 31, 1961. "Muzei dereviannogo zodchestva Vitoslavlitsy," http://tk-podvorie.ru/wheretogo/9/4855.

30. For a full list of the museums of folk architecture that opened between 1964 and 1990, see Golubev, 145.

31. See Decree No. 190/14 of 5 June 1964 "On the Organization of a Reserve of Objects of Wooden Folk Architecture," NGOM, op. 1, d. 440 (Materials on the preservation and restoration of architectural monuments [orders, information, acts, correspondence]), 40–41.

32. Cf. the discussion of Spegal'skii's writings on architectural preservation in chapter 1.

33. See Krasnorech'ev's keynote speech at the regional conference "The Discovery, Propaganda, and Preservation of the Historical and Cultural Monuments of the Novgorod Region," NGOM op. 2, d. 973 (Documents on the regional conference "The Discovery, Propaganda, and Preservation of the Historical and Cultural Monuments of the Novgorod Region" [plan, propaganda, recommendations]), 16.

34. "Novgorodskii muzei Vitoslavlitsy. Sozdannaia chast' i proekt," Jur-portal.ru, http://www.jur-portal.ru/work.pl?act=law_read&subact=sudja&id=54746.

35. Ibid.

36. GANO, f. R-4563, op. 1–4, d. 40 (Reports on regional departments for 1979–1980), 2.

37. Questions arising in connection with the reconstruction of the interiors of the folk churches at Vitoslavlitsy were discussed at a conference held at the Novgorod Museum in 1981. NGOM, op. 3, d. 1057 (Theses of papers presented at conference [on the basis of scientific-research work]), 9.

38. "Novgorodskii muzei Vitoslavlitsy. Sozdannaia chast' i proekt," Jur-portal.ru, http://www.jur-portal.ru/work.pl?act=law_read&subact=sudja&id=54746.

39. NGOM, op. 2, d. 973, 16.

40. Ibid.

41. For a detailed biography of the restorer, see "Pamiati L.E. Krasnorech'eva," Federal'noe gosudarstvennoe biudzhetnoe ucherezhdenie kul'tury "Novgorodskii gosudarstvennyi ob'edinennyi muzei-zapovednik," http://novgorodmuseum.ru/novosti/431-pamyati-l-e-krasnorecheva.html.

42. NGOM, op. 2, d. 973, 34

43. Ibid.

44. For a discussion of folk themes in postwar Soviet classical music, see Sidney Walter Finkelstein, *Composer and Nation: The Folk Heritage in Music* (London: Lawrence & Wishart, 1960), 280–301.

45. "V Vologdu za pesnei," *Krasnyi sever*, March 3, 1977, 4.

46. GAVO, f. 4795, op. 6, d. 108 (Surveys, information and reports, and other perspectives of regional museums about their work in 1965), 157.

47. GAVO, f. 4795, op. 6, d. 175 (Surveys, information and reports, correspondence with regional museums about their work, Feburary 10, 1967–January 25, 1968), 19.

48. VOKM, op. 1, d. 678 (Reports and information about the work of the museum and its filials in 1970), 70.

49. VOKM, op. 1, d. 768 (Thematic plan for the exhibition "Folk Art," The museum's fiftieth anniversary), 13–14

50. VOKM, op. 1, d. 998 (Reports on the work of the Vologda Regional Kraevedenie Museum, 1979), 5.

51. VOKM, op. 1, d. 942 (Report on the work of the Vologda Regional Kraevedenie Museum in 1977), 10–11.

52. "O kruzheve i kruzhevnitsakh," *Krasnyi sever,* January 25, 1977, 4.

53. GAVO, f. 134, op. 4, d. 275 (Program and scenario for the performance and organization of festivals and mass events), 126.

54. Ibid., 130.

55. See, for example, the correspondence with the Ministry of Culture on the subject of the wooden Trinity-Annunciation Church and belfry in the village of Pustyn' in the Chagodoshchenk region of the Vologda oblast, both of which were destroyed by fire in 1960. GAVO, f. 4795, op. 1, d. 230 (Correspondence with the Ministry of Culture of the RSFSR about the work of cultural institutions), 150; see also the report on the condition of the wooden Ilin Church in the Kirillov region, which, as a result of a storm, had lost two of its outer tiers and its roof. GAVO, f. 4795, op.6, d. 42 (Surveys, information and reference material about the condition of regional cultural monuments in 1963), 24.

56. GAVO, f. 4795, op. 1, d. 231 (Correspondence with Ministry of Culture of the RSFSR and other institutions working with museums and the preservation of architectural monuments. 1960), 167.

57. GAVO, f. 4795, op. 6, d. 42, 23.

58. GAVO, f. 4795, op. 6, d. 76 (Surveys, information, reference materials and other correspondence on the condition of regional cultural monuments. 1964), 128–130.

59. Ibid.

60. Reshenie ot 14.12.79 No. 747 "O sozdanii muzeia dereviannogo zodchestva Vologodskoi oblasti," Semenkovo Museum website, "Istoriia muzeia" page, https://www.semenkovo.ru/ru/o-muzee/istoriya-muzeya.

61. Ibid.

62. P. I. Dmitrii Mukhin, head of the exhibition sector at the Semenkovo museum. Vologda, March 2009.

63. V. D. Parmenov, *Portret na fone Vologdy. Vospominaniia, razmyshleniia, dokumenty* (Vologodskaia gorodskaia duma i administratsiia goroda Vologdy: Vologda, 2007), 84–85.

64. Ibid.

65. Golubev, "'A Wonderful Song of Wood,'" 159.

66. For a comprehensive guide to Vologda's merchant architecture, see A. Sazonov, *Takoi gorod v Rossii odin* (Vologda: PF "Poligrafist," 1993). The contents of the book can be viewed online at http://www.booksite.ru/fulltext/such/town/in/rus/sia/index.htm.

67. On the urban modernization of Vologda in the 1960s and 1970s, see Parmenov, *Portret na fone Vologdy*, 88–95.

68. Iu. K. Nekrasov, ed., *Vologda v minuvshem tysiacheletii: Ocherki istorii goroda*, 2nd ed. (Vologda: Drevnosti Severa, 2006), 220–224.

69. Parmenov, *Portret na fone Vologdy*, 3.

70. See "Instruktsiia o poriadke ucheta registratsii soderzhaniia i restavratsii pamiatnikov arkhitektury, sostoiashchikh pod gosudarstvennoi okhranoi. Utverzhdena predsidatelem Komiteta po delam arkhitektury pri Sovete Ministrov SSSR. 8 aprelia 1949," *Okhrana pamiatnikov istorii i kul'tury: Sbornik dokumentov* (Moscow: Sovetskaia Rossiia, 1973), 103–115.

71. Postanovlenie SM RSFSR No.1327 ot 30.08.60. Upravlenie kul'tury ispolnitel'nogo komiteta Vologodskogo oblastnogo soveta narodnykh deputatov (Vologodskoe otdelenie vserossiiskogo obshchestva okhrany pamiatnikov istorii i kul'tury Vologodskoi oblasti. Vologda. 1989).

72. Aleksandr Rybakov, "Sokhraniaem istoricheskii oblik goroda," in Parmenov, *Portret na fone Vologdy*, 86–88.

73. "Etazhi Vologdy," *Krasnyi sever*, August 11, 1968, 2.

74. N. Volkhov, "Nov' starykh kvartalov," *Krasnyi sever*, February 28, 1969, 3.

75. V. M. Malkov, *Vologda* (Vologda: Vologodskoe knizhnoe izdatel'stvo, 1964), 3.

76. GAVO, f. 4795, op. 6, d. 257 (Information, surveys, and other correspondence on the condition of historical and cultural monuments, January 2, 1972–December 12, 1972), 15.

77. Rybakov, "Sokhraniaem istoricheskii oblik goroda," 87.

78. Reshenie oblispolkoma No.257 ot 27.04.77. (Upravlenie kul'tury ispolnitel'nogo komiteta Vologodskogo oblastnogo soveta narodnykh deputatov. Vologodskoe otdelenie vserossiiskogo obshchestva okhrany pamiatnikov istorii i kul'tury. Spisok pamiatnikov istorii i kul'tury Vologodskoi oblasti. Vologda. 1989).

79. GAVO, f. 4795, op. 6, d. 138 (Surveys, information, reports and other correspondence on the condition of local cultural monuments for 1966), 49.

80. GAVO, f. 843, op. 1, d. 213 (Documents on questions of restoration and exploitation of historical and cultural monuments, letters, complaints, and declarations), 163.

81. For an account of the fate of Vologda's wooden merchant mansions in the 1980s and 1990s, see A. I. Sazonov and E. A. Starikov, *Moia Vologda: Gorod nashei pamiati* (Vologda: Drevnosti Severa, 2007), in particular part 4, "Progulka po Zarech'iu," 252–260.

82. B. Chulkov, "Nash gorod stal neuznavaemym," in Sazonov, *Takoi gorod v Rossii odin*, 52.

Notes to Chapter 4

1. On the emergence of social justice as a pillar of perestroika politics, see Richard Sakwa, *Gorbachev and His Reforms, 1985–1990* (New York: Philip Allan, 1990), 8–9; and Stephen Lovell, *Destination in Doubt: Russia Since 1989* (New York: Zed Books, 2006), 76.

2. GANO, f. R-4563, op. 1–9, d. 176 (Documents on the work of the public inspectorate for matters pertaining to the preservation and the exploitation of monuments [plans, reports, lists]), 13.

3. The case was discussed at a meeting of the Presidium of the regional VOOPIiK on July 3, 1990. GANO, f. R-4563, op. 1–10, d. 211 (Protocols from the meeting of the presidium of the regional soviet), 77–83.

4. GANO, f. R-4563, op. 1–10, d. 211, 77.

5. Oxf/AHRC-SPb-08 AP PF. Aleksandr Davidovich Margolis.

6. G. Alimov and R. Lynev, "Kuda uvodit pamiat," *Izvestiia*, June 3, 1987, 3.

7. I found no archival evidence that regional branches of "Memory" had ever existed in Novgorod, Pskov, or Vologda. Local museum workers and representatives of the authorities for the preservation of heritage likewise had no knowledge of the organization being active in the region at this time.

8. See the webpage of the *Rossiiskii fond kul'tury*, http://fond.culture.ru/ru/about/history.

9. Ibid.

10. For a more detailed discussion of the strategic relations between the post-Soviet Russian state and the Orthodox Church under Gorbachev and Yeltsin, see Geoffrey A. Hosking, *The Awakening of the Soviet Union* (Cambridge, Mass.: Harvard University Press, 1991), 117–136; and Ronald Grigor Suny, *The Revenge of the Past: Nationalism, Revolution and the Collapse of the Soviet Union* (Stanford: Stanford University Press, 1993), 15–16, and 49–62; for a broader discussion of the Orthodox revival and the role of the church in post-Soviet Russian life, see Zoe Knox, *Russian Society and the Orthodox Church: Religion in Russia after Communism* (Oxford: Routledge, 2005).

11. Suny, *The Revenge of the Past*, 54.

12. On Yeltsin's populist tactics and appeals to various lobbies in Russian society in the run-up to the 1996 election, see Robert William Davies, *Soviet History in the Yeltsin era* (Basingstoke: Macmillan, 1997), 60–79.

13. On the reconsecration of churches in Russia after 1991, see "Conclusion" in Catriona Kelly, *Socialist Churches: Radical Secularization and the Preservation of the Past in Petrograd and Leningrad, 1918–1988* (DeKalb: Northern Illinois University Press, 2016).

14. Local lists of federally significant architectural monuments were compiled following the adoption of the Resolution of the Council of Ministers of the RSFSR No. 1327 of 30 August 1960 "On the Further Improvement of Work for the Preservation of Cultural Monuments in the RSFSR," *Okhrana pamiatnikov istorii i kul'tury: Sbornik dokumentov* (Moscow: Sovetskaia Rossiia, 1973).

15. NGOM, op. 1, d. 407 (Report on the work of the Novgorod historical-architectural museum-zapovednik in 1961), 16; NGOM, op. 1, d. 398 (Materials on the preservation and restoration of architectural monuments [extracts from orders, protocols, enclosure of correspondence]), 53.

16. Decision of 26.06.91 No. 257 "On the Transference of the St. Sophia Cathedral, St. George's Monastery in Perin Skete, Khutyn Monastery and the Our Lady of the Sign Icon to the Novgorod Diocese Authorities," GANO, f. R-4563, op. 1–11, d. 222 (Decisions of the ispolkoms of the Novgorod Regional and Town Council of People's Deputies for the preservation, use and transference of historical and cultural monuments), 3.

17. GANO, f. R-4563, op. 1–11, d. 222, 7.

18. GANO, f. R-4563, op. 1–11, d. 222, 11.

19. "Novgorodskii sofiiskii sobor," *Drevo: Otkrytaia pravoslavnaia entsiklopediia*, http://drevo-info.ru/articles/3535.html.

20. GAPO, f. R-1855, op. 1, d. 2000 (Documents on the preservation and equipment of historical and cultural monuments), 88–90.

21. GAPO, f. R-1855, op. 1, d. 328 (Correspondence with the Ministry of Culture about the preservation of historical and cultural monuments), 3.

22. GAPO, f. R-1855, op. 1, d. 2000, 88–90. Other museum objects transferred to the diocese at this time included the fifteenth-century Pskov-Caves Monastery complex and the St. Nicholas the Miracle Worker church (1412) in Porkhov. GAPO, f. R-1855, op. 1, d. 2143 (Correspondence with the Ministry of Culture of the RF and organizations for museum work and the preservation of monuments), 3–7.

23. I. B. Golubeva, V. D. Sarab'ianov, *Sobor Rozhdestva bogoroditsy Snetogorskogo monastyria* (Moscow: "Severnyi palomnik," 2002), 20.

24. "Vlasti davno soglasny otdat' sobor . . .," *Prem'er*, July 19–25, 2000, http://premier.region35.ru/gazeta/np151/3s.html.

25. Liudmila Martova, "Krestovyi pokhod," *Prem'er*, July 12–18, 2000, 1.

26. Ibid.

27. Kelly, *Socialist Churches*, 264.

28. Perhaps the best-known example from this time was the reconstruction and reconsecration of the Church of Christ the Savior in Moscow, which was took place between 1995 and 2000. For a discussion of this case, see Kathleen E. Smith, "An Old Cathedral for a New Russia: The Symbolic Politics of the Reconstituted Church of Christ the Saviour," *Religion, State and Society: The Keston Journal* 25, no. 2 (1997): 163–175.

29. "Vlasti davno soglasny otdat' sobor . . ." The debate over the church's status nevertheless continued in the decades that followed. In 2015, after a long and protracted debate, the building was finally returned to the Vologda diocese, resulting in the eviction of the Museum Gallery after half a century's residence in the historic cathedral. "Vologodskoi mitropolii peredadut Voskresenskii sobor, v kotorom polveka nakhodilas' gallereia," *tass.ru*, July 2, 2015, http://tass.ru/vologodskaya-oblast/2088130.

30. Adrian Forty and Susanne Küchler, eds., *The Art of Forgetting* (Oxford: Berg, 1999), 9.

31. A. I. Sazonov and E. A. Starikov, *Moia Vologda: Gorod nashei pamiati* (Vologda: Drevnosti Severa, 2007), 302.

32. Sazonov and Starikov, *Moia Vologda*, 123.

33. Ibid.

34. See the entry on the church in the online *Solvari i entsiklopedii na Akademike*: http://dic.academic.ru/dic.nsf/ruwiki/1334917.

35. I discuss the collective memory of the church's destruction in more detail in chapter 6.

36. Andrei Sal'nikov, "Gospodi, uslishi rab tvoikh, moliashchikhsia tebe," *Krasnyi sever*, November 3, 1998, 2.

37. Ibid.

38. Andrei Sal'nikov, "Stroim ploshchad' soglasiia," *Krasnyi sever*, November 4, 1997, 4.

39. Ibid.

40. Sal'nikov, "Gospodi, uslishi rab tvoikh, molyashchikhsya tebe."

41. Rasporiazhenie ot Gosudarstvennogo komiteta RF po upravleniiu gosudarstvennym imushchestvom, December 28, 1994. Reprinted in *Rossiiskaia gazeta*, December 3, 1994.

42. Evgenii Arsiukhin, "Operatsiia 'Vyshnevyi sad': V Rossii s 1 marta nachinaetsia privatizatsiia pamiatnikov kul'tury," *Rossiiskaia gazeta*, February 26, 2008, http://www.rg.ru/2008/02/26/pamatnik.html.

43. GAPO, f. R-1855, op. 1, d. 2290 (Correspondence with the RF Ministry of Culture and organizations for museum work, the preservation of historical and cultural monuments), 11.

44. Ibid., 15.

45. Galina Filimonova, "Kul'turnaia privatizatsiia," *Poleznaia ploshchad'*, February 6, 2008, http://gttp.ru/text/136.htm.

46. See the Federal Law of the Russian Federation of 29 December 2006 No. 258-F3, http://www.rg.ru/2006/12/31/izmeneniya-dok.html.

47. Elena Kuznetsova, "Otdam v dobrye ruki," *RG-Nedele-Severo-Zaoada*, October 21, 2010, http://www.rg.ru/printable/2010/10/21/reg-szapad/novgorod.html.

48. Arsiukhin, "Operatsiia 'Vyshnevyi sad.'"

49. See the estate website: "Usad'ba 'Nesvoiskoe': Otdykh v pomest'e XVIII veka," http://www.nesv.ru/.

50. "Rukopisi ne goriat. A pamiatniki?," *Russkii sever*, February 22, 2001, 3.

51. Tat'iana Okhotnikova, "Goriat . . . kvartiry . . . doma . . . sklady," *Russkii sever*, September 29, 2000, 3.

52. *Sotsial'nyi zakaz* is a quintessentially Soviet phrase, dating back to the 1920s, which has the meaning of a social prompt or mandate that is issued by the proletariat or Party or society generally to do, create, or write something. The introduction of the term into Soviet parlance is generally linked with the work of the avant-garde Left Front of Arts (LEF) group. See Nikolai Berdiaev, "Literaturnoe napravlenie i 'sotsial'nyi zakaz,'" *Put'* 29 (1931): 80–92.

53. Natal'ia Leuta, "Vologodskaia starina ili skazochka pro belogo bychka," *Khronometr*, October 12, 1999, 5.

54. Svetlana Vetrova, "Spaset li pamiatniki kul'turnaia revoliutsiia?," *Vologodskaia nedelia,* March 1–8, 2001, 4.

55. Andrei Sychev, "Razrukha," *Nash region,* March 7, 2001, 4.

56. Robert Balakshin, "Vologda, kotoruiu my teriaem," *Russkii sever,* May 26, 1995, 4.

57. Viktor Filippov, "Moskva zashchishchaet chestnogo chinovnika," *Izvestiia,* July 14, 1995, 6.

58. This scandalous episode was reported by various national and local news sources at the time. See, for example, Viktor Filippov, "Byt' chestnym chinovnikom opasno dlia zhizni," *Izvestiia,* March 22, 1995, 5; Aleksandr Petrov, "Neprikasaemy?," *Prem'er,* December 30, 1998, 9; Filippov, "Moskva zashchishchaet chestnogo chinovnika."

59. Sychev, "Razrukha."

60. Petrov, "Neprikasaemy?"

61. Balakshin, "Vologda, kotoruiu my teriaem."

62. Svetlana Prokop'eva, "Pozolochennaia naberezhnaia: Arkhitekturnyi labirint dlia pskovskikh patriotov," *Pskovskaia guberniia,* October 31–November 6, 2002, reprinted in *Pskovskaia guberniia. Izbrannye stranitsy, 2000–2005* (Pskov: ANO "Svobodnoe slovo," 2005), 475–481.

63. Brokhman discussed the project and its positive impact on the Pskov landscape in an interview with *Ekho Moskvy* in 2014. For the transcript of the interview, see "Iurii Brokhman o zhilishchnom stroitel'stve v Pskove i za ego predelami," *PLO Dom,* http://dom.pln24.ru/blogers/187286.html.

64. Prokop'eva, "Pozolochennaia naberezhnaia."

65. Ibid.

66. Federal Law of 25 June 2002 No. 73-F3 "On Objects of Cultural Heritage (Historical and Cultural Monuments) of the Peoples of the Russian Federation," https://www.consultant.ru/document/cons_doc_LAW_37318/.

67. Prokop'eva. "Pozolochennaia naberezhnaia."

68. See, for example, G. Melomedov's 1967 letter to *Novgorodskaia pravda* concerning the plans to limit the number of stories on local hotels in Novgorod, discussed in chapter 2.

69. Prokop'eva.

70. Sazanov and Starikov, *Moia Vologda: Gorod nashei pamiati.*

71. A. I. Sazanov, *Takoi gorod v Rossii odin* (Vologda: PF "Poligrafist," 1993).

72. "Rukopisi ne goriat. A pamiatniki?"; "Goriat . . . kvartiry . . . doma . . . sklady."

73. See the discussion of this issue on the online forum *Vabla.ru* on the theme "davaite iskat' po gorodu priznaki skorogo priezda Putina," *Vabla.ru,* http://wobla.ru/forum/Default.aspx?postid=214558.

Notes to Chapter 5

1. On the promotion of state patriotism in the Putin era, see, for example, Marlène Laruelle, *In the Name of the Nation: Nationalism and Politics in Contemporary Russia* (New York: Palgrave Macmillan, 2009), and *Russian Nationalism and the National Reassertion of Russia,* ed. Marlène Laruelle (London: Routledge, 2009), in particular part 4, "Construction of an Official Patriotism: in search of a new ideology?"; for an informed commentary on the surge of state-sponsored patriotic consciousness since the 2014 annexation of Crimea, see Ilya Rozhdestvensky, "Russia's Littlest Soldiers: How the Government Teaches Kids to Love the Motherland and Fight for It," *Meduza,* July 16, 2015, https://meduza.io/en/feature/2015/07/16/russia-s-littlest-soldiers.

2. On politics as a form of "spectacle" in Putin's Russia, see Peter Pomerantsev's much discussed portrait of the post-Soviet regime, *Nothing is True and Everything is Possible: Adventures in Modern Russia* (London: Faber and Faber, 2015), and Mark Lipovetsky, "Anything Goes: How the Russian News Became a Postmodern Game Without Rules," *The Calvert Journal,* March 10, 2015, http://calvertjournal.com/comment/show/3736/political-steampunk-postmodern-game-mark-lipovetsky; for excellent analyses of World War II commemorations as spectacle, see Stephen Hutchings and Natalia Rulyova, "Commemorating the Past/Performing the Present: Television Coverage of the Second World War Victory Celebrations and the (De)construction of Russian Nationhood," in *The*

Post-Soviet Russian Media: Conflicting Signals, ed. Birgit Beumers, Stephen Hutchings and Natalia Rulyova (London: Routledge, 2009), 137–155; and Serguei A. Oushakine, "Remembering in Public: On the Affective Management of History," *Ab Imperio* 1 (2013): 269–302.

3. On early Soviet propaganda and theatrical performance, see, for example, *Street Art of the Revolution: Festivals and Celebrations in Russia, 1918–1933,* ed. Vladimir Tolstoy, et al. (London: Thames and Hudson, 1990); and Brandon Taylor, *Art and Literature under the Bolsheviks* (Concord, MA: Pluto Press, 1991–1992). I discuss the methods of early-Soviet propaganda and their revival in the Putin era in greater detail below.

4. Lyudmila Parts, "'How is Voronezh not Paris?' City Branding in the Russian Provinces," in *Russia's Regional Identities: The Power of the Provinces,* ed. Edith W. Clowes, Gisela Erbslöh, Ani Kokobobo (London: Routledge, 2018), 120–140.

5. M. L. Spivak, "'Provintsiia idet v region': O nekotorykh osobennostiakh sovremennogo upotrebleniia slova *provintsiia,*" in *Geopanorama russkoi kul'tury: Provintsiia i ee lokal'nye teksty,* ed. L. O. Zaionts (Moscow: Iazyki slavianskoi kul'tury, 2004).

6. Parts, "'How is Voronezh not Paris?'"

7. Ekaterina Melnikova, "Celebrating Locality in an Era of Territorial Branding: Rituals and Symbols of Local Solidarity after 1992," unpublished conference paper presented at ASEEES Annual Convention in San Antonio, November 2014.

8. Anne Lounsbery has explored the historical and literary construct of the Russian province in "'No, this is not the provinces!': Provincialism, Authenticity, and Russianness in Gogol's Day," *The Russian Review* 64, no. 2 (2005): 259–280; and "'To Moscow, I Beg You!': Chekhov's Vision of the Russian Provinces," *Toronto Slavic Quarterly* 9 (2004), http://sites.utoronto.ca/tsq/09/lounsbery09.shtml.

9. Parts, "'How is Voronezh not Paris?'"

10. Of relevance to this discussion is Nicolai N. Petro's work on symbolic politics and democratic transition in post-Soviet Novgorod: *Crafting Democracy: How Novgorod Has Coped with Rapid Social Change* (New York: Cornell University Press, 2004).

11. For a description of Altman's work in Petrograd by the artist himself, see N. Altman, *Vospominaniia (Reminiscences),* in the Manuscript Department of the Saltykov-Shchedrin Public Library, Leningrad, f. 1126, republished in English translation in *Street Art of the Revolution,* 71.

12. On the staging of Evreinov's *Storming of the Winter Palace,* see Frederick C. Corney, *Telling October: Memory and the Making of the Bolshevik Revolution* (Ithaca: Cornell University Press, 2004), 75–82; and James von Geldern, *Bolshevik Festivals, 1917–1920* (Berkeley: University of California Press, 1993), 200–205.

13. A. V. Lunacharsky, "On Popular Festivals," *Vestnik teatra [Theatre Courier]* 62 (April 27–May 2, 1920): 13, republished in English translation in *Street Art of the Revolution.*

14. "Gorod gotovitsia k iubileiu," *Velikii Novgorod—rodina Rossii,* http://1150.novgorod.ru/read/press/gorod_preparing.

15. Melnikova, "Celebrating Locality."

16. "Kontseptsiia programmy iubileinykh torzhestv, posviashchennykh 1150-letiiu osnovaniia g. Velikii Novgorod. 19–22 sentiabria 2009 goda," Velikii Novgorod 1150 website, http://1150.novgorod.ru/read/jubilee/.

17. Dmitrii Likhachev, *Zemlia rodnaia: Kniga dlia uchashchikhsia* (Moscow: "Prosveshchenie," 1983), quoted in the "Kontseptsiia programmy."

18. Quoted in an article by Alisa Romanova, "Iubilei Velikogo Novgoroda prazdnuiut s razmakhom," *Vesti.ru,* September 19, 2009, http://www.vesti.ru/doc.html?id=316034.

19. "Kontseptsiia programmy."

20. Ibid.

21. The following details are drawn from information available from local posters and publications during the festival. Pskov, July 2009.

22. On ritualistic expressions of gratitude at Soviet public festivals, see Jeffrey Brooks, *Thank You, Comrade Stalin!: Soviet Public Culture from Revolution to Cold War* (Princeton, NJ: Princeton University Press, 2000).

23. These techniques bore notable resemblance to the methods employed by the Soviet state to associate historic monuments with modern socialist architecture in the 1950s and 1960s. Cf. chapter 1.

24. I discuss the local mythology of St. Ol'ga of Kiev and its role in Pskov's cultural life in greater detail below.

25. GAPO, f. R-1855, op. 1, d. 1892 (Programs and documents for the federal financing of the program "Preservation and Development of Culture and Art" in 1993), 72.

26. Ibid., 70.

27. Ibid.

28. GAPO, f. R-1855, op. 1, d. 1895 (Informative reports on the work of town and regional cultural departments in 1993), 62.

29. Ibid.

30. N. K. Terenina, "Promyshlennost' Pskovskoi oblasti: sovremennoe sostoianie i perspektivy razvitiia," *Pskovskii regional'nii zhurnal* 2 (2006), http://cyberleninka.ru/article/n/promyshlennost-pskovskoy-oblasti-sovremennoe-sostoyanie-i-perspektivy-razvitiya.

31. "Ozhidaemaia prodolzhitel'nost' zhizni pri rozhdenii, let, god, znachenie pokazatelei za god, vse naselenie, oba pola," *Federal'naia sluzhba gosudarstvennoi statistiki,* http://www.gks.ru/dbscripts/cbsd/dbinet.cgi; the population change per 1000 inhabitants in 2005 was 15.7 fewer inhabitants in Pskov; this figure compared to 13.2 fewer in Novgorod, 8.3 fewer in Vologda, and 5.9 fewer in Russia as a whole. "Rozhdaemost', smertnost', i estestvennyi prirost naseleniia po sub"ektam Rossiiskoi federatsii," http://www.gks.ru/bgd/regl/b07_13/IssWWW.exe/Stg/d01/04-22.htm.

32. Ibid.

33. The letter was recorded among the documents relating to the organization of the ten-day festival "Without Pskov there is no Russia," held in Pskov to mark the anniversary in 2003: GAPO, f. R-1855, op. 1, d. 2288 (Documents on the organization of the festival "Without Pskov there is no Russia), 9.

34. Ibid.

35. For an account of the Ol'ga myth and its evolution, see, for example, N. N. Bedina, "Obraz sviatoi kniagini Ol'gi v drevnerusskoi knizhnoi traditsii (XII-XVI v.)," *Drevniaia Rus'. Voprosy medievistiki* 4, no. 30 (2007), 8–12.

36. See Vasilii Surikov's painting *Kniaginia Ol'ga vstrechaet telo kniazia Igoria* (1915) and Mikhail Nesterov's *Sviataia ravnoapostol'naia kniaginia Ol'ga* (1927).

37. For details of the society's activities, see "Vserossiiskoe Ol'ginskoe obshchestvo," on the website *Drevnii gorod Pskov. 903–2017 gody,* http://www.old-pskov.ru/olga_ob.php.

38. This declaration was adopted as part of a far-reaching program of activities dedicated to developing the cultural sphere in the Pskov region between 1994 and 1998. See GAPO, f. R-1855, op. 1, d. 1930 (Program for the development of the cultural sphere in the Pskov region, 1994–1998), 17.

39. The landlady of the flat I rented in Pskov, who owned a dacha in the Vybuty area, described the bureaucratic hurdles that had been erected to prevent further construction in the region following the 1995 preservation order.

40. GAPO, f. R-1855, op. 1, d. 1930, 17.

41. For a full account of the chapel's destruction and reconstruction in the post-Soviet period, see "Ol'ginskoi chasovne v Pskove—15 let," Pskov Library website, http://bibliopskov.ru/zip/olga_chasovnya15let.pdf.

42. "Vserossiiskoe Ol'ginskoe obshchestvo."

43. Ibid.

44. See, for example, the description of the reconstructed chapel in T.V. Shulakov, *Khramy Pskova. Arkhitekturnyi putevoditel'* (Pskov, Pskovskii Volnyi institut, 2005), 25–26.

45. Ibid.

46. GAPO, op. 1., d. 513 (Materials pertaining to the preservation and restoration of historical and cultural monuments, March 30, 1970–October 23, 1970), 7–15.

47. Shulakov, *Khramy Pskova. Arkhitekturnyi putevoditel'*.

48. For a discussion of Tsereteli's contribution to Moscow's sculptural landscape, see Bruce Grant, "New Moscow Monuments, or, States of Innocence," *American Ethnologist* 28, no. 2 (2001): 332–362.

49. Svetlana Prokop'eva, "Povest' o tom, kak vstretilis' Ol'ga Evgen'evna i Ol'ga Mikhailovna," *Pskovskaia guberniia*, August 5, 2003, reprinted in *Pskovskaia guberniia. Izbrannye stranitsy, 2000–2005* (Pskov: ANO "Svobodnoe slovo," 2005), 625–629.

50. *Pskovskaia pravda* published regular editorials and collections of readers' letters in the run-up to the 1100th anniversary celebrations, in which the monuments' location was a frequent subject of debate.

51. Prokop'eva, "Povest' o tom, kak vstretilis' Ol'ga Evgen'evna i Ol'ga Mikhailovna."

52. Contrast, for example, the fruitless efforts of the Pskov "Memorial" Society to commission a suitable monument to the local victims of political repression in the Soviet period. "Pominal'nyi priblizilsia chas," *Pskovskaia guberniia*, July 29–August 4, 2007, http://gubernia.pskovregion.org/number_352/02.php.

53. These different phases in the monument's construction were described by Aleksandr Prokhanov in a television broadcast that aired on *Rossiia 24* on October 3, 2014: "Sviashchennyi kholm: Replika Aleksandra Prokhanova," *Vesti.ru*, October 3, 2014, http://www.vesti.ru/doc.html?id=2018082. The broadcast is discussed in greater detail below.

54. Aleksandr Prokhanov, *Kholm: Roman* (Moscow: Vagrius, 2008).

55. Sander Brouwer has discussed the novel in an unpublished conference paper, "Centre and Borders in Dugin and Prokhanov," presented at the interdisciplinary workshop "Russia on Edge: Reclaiming the Periphery in Contemporary Russian Culture," December 11–12, 2009 (CRASSH, University of Cambridge).

56. For a more detailed discussion of Prokhanov's ultranationalist writings and philosophy, see Keith Livers, "The Tower or the Labyrinth: Conspiracy, Occult, and Empire-Nostalgia in the Work of Viktor Pelevin and Aleksandr Prokhanov," *The Russian Review* 69, no. 3 (2010): 477–503.

57. Aleksandr Prokhanov, "Ne kniaz' Vladimir vybral, eto pravoslavie izbralo ego i Rus," *Izborskii klub*, http://www.dynacon.ru/content/articles/7282/.

58. "1150 let Izborsku: prolivnoi dozhd', anshlag i Izborskii klub," *Regnum informatsionnoe agentstvo*, September 10, 2012, https://regnum.ru/news/polit/1569497.html. On the "About the Club" page of the Izborsk Club website, it also states, somewhat cryptically, that Turchak "played an important role in the creation of the club," *Izborskii klub*, https://izborsk-club.ru/about.

59. See the individual biographies of the club's members on the website: https://izborsk-club.ru/.

60. "Novorossiia" is a historical term of the Russian Empire denoting a region north of the Black Sea (now part of Ukraine). The term regained popularity in Russia following a statement by President Putin in an interview, on April 17, 2014, that the territories of Kharkiv, Luhansk, Donetsk, Kherson, Mykolaiv, and Odessa were part of a territorial entity called "Novorossiia." The transcript of this interview can be found on the website of the *Washington Post*: https://www.washingtonpost.com/world/transcript-vladimir-putins-april-17-qanda/2014/04/17/ff77b4a2-c635-11e3-8b9a-8e0977a24aeb_story.html?utm_term=.ff88a881b3bb. In May 2014, the self-proclaimed Donetsk People's Republic and Luhansk People's Republic declared themselves part of the confederation of Novorossiia and independent from Ukraine. For a discussion of this term in the context of Aleksandr Prokhanov's ultraconservative thinking, see Edith Clowes, "Provinces, Piety, and Promotional Putinism: Mapping Aleksandr Prokhanov's Imagined Russia," in *The Post-Soviet Politics of Utopia: Language, Fiction and Fantasy in Russia*, ed. Mikhail Suslov and Per-Arne Bodin (London: I.B. Tauris, 2018).

61. "Izborskii klub sobral krymskie zemli dlia sviashchennogo kholma v Izborske i obsudil fenomen Kryma kak Russkogo chuda," *Izborskii klub*, http://www.dynacon.ru/content/articles/7607/?sphrase_id=17799.

62. "Sviashchennyi kholm: Replika Aleksandra Prokhanova."

63. Edith Clowes has noted parallel tendencies toward the language of the sacral in the work of Aleksandr Dugin in her chapter "Postmodernist Empire Meets Holy Rus': How Aleksandr Dugin Tried to Change the Eurasian Periphery into the Sacred Center of the World," in *Russia on the Edge: Imagined Geographies and Post-Soviet Identities* (Ithaca, NY: Cornell University Press, 2011), 43–67.

64. The articles on the burials can be found in the archives of the newspaper's online site. See Lev Shlosberg, "Mertvye i zhivye," *Pskovskaia guberniia,* August 26–September 2, 2014, web.archive.org/web/20140831012426/http://gubernia.pskovregion.org/number_705/01.php?; and Aleksei Semenov, "Voina spishet vse," *Pskovskaia guberniia,* August 26–September 2, 2014, http://web.archive.org/web/20140903102603/http://gubernia.pskovregion.org/number_705/00.php.

65. "Russian Opposition Deputy Expelled from Regional Assembly," *Radio Free Europe. Radio Liberty,* http://www.rferl.org/a/russia-lev-shlosberg-yabloko-expelled/27267911.html.

66. "Krymskaia zemlia stala chast'iu Sviashchennogo kholma v Pskovskom Izborske," *Regnum: informatsionnoe agentstvo,* August 27, 2014, http://www.regnum.ru/news/polit/1841042.html.

67. For more on the historical reenactment projects of the "Night Wolves," see the club's webpage, accessed August 8, 2017, http://www.nightwolves.ru/nw/; on the activities of Vladimir Medinskii's "Russian Military Historical Society," see the "Projects" page of the website, accessed August 8, 2017, http://rvio.histrf.ru/activities/projects.

Notes to Chapter 6

1. Elaine J. Lawless, *Holy Women, Wholly Women: Sharing Ministries of Wholeness through Life Stories and Reciprocal Ethnography* (Philadelphia: University of Pennsylvania Press, 1993).

2. Alessandro Portelli, *The Battle of Valle Giulia: Oral History and the Art of Dialogue* (Madison: The University of Wisconsin Press, 1997), 24.

3. Marina Loskutova, *Pamiat'o blokade. Svidetel'stva ochevidtsev i istoricheskoe sozdanie obshchestva* (Moscow: Novoe izd-vo, 2006); Svetlana Alexievich, *Vremia sekond khend* (Moscow: Vremia, 2014).

4. Nancy Ries, *Russian Talk: Culture and Conversation During Perestroika* (Ithaca: Cornell University Press, 1997), chapter 3.

5. Dale Pesmen, *Russia and Soul: An Exploration* (Ithaca: Cornell University Press, 2000).

6. Darya Tsymbalyuk, "Agency, Meaning-Making and Displacement in Two Stories from Donbas, Ukraine" (Erasmus Mundus MA diss., University of St Andrews—Perpignan, 2017).

7. Judith Stacey, "Can There Be a Feminist Ethnography?," in *Women's Words: The Feminist Practice of Oral History,* ed. Sherna Gluck Berger and Daphne Patai (London: Routledge, 1991), 111–121 (114).

8. Julian Wolfreys, *Readings: Acts of Close Reading in Literary Theory* (Edinburgh: Edinburgh University Press, 2000), ix.

9. A number of transcribed interviews with residents of the Russian Northwest can be accessed at the *Oxford Russian Life History Archive,* http://www.ehrc.ox.ac.uk/lifehistory/archive.htm.

10. European heritage organizations, such as the National Trust in Britain, have long been preoccupied with the bias in their membership. See, for example, the studies highlighting the gap between participation in heritage between the most and least deprived areas of England on the "Historic England" website: https://historicengland.org.uk/whats-new/news/new-data-surge-in-heritage-interest.

11. See the *LiveJournal* "town groups" pages: http://www.livejournal.ru/communities/.

12. On the representation of northwestern history and heritage in the national media, see the state-funded Russian historical drama television series set in the second half of the fifteenth-century, "Sofiia," directed by Aleksei Andrianov (Moskino, 2016).

13. The responses to this survey, provided by university students in Lipetsk and Voronezh, were collated by Dmitry Shatalov in March 2018.

14. For a detailed history of the site, see the report on the removal of the workshops and residential accommodation from the corpus in 1984. NGOM, op. 3, d. 1295 (Reports on the work of the museum-zapovednik in 1984).

15. GANO, op. 6–81, d. 47 (Materials about the preservation of architectural monuments [orders, plans, information and correspondence]), 163.

16. On the adaptation of church architecture for cultural and scientific purposes in the Soviet period, see Catriona Kelly, *Socialist Churches: Radical Secularization and the Preservation of the Past in Petrograd and Leningrad, 1918–1988* (DeKalb: Northern Illinois University Press, 2016).

17. Marina Tsvetaeva, *A Captive Spirit: Selected Prose*, trans. J. Marin King (London: Virago, 1983), 326.

18. On Soviet childhood as a focus of popular nostalgia, see Catriona Kelly "A Joyful Soviet Childhood: Licensed Happiness for Little Ones," in *Petrified Utopia: Happiness Soviet-style*, eds. Marina Balina and Evgeny Dobrenko (London: Anthem Press, 2009), 3–18.

19. Stoves are a frequent motif in memories of domestic life in Russia and Ukraine. For a discussion of the stove as a focus of diasporan memory among displaced migrants from Donbas in post-2014 Ukraine, see Tsymbalyuk, "*Agency, Meaning-Making and Displacement*."

20. On the crash modernization of the northwestern periphery, see Victoria Donovan, "The 'Old New Russian Town': Modernization and Architectural Preservation in Russia's Historic North West, 1961–1982," *Slavonica* 19, no. 1 (April 2013): 18–35; for an associated study of urban transformation and popular dissent in Khrushchev-era Moscow, see Stephen Bittner, *The Many Lives of Khrushchev's Thaw: Experience and Memory in Moscow's Arbat* (Ithaca: Cornell University Press, 2008).

21. NGOM, op. 3, d. 1295 (Information on the work of the museum-zapovednik in 1984). See, also, the historical information available on the monastery's website. "Sovremennost'," *Sviato-Iur'ev muzhskoi monastyr'*, http://georg.orthodoxy.ru/history.htm.

22. On war memory in the Putin era, see Serguei Oushakine, "Remembering in Public: On the Affective Management of History," *Ab Imperio* 1 (2013), 269–302; Stephen Hutchings, "V-Day: The (De-)construction of Nationhood on Russian TV," *Art Margins* [online], August 14, 2009, http://www.artmargins.com/index.php/8-archive/489-v-day-the-de-construction-of-nationhood-on-russian-tv-.

23. Cultural memory, as Jan Assmann and John Czaplicka have defined it, is the crystallization of once living memory into objective culture, or, to put it another way, the transformation of individual recollection into collective belief. Jan Assmann and John Czaplicka, "Collective Memory and Cultural Identity," *New German Critique* 65 (1995): 125–133.

24. Kukryniksy, *Flight of the Fascists from Novgorod* (1944–46). I discuss this painting, among other artistic representations of the wartime destruction of the Northwest, in chapter 1.

25. The speaker is referring here to the November 1945 declaration "On Measures to Reconstruct the Towns of the USSR Destroyed by the Nazi Invaders." The declaration underlined the need for urgent restoration work to historic architecture in Russia's fifteen oldest towns, including Novgorod and Pskov. I discuss this ruling and its consequences for the architectural landscape in more detail in chapter 1.

26. *Pskov: Art Treasures and Architectural Monuments*, ed. Savely Yamshchikov et al. (Leningrad: Aurora Art Publishers, 1978), 141.

27. On the militarization of youth culture in the postwar and Brezhnev eras, see Juliane Fürst, *Stalin's Last Generation: Soviet Post-War Youth and the Emergence of Mature Socialism* (Oxford: Oxford University Press, 2010), in particular chapters 1 to 4; see also Nina Tumarkin, *The Living and the Dead: The Rise and Fall of the Cult of World War II in Russia* (New York: Basic Books, 1994).

28. Marianne Hirsch, "The Generation of Postmemory," *Poetics Today* 29, no. 1 (2008): 103–128 (103).

29. *Domiki s znakom porody, / S vidom ee storozhei, / Vas zamenili urody, - / Gruznye, v shest' etazhei. / Domovladel'tsy - ikh pravo! / I pogibaete vy, / Tomnykh prababushek slava, / Domiki staroi Moskvy.* Marina Tsvetaeva, "Domiki staroi Moskvy" (1906–1920).

30. G. Melomedov in "O gorode moem rodnom," *Novgorodskaia pravda*, January 6, 1967, 4.

31. svc63 and Navaialy, January 11, 2009, *LiveJournal: Novgorod*, January 11–30, 2009, http://novgorod.livejournal.com/227875.html.

32. karakatizza and Navaialy, January 11, 2009, *LiveJournal: Novgorod.*

33. P. I. Elizabeth (b. 1983), St. Petersburg, Summer 2010.

34. Alena (b. 1983). Vologda. Summer 2009.

35. Dmitrii (b. 1979). Pskov. Summer 2009.

36. Valentina (b. 1958). Vologda. Winter 2009.

37. V. Gippenreiter, E. Gordienko, and S. Iamshchikov, *Novgorod (Fotoal'bom)* (Moscow: Planeta, 1976).

38. See, for example, the discussion of Pskov's architectural landscape in the introduction to *Pskovskii krai v istorii Rossii*, ed. E. P. Ivanov (Pskov: izd-vo Pskov. Obl. In-ta povysheniia kvalifikatsii rabotnikov obrazovaniia, 2000), 1–7.

Notes to Conclusion

1. Ivan Leshchinskii, "Novye Liudi," *Nauchno -prosvetitel'skii zhurnal Skepsis*, August 2008, http://scepsis.ru/library/id_2149.html.

2. D. S. Likhachev, "Pamiat' istorii sviashchenna," *Ogonek* 29 (July 1982): 18.

3. "Trebuet neusypnogo vnimaniia," *Ogonek* 7, no. 12 (Feb 1983): 19–20.

4. A popular online forum for the expression of regional frustrations with inadequate preservationist institutions was the *LiveJournal* "town groups" pages: http://www.livejournal.ru/communities/.

5. Michael Hunter, ed., *Preserving the Past: The Rise of Heritage in Modern Britain* (Stroud, Gloucestershire: Alan Sutton Publishing Limited, 1996), 10.

6. For a comprehensive account of postwar legislation on historic preservation in Europe, including the cases of Austria, Bavaria, Belgium, Denmark, and Finland, see Denis Rodwell, "Conservation Legislation," in *Architectural Conservation in Europe*, ed. Sherban Cantacuzino (Bedford: The Architectural Press Ltd., 1975), 131–138.

7. For a discussion of postwar social transformation in other European contexts, see, for example, Jonathan Dunnage, *Twentieth Century Italy: A Social History* (Pearson Education Limited: London, 2002); Martin Clark, *Modern Italy 1871–1995* (London: Longman, 1996); and Friedrich Lenger, ed., *Towards an Urban Nation: Germany since 1780* (Oxford: Berg, 2002); on the transformation of the urban sphere in postwar London, see Michael Young and Peter Willmott, *Family and Kinship in East London* (London: Routledge and Kegan Paul, 1986).

8. On the French Revolution as a civilizational rupture and its consequences for national memory, see Pierre Nora, "Between Memory and History: Les Lieux de Memoire," *Representations* 26 (1989): 7–24; on the rupturing effect of the Industrial Revolution, see Peter Fritzsche's *Stranded in the Present: Modern Time and the Melancholy of History* (London: Harvard University Press, 2004); for some insightful commentary on strategies of memorialization within the domestic sphere, see Raphael Samuel, *Theatres of Memory: Past and Present in Contemporary Culture*, rev. ed. (London: Verso, 2012); and, on the Russian case, Catriona Kelly, *St Petersburg: Shadows of the Past* (New Haven: Yale University Press, 2014).

9. "National Trust Membership Soars to Four Million," *BBC News*, October 6, 2011, http://www.bbc.co.uk/news/uk-15187147.

10. GANO, f. R-4563, op. 1–4, d. 40 (Information about work of the regional VOOPIiK department, 1979–1980), p. 1; GAVO, f. 843, op. 1, d. 157 (Correspondence with party and soviet organs and state institutions about issues connected with the preservation and propaganda of monuments, February 26, 1982–December 10, 1982), 27.

11. See Yitzhak M. Brudny, *Reinventing Russia: Russian Nationalism and the Soviet State, 1953–1991* (Cambridge, MA: Harvard University Press, 1998); John B. Dunlop, *The Faces of Contemporary Russian Nationalism* (Princeton, NJ: Princeton University Press, 1983); Nikolai Mitrokhin, *Russkaia partiia: Dvizhenie russkikh natsionalistov v SSSR 1953–1985 gody* (Moscow: Novoe literaturnoe obozrenie, 2003).

12. David Brandenberger, *National Bolshevism: Stalinist Mass Culture and the Formation of Modern Russian National Identity, 1931–1956* (Cambridge, MA: Harvard University Press, 2002).

13. Cf. Alexander Etkind's argument concerning the processes of "self-colonization" in the Russian Empire in *Internal Colonization: Russia's Imperial Experience* (Cambridge, MA: Polity, 2011).

INDEX